W9-DHG-553

A Journey of Heart and Mind

Transformative Jewish Learning
in Adulthood

The Jewish Education Series:

Textual Knowledge: Teaching the Bible in Theory and in Practice by Barry W. Holtz

A Journey of Heart and Mind: Transformative Jewish Learning in Adulthood by Lisa D. Grant, Diane Tickton Schuster, Meredith Woocher, and Steven M. Cohen

A Journey of Heart and Mind

Transformative Jewish Learning in Adulthood

Lisa D. Grant, Diane Tickton Schuster, Meredith Woocher, and Steven M. Cohen

The Jewish Theological Seminary of America

The publication of this volume was made possible
by generous support from the Kazis Family Publication Fund.

THE JEWISH
EDUCATION
SERIES

Contents

Introduction

In rabbinic literature, a story is told about how Rabbi Yochanan spent eighteen days studying with a renowned teacher, Rabbi Oshaya Beribi, but confessed to having only learned one small detail, about the proper spelling of a certain word. While he learned little from his teacher, Rabbi Yochanan went on to say that he learned "the heart and mind" of each of the other twelve students who studied at Rabbi Oshaya Beribi's table (Eruvin 53a).

This short tale has great relevance for teaching Jewish adults. It tells us that the process and experience of learning for adults goes beyond mastering a certain body of literature. Equally important to the content is creating a safe and welcoming space for learners to learn "the heart and mind" of the other students around the study table. While Rabbi Oshaya Beribi may have been the most learned teacher in his community, ultimately he failed to help his students find meaning in the text. His teaching style was too inaccessible for his students to grasp. A message of this story is that knowledge of subject matter alone is inadequate for teaching adult Jewish learners. Teachers must also know their learners, their needs, their questions, and their motivations for learning. Ultimately, they must be aware that their students are looking for meaning and want to find it in Jewish study.[1]

Twenty years ago, there were few serious and sustained adult Jewish learning opportunities in the non-Orthodox Jewish community. Most

[1]Eruvin 53a was cited by Mark Hirshman, director of the Melton Centre for Jewish Education at the Hebrew University during a session at the 2001 conference for site directors of the Florence Melton Adult Mini-Schools.

programs for Jewish adults consisted of an occasional guest lecturer and a few short-term programs at synagogues and Jewish Community Centers. Since the mid-1980s, however, the number of long-term, substantive programs of adult Jewish learning has grown exponentially in the United States and other countries. Today, Jewish adults engage in Jewish study at synagogues, Jewish Community Centers, Bureaus of Jewish Education, independent schools and retreat centers, movement-sponsored programs, museums, and informal networks (including book groups, *havurot, rosh hodesh* groups, and other study circles). Programs range in length and venue, taking place in formal classrooms, downtown offices, people's homes, out in nature, through travel programs, and in cyberspace.

While the range and variety of Jewish adult learning programs continue to grow, little research has been conducted about the nature and impact of these programs in terms of their individual characteristics and contributions, and in how they compare with one another. This book constitutes the first in-depth examination of the contemporary adult Jewish learning scene in North America. Through a focused examination of one program, the Florence Melton Adult Mini-School, a two-year program of formal Jewish study, it explores an array of issues and challenges that any adult Jewish educational enterprise must consider as it plans programs and instruction for its learners. It asks: How does this learning experience make a difference in the lives and learning of its students? And how do the program leaders, curriculum planners, and teachers make decisions about what to transmit and how to teach the complex and multifaceted topics of Judaism to mature adults?

Using data from interviews, classroom observations, and surveys, as well as a careful examination of teaching materials and other documents, we present a vivid portrait of an established Jewish adult learning institution. Our findings about the Mini-School provide us with a picture of a much broader terrain, namely, the cultural and sociological factors contributing to the emergence of this form of adult Jewish learning at this point in American Jewish life. The successes and challenges faced by Mini-School planners, administrators, and teachers, as well as the learning experiences of more than twelve thousand alumni, provide a framework for addressing important questions about adult Jewish literacy as a priority in the contemporary Jewish community. The call for such literacy is growing (Yoffie 1997; Shrage 1996), and communities are trying to respond without adequate data about what works, what makes a difference, and what has been learned by pioneers in this emerging field. This book sheds light on how the Mini-School's eighteen years of experience can inform new endeavors on the adult Jewish learning horizon.

The Context

The current renaissance of adult Jewish education has been shaped by a number of sociological factors that help explain the context in which the Mini-School has successfully evolved. As happened during the "Great Awakening" at the turn of the twentieth century (Sarna 1995), the 1980s and 1990s were a time when internal and external societal forces pushed American Jews to question how well they understood their religion and whether they were in a position to authentically transmit their heritage to succeeding generations. Increasingly, communal leaders expressed concern about the likelihood of Jewish continuity and also despaired that most post-Holocaust Jews had received only a "pediatric" Jewish education (Cowan 1994; Hoffman 1996; Poupko 1999). In response, in diverse segments of the American Jewish community, increasing numbers of adults supported expanded enrollments in Jewish preschools, day schools, overnight camps, Israel Experience programs, Jewish studies on college campuses, and a range of adult Jewish learning programs.

The context was shaped by other factors as well. By the 1980s, a substantial majority of Jewish adults had acquired a college education, as well as the critical thinking skills honed through higher learning and professional success. However, as they matured, these well-educated individuals began to discern the gap between their secular knowledge and their understanding of their religion and their identities as Jews. Accustomed to a sense of mastery in other domains, these adults were motivated to use their intellectual capabilities to achieve an authentic knowledge base about their heritage. Moreover, in response to the challenges of modernity—to a society buffeted by industrialization, urbanization, mass social mobility, and technology—contemporary Jewish adults (like others of their generation) were profoundly shaken in many ways. They experienced a loss of social location (not being sure where they belonged), a loss of given truths (not being sure of what was right and wrong), and a loss of established norms and purpose (not being sure of what they should do and what they were about) (Cohen and Eisen 2000). Their lives required them to make more changes more often (in residence, occupation, station in life, family situation, cultural environment, religious affiliation, and so on) and to adapt to the multiple demands of modern life in more flexible ways (Kegan 1994).

As sociologist Robert Wuthnow (1999) points out, compared with the past, today's society is much more porous; people, goods, and ideas flow more freely and rapidly between and among families, regions, companies, countries, groups, ethnicities, and so forth. When a society becomes more porous and mobile, people find that they have more choices. In exercising these choices, they tend to become more individuated, individualized, and individualistic—looking out more for themselves than for their communities (Putnam 2000), and less bound by communal structures and traditions. This freedom impels many adults to embark upon personal journeys, to search for a clearer understanding of who they are, where they fit in, and what sorts of lives they should lead. These adults are looking for meaning: about themselves, their values, their religious commitments, and what gives them a sense of place and connection in a world characterized by upheaval and change.

In many cases, a quest for meaning prompts adults—especially well-educated adults—to look for new learning experiences that can clarify unanswered questions or provide new structures for understanding. Many seekers perceive adult education as a viable avenue for personal and intellectual growth. They are attracted to activities that offer them the opportunity to deliberately explore and struggle with ideas rather than require them to conform to any absolute "truth."

Relatively little is known about contemporary adult Jewish learners (Schuster 2003), but when we began our research we assumed that the learners at the Mini-School would share a number of commonalities with the moderately affiliated Jews interviewed for *The Jew Within: Self, Family, and Community in America* (Cohen and Eisen 2000). On the whole, Cohen and Eisen found that, in the non-Orthodox community, Jewish adults no longer look to outside authority (such as traditional ideological systems or the rabbis who interpret them) to tell them what they should or should not do as Jews. They see Judaism as a voluntary cultural resource, rather than as an obligatory, normative tradition. As such, the only source of obligation comes from within the self, not from the tradition, or from its expert and learned interpreters, and not from the sanctions of community or other such forces external to the self.

Moreover, these adults also regard the practice of Judaism as a matter of personal choice that is driven by an individual's conception of meaning rather than as an obligatory compliance with divinely ordained commands. For them, being Jewish doesn't necessarily mean "doing what the group expects" so as to ensure ongoing communal membership. Practice may take on different meaning—or none at all—and group membership is less important than the freedom of choice about how, when, and why one practices Judaism at all. Just as Cohen and Eisen's insights about moderately affiliated Jews helped Jewish communal leaders to understand how better to meet the needs of the contemporary Jewish population, research about a successful adult Jewish learning program can reveal important indicators about what contributes to the vitality of an increasing and important segment of the Jewish community. Moreover, inquiry into the impact of the Mini-School provides a useful perspective about the core issues and challenges that any adult Jewish educational enterprise must consider as it plans programs and instruction for its learners. It may also point to ways in which increased Jewish literacy among adults may effect enduring change in the Jewish community.

The Mini-School: A Focus for Research

While the "field" of adult Jewish learning has expanded and diversified in recent years, this growth has not been systematically documented. Nor has the experience of learners, teachers, or adult education programs been analyzed. Thus, in 1999, when we were invited to conduct a formal study of the impact of the Mini-School on its learners and alumni, we created a research design that would enable us to focus on the participants' learning and would help us explore larger issues in adult Jewish education as well. By making the Mini-School model the focus of our research, we were able to investigate how a serious Jewish educational institution makes choices about its educational philosophy and curriculum and how it provides direction to and collaborates with the many local coordinators (called "site directors") and teachers who are involved in carrying out its mission. We were particularly interested in the Mini-School because of its commitment to promoting Jewish literacy through a sequential, systematic introduction to Jewish sources, to helping adults apply traditional texts to their lives, to employing a pluralistic faculty, and to welcoming all students without judging these learners' choices with regard to belief or practice. Beyond our case study, we were eager to place the experience of this two-year adult Jewish learning program in a broader social and educational context and to assess the relevance of the Mini-School approach to other endeavors in the Jewish community.

Genesis and Development

The genesis of the Mini-School dates back to 1980, when Florence Melton, an entrepreneur and philanthropist active in Jewish educational initiatives, decided that she needed a better Jewish education. As she related: "I knew how we did everything as Jews but I didn't have a clue as to *why* we did it!" She soon discovered that there was no comprehensive, sequential, sustained program of Jewish education for adults to help her answer the "why." In fact, at the time, aside from a few short-term programs at synagogues and Jewish Community Centers and an occasional guest lecturer, there were few adult Jewish learning opportunities in most non-Orthodox Jewish communities.

Melton sensed that she was not alone in her thirst for Jewish knowledge. She surmised that many other Jewish adults, though competent and successful in their personal and professional lives, felt that their Jewish educational background was inadequate to transmit even the basic essentials of Jewish history, culture, ideas, and values to their children, or to make much meaning out of Judaism for themselves.

Initially, in trying to market her idea of a sustained course of adult Jewish study to a variety of institutions, most Jewish educational leaders assumed that adults would refuse to make a long-term commitment to Jewish learning. As Melton noted:

> In 1980 it was unheard of in Jewish education to even consider that adults would participate in formalized education, where they would go to a school on a regular basis and pay tuition and have a pluralist environment in a classroom. But I knew it was going to fill a human need that was not being met.

Ultimately, the Melton Centre for Jewish Education in the Diaspora at the Hebrew University in Jerusalem agreed to develop these ideas. In the early 1980s, a team of scholars and educators at the Hebrew University gathered to develop a prototype curriculum entailing four courses to be taught over two years, for a total of 120 hours of study. From its inception, the central goal of the Mini-School was to increase Jewish literacy among participants. An early planning document described this goal:

> [The objective is] to give adults mastery of basic Jewish literacy, in a systematic and stimulating manner. Students move from encountering basic Jewish vocabulary, including Hebrew reading, to an intellectual, experiential and spiritual exploration of the four core areas of Jewish knowledge: Bible, History, Rabbinics, and the Jewish calendar. (Melton Centre for Jewish Education in the Diaspora 1985, 2–3)

Three pilot sites opened in 1986 in Chicago, New York, and Commack, Long Island. In 1989, the North American office opened, designed to oversee site development and serve as a liaison between the American sites and the academic resources based at the Hebrew University. Since that time, as the number of sites and students have grown substantially, the curriculum has undergone continual evaluation and revision. As of spring 2003, sixty-five sites operated in North America, Great Britain, Australia, and Israel. A range of communal institutions, including Jewish Federations, Jewish Community Centers, Bureaus of Jewish Education, and, in a few select cases, synagogues sponsor these sites. In the United States, Mini-School communities range in size from just a few thousand Jews, such as Des Moines, Iowa, and Akron, Ohio, to major Jewish population centers such as Chicago, St. Louis, Baltimore, Philadelphia, and Miami. To date, an estimated twelve thousand students have "graduated" from the Mini-School, and approximately 4,500 students were enrolled for the 2002–03 academic year.

The Organizational Structure

The Mini-School is a not-for-profit organization, based on a franchise model. Accordingly, it operates as a confederation of sites that function at the local level with central office support and oversight. The organizational structure consists of three layers that form a collaborative partnership.

The top level of the organizational structure is the international office (also called the Florence Melton Adult Mini-School Institute), which is based at the Melton Centre for Jewish Education at The Hebrew University. This institute, directed by Jonathan Mirvis, is responsible for the Mini-School's curriculum development and oversight, as well as site development and expansion outside of North America.

At the second level is the North American office, located outside of Chicago. Betsy Katz, North American director, and her staff are responsible for North American site development and expansion and for providing ongoing organizational support and professional development for site directors and faculty. This office also has developed customized Mini-Schools for specific groups such as Jewish educators, community leaders, and parents of day school children.

The third layer of the organizational structure is the sites themselves. These sites purchase a licensing agreement and curriculum and are entitled to a variety of benefits, including professional development and organizational consultation. Sites are sponsored by a variety of nondenominational local Jewish communal agencies such as Jewish Federations, Jewish Community Centers, and Bureaus of Jewish Education. In a few situations, synagogues serve as a sponsoring site with the stipulation that the congregational rabbis may not teach in the school, so as to maintain an independent institutional identity.

Sponsoring agencies are responsible for establishing an advisory board and hiring a site director. The director hires and supervises faculty (with guidance from the advisory board and North American office) and handles the management of the school, including marketing and recruiting students, setting the calendar, budgeting, fund-raising in conjunction with the advisory boards, supplying classrooms and study materials, and planning extracurricular events.

The Curriculum

The Mini-School's curriculum consists of four yearlong courses designed to excite students about the intellectual and community-building benefits of Jewish study. Students take two classes at a time, meeting for two hours a week, thirty weeks each year. Each course includes the phrase "of Jewish living" in its title. As Betsy Katz stated: "The intention is to attach learning to life. Sharing this process links people to one another." As can be seen from the following brief descriptions, each course focuses on helping learners connect their personal experience to and make meaning from Jewish tradition, Jewish thought, and Jewish history.[2]

Year One

- The Rhythms of Jewish Living: This course aims to introduce students to the ideas, beliefs, and practices that shape a Jewish life. It covers the Jewish calendar in terms of the holidays and life-cycle events. A fundamental objective is to create awareness of *kedusha*—separateness, holiness, specialness—of Jewish living. Teachers are encouraged to focus on the theoretical issues upon which religious practice and ritual are based, rather than on the particulars of religious observance.
- The Purposes of Jewish Living: This course provides an overview of the theological foundations of Jewish life and religious practice. Whereas many adult Jewish education classes answer the questions of who, what, where, when, and how, this course is devoted to the question *why*. It seeks to identify the ultimate purposes of Judaism as they arose out of the historical experience. This course is the one where conversation about God is most likely to occur. The curricular materials are rooted in the principle of "suspended belief." In other words, teachers are urged to ask participants to let the texts speak for themselves. As the introduction to the course explains:

   If, for example, the texts assume God's existence and His intervention in human affairs, an assumption which may be highly problematic for many, we ask that the participants study those texts, even if they don't accept their premise, in the hope that they will discover ideas and messages that are relevant and meaningful nonetheless. ("Purposes of Jewish Living," *Introduction to the Teacher*, 2)

---

[2]Course descriptions are summarized from Katz and Shapiro, *Madrich: Coordinator's Manual* (1998).

Year Two

- The Dramas of Jewish Living through the Ages:[3] This course focuses on specific dramatic events, experiences, and issues from different periods of Jewish history in order to help strengthen the students' connection to Jewish memory. As the introduction to the course states, "Jewish memory is not just about acquiring information of the past, but about utilizing the past in order to help us make sense of our lives and to deepen our individual and collective identities in the present" ("Dramas of Jewish Living," *Introduction to the Curriculum*, 1). The curriculum is organized chronologically and includes historical events from the biblical, Second Temple rabbinic, medieval, modern, and contemporary periods. Each lesson contains primary texts from the period in question as well as a variety of supporting material such as maps, timelines, and a summary of the historical context in which the drama occurred. Teachers are encouraged to "bring the drama to life" by facilitating a challenging and meaningful discussion.
- The Ethics of Jewish Living: This course is a text-centered approach to the study of Jewish ethics. Students learn how rabbinic literature views human behavior and how to debate and think about practical dilemmas in life. To some extent, this course goes hand-in-hand with the Purposes of Jewish Living. *Purposes* tries to answer the question, "What is the meaning of a Jewish person's life?" *Ethics* tries to answer the question of how to act on those ideas. The curriculum emphasizes God and commandment as the source of Jewish ethics. The course is divided into three parts: introductory lessons called "Foundations" describe core principles that guide Jewish ethical thinking; the core of the curriculum, "Applications," focuses on specific, practical areas of daily human conduct; the final part of the course, "Challenges," explores controversial moral issues confronting contemporary society, such as abortion, euthanasia, homosexuality, and suicide.

Beyond the four courses that form the common core of the learning experience, many sites offer extracurricular and informal programs. These

---

[3]Formerly called "Dilemmas of Jewish Living," this course title was changed in 2000 to reflect its most recent revision.

may include holiday parties, field trips, Shabbat dinners, workshops, and speakers. Many sites also offer short-term and ongoing continuing education beyond the two years in areas such as Hebrew language, rabbinic literature, Israel, and modern Jewish thought. Another key component of programming beyond the fixed curriculum is the Israel Seminar, an eleven-day study tour for students, alumni, and their spouses. Large sites typically organize their own trips, while smaller sites may combine with others. While in Israel, the text-centered classroom approach is adapted and expanded, with students learning "texts in context" at different locations throughout the country.

Conceptual Frameworks

Our case-study analysis of the Mini-School was informed by a variety of conceptual frameworks. Scholarship about adult education, adult religious education, the teaching process (specifically, the relationship between teachers, learners, and curriculum), Jewish identity education, and adult cognitive development (specifically, perspective transformation) all contributed to our understanding of teaching and learning at the Mini-School. As we reviewed the pertinent literatures, we continually asked ourselves five questions about how adult Jewish learning is shaped, in terms of process and impact:

1. How do an adult Jewish learning program's educational philosophy and instructional approaches conform to empirical findings about adult learners and their preferred experiences in adult education?
2. In what ways is the institutional agenda of an adult Jewish learning program consistent with principles of adult religious education?
3. What characterizes interactions between the teacher, learner, and curriculum in adult Jewish learning activities?
4. In what way does the adult Jewish educational experience shape and strengthen Jewish identity?
5. In what ways and to what extent does learning transform learners' perspectives about Judaism or themselves as Jews?

As we detail below, in addition to insights from adult education and adult religious education, our thinking was informed by recent literature about the rise in spiritual seeking and religious affiliation among the general American population (Bellah et al. 1985; Roof 1993, 1999; Wuthnow 1994) and about the need for increased Jewish communal support for educational programs that enhance Jewish identity (London and Chazan 1990; Cohen 1995; Shrage 1996).

Findings about Adult Learners

Our starting point for studying the impact of an adult Jewish learning experience was to review the extensive literature on adult learners and successful adult learning. We assumed that people who enroll in the Mini-School would resemble the growing population of adults who now attend intellectually demanding programs at colleges, community lecture series, Elderhostels, and in the workplace. Because little has been written specifically about the experience of contemporary Jewish adult learners—either in secular or religious settings—we focused on trends in the general community of "lifelong learners."

Studies of lifelong learners consistently have found that adult "growth" can be significantly shaped by participation in meaningful educational experiences (Apps 1994; Tennant and Pogson 1995). The more that people enroll in adult education programs, the more they see adult learning as an asset to personal development and seek new learning opportunities (Cross 1981). Throughout the adult years, when people are in times of transition, they look to educational institutions for assistance and support (Aslanian and Brickell 1980). This includes individuals who are making the transition to retirement or post-parental responsibilities.

Participation in formal and informal adult educational activities is at an all-time high and continues to expand; lifelong learning has become ubiquitous in most segments of the American population (Kim and Creighton 2000). Given the lengthening life span of middle-aged adults, as well as the already high level of education of baby boomers, adult learning program planners now anticipate that the demand for quality adult education programs will only continue to grow (Caffarella 2002).

As more and more people engage in adult learning, scholars have asked two important, related questions: What constitutes effective adult education? And what helps adults to learn? Some have debated whether, as learners, adults are different from children and adolescents, and whether there might be a field of "andragogy" (teaching and learning unique to adults) that is distinguishable from pedagogy (literally, the instruction of children) (Knowles 1980). After years of discourse, these thinkers have concluded that "good teaching is good teaching" and what works well for adults should also work for children (and vice versa) (Knox 1986; Merriam and Caffarella 1999). However, these experts also acknowledge that adults bring more experience and self-determination to the educational setting and, when they elect to learn, will respond differently from children.

Moreover, unlike children, adults are fully independent actors, learners, and consumers. They choose whether to enroll in learning experiences, which sorts of subject matter to pursue, what sorts of learning environments they find most appealing, when they wish to learn, and with whom. They are motivated, or alienated, by such matters as intellectual curiosity and engagement, need for companionship, comfort, social prestige, utility, learning style, cost, and convenience. These considerations influence the voluntary decisions to seek out learning opportunities, to enroll in particular programs, and to remain once they are enrolled. In interaction with their experiences in the classroom (or other learning environment), these factors influence their cognitive and affective experiences, as well as the extent and nature of their satisfaction with the program.

Adults prefer learning environments that support the development of personal mastery and a sense of personal authority (Daloz 1999). These environments typically feature teachers who are respectful of the learner's experience and acknowledge the diversity and complexities of contemporary lives. Such teachers are committed to helping learners critically assess and reflect on assumptions, consider alternative ways of thinking, and find relevance or applicability in new knowledge (Brookfield 1987; Cranton 1994). They take the position that knowing is a "dialogical process" that stretches learners toward "inquiring into and responding openly to others' ideas" and "surfacing and questioning assumptions underlying beliefs, ideas, actions and positions" (Taylor, Marienau, and Fiddler 2000, 32). They develop curricula with the needs of the learner in mind and adapt the curriculum in response to learners' developmental and intellectual needs.

Rather than coddling adult learners, respected teachers interact authentically and encourage the evolution of the learner's own ideas (Belenky et al. 1986). They neither present themselves as the only expert in the room nor do they dominate by "depositing" information into learners' heads (Freire 1971). Ultimately, effective teachers help learners utilize multiple resources for meaning-making and ongoing inquiry

(Brookfield 1991). We wondered whether the motivations and experiences of the learners we interviewed and surveyed would correspond to this more generic picture of lifelong learners.

Principles of Adult Religious Education

In traditional Jewish circles, Jewish study is understood, fundamentally, as a religious activity. Yet curiously, few Jewish adult educators employ the term "religious education" to characterize what they teach. In fact, recent writings about adult Jewish learning (such as the winter 2001 issue of *Jewish Education News,* which was devoted to adult education) make no mention of a "religious education agenda" among either teachers or learners.

Mindful of this gap, we consulted key works in adult religious education to evaluate whether and how a two-year Jewish literacy program might be considered an experience of religious education. We concluded that "religious education" is a term more frequently connected to Christian circles than to Jewish ones. Indeed, Christian education typically is associated with the goal of helping people to "live their faith" (Deboy 1979) or with creating a context "in which faith can be awakened, supported and challenged" (Osmer 1992). Even when we delimited the discussion to the more focused experience of "text study," we concluded that the goal of adult learning for Christians typically centers more on the "finding and proclaiming of God" through "the Word" (Krych 1997) than on acquiring pluralistic perspectives on texts or discussing divergent views of religious practice. This language is not readily embraced in the world of Jewish education, where adult Jewish learning is generally conceptualized as a multidimensional process that can help learners to gain an appreciation of Jewish history, culture, literature, practice, and belief. Such a broad agenda is especially true for the Florence Melton Adult Mini-School, which defines itself as an experience of studying texts to acquire and deepen Jewish literacy, rather than as one of spiritual or religious growth.

A more expansive reading of Christian adult religious education literature, as well as recent works in the sociology of religion (Wuthnow 1994; Roof 1993), points to another reason that adults of all faiths may seek adult learning opportunities: the quest for increased understanding of religious teachings and the desire for greater personal meaning in life. In a thoughtful discussion of the purposes and scope of adult religious education, Leon McKenzie (1986) argues that all humans find the "notion of meaning" crucial to their existence: we all come into the world striving for "intelligibility and purpose," seeking a "perspective or framework for our being-in-the-world" (11). Accordingly, McKenzie suggests, the work of religious education is to help people develop such a framework:

> Religious education [is] a process that enables persons: 1) to acquire meaning, 2) to explore and expand meaning, and 3) to express meaning in a productive manner. The religious educator is a facilitator who helps people gain meaning, explore and expand the meaning structures they possess, and express their meanings effectively. (10–11)

Most important, religious education can help adults to critically reflect and evaluate religious commitments—and thus to develop a mature and reasoned set of beliefs rather than an adherence to "blind faith" (McKenzie 1986). Jewish adults who feel Jewishly illiterate may hunger for a religious education that can help them connect more thoughtfully, on their own terms, to Judaism and its lessons for modern life. In their curiosity, they bring to their learning a readiness to reflect upon, and conceivably change, their religious lives. Many such adults discover through texts the relevance of Judaism to their own experience and also encounter questions that they perceive as having religious significance.

Accordingly, although religious growth is not an expressed goal of the Mini-School, we assumed that the adults who attend might be seeking to make religious meaning for themselves. In our research, we paid particular heed to what the learners, teachers, directors, and program planners had to say about experiences of meaning-making and other aspects of religious development.

Teacher-Learner-Curriculum Interactions

As we explored how text-based, literacy-focused Jewish learning compared with other forms of religious education, we realized that we also needed to explore the process of curriculum development and its subsequent use and adaptation by the teachers. Jewish education of any sort is usually a complex mixture of history, knowledge, beliefs, competencies, and behaviors. At the same time that educators hope that their students will master the subject matter, most also hope to inspire or initiate their students into a deeper, more meaningful connection to being Jewish (Holtz 1999). Any Jewish educational institution and its teachers must grapple with how to balance these two goals. Teachers continually must make choices about the content and sequence of material, as well as choices about the aims and methods of instruction. At first, these choices are manifested in the content, values, and intentions conveyed by the curriculum. Then the curriculum is mediated, interpreted, and adapted by the faculty who teach it, based on their own knowledge, beliefs, interests, values, and personality.

Broadly speaking, curriculum is the translation of knowledge into learning experiences. It functions at three different levels. The *formal* curriculum is represented by the written materials, texts, lesson plans, and guidelines that express their designers' values and intentions. As Joseph Schwab warns us, however, readers and users of curriculum can only partially know the curriculum designer's values and intentions (1977). Thus, the formal curriculum per se is never taught. What is taught is the *enacted* curriculum; that is, the teacher's interpretation and, at times, modification of the curriculum developer's intentions and values. The enacted curriculum is influenced by the teacher's beliefs as well as by how the teachers and students interact when they try to make meaning out of the materials. Ultimately, it is the *received* curriculum that matters to the learners.

One view of teaching is that the enacted curriculum should be the same as, or as close as possible to, the formal curriculum. According to this view, the curriculum is essentially "teacher-proof." That is, detailed instructions are provided and teachers are cautioned to follow a structured sequence and avoid improvising or adding to the material (McCutcheon 1988). Obviously, such an approach limits teachers' creativity and interpretive capabilities. An alternative view of curriculum use is referred to as the "deliberationist" approach in which teachers constantly assess, adapt, and transform curriculum to fit their particular students in their particular setting (McCutcheon 1988).

Education scholars and practitioners have come to realize that a quality educational experience cannot just consist of the first model, in which the teacher follows the lockstep directions of a textbook or curriculum guide. Every educational experience is a product of the interaction between the content of the curriculum and its interpretation by the teachers and the learners (Gudmundsdottir 1991). A good curriculum will be flexible enough to allow teachers to adapt and transform it to fit the realities of their particular learners' needs (Shulman 1990). Likewise, to be effective, teachers must develop the skills to make these creative interpretations and reconstructions (Ben-Peretz 1990).

In studying the impact of the Mini-School on learners, we wanted to understand the relationship between the formal, enacted, and received curricula at a well-established institution of adult Jewish learning. We wanted to discern the nature of the educational philosophy that was embedded in the curriculum and how that philosophy was conveyed to the site directors and faculty who interact with the learners in the hundreds of Mini-School classrooms around the world. We also wanted to explore how the teachers understood and interpreted this philosophy through the instructional methods they choose and their interactions with their students. Toward the second objective, we looked to the literature on the "teaching-learning process," especially as described by Philip Jackson (1986).

According to Jackson, for centuries two different traditions have shaped thinking about teaching and learning. The "mimetic" tradition focuses on the transmission of knowledge from teacher to student through an imitative process. In this tradition, knowledge is " 'presented' to a learner, rather than 'discovered' by him or her" (117). Mimetic knowledge is largely procedural and additive. There is a presumption that the teacher possesses the knowledge or skills to direct the learner in the correct way of knowing or doing. Certainly, Jewish literacy requires mastery of a base of knowledge of Jewish ideas, history, and traditions that are most often conveyed through such a mimetic approach.

However, most Jewish educators hope their influence on their learners will go beyond the acquisition of knowledge and move toward personal growth and a stronger Jewish identity. They want their students to engage in Jewish life and Jewish practice on some level. This aim of education is translated into what Jackson called the "transformative" tradition. Here, teaching is about effecting a qualitative and fundamental change in the person being taught. Transformative teachers are less focused on imparting knowledge and more focused on helping learners develop their human potential. As Jackson wrote:

> The transformations aimed for within this tradition are typically conceived of as being more deeply integrated and ingrained within the psychological makeup of the student—and therefore perhaps more enduring—than are those sought within the mimetic . . . outlook. (121)

Generally speaking, the mimetic and transformative traditions are often seen as polar opposites; however, Jackson argued that the two systems should complement and actually function in close relationship to each other. Few educational experiences should rely exclusively on one or the other approach. Nonetheless, Jackson ruefully admitted that his idealized blending of the two traditions occurs rarely in practice and is most likely to be resolved at the individual classroom level by individual teachers, rather than through written guidelines or a policy directive.

We wanted to understand how these two teaching traditions played out in the adult Jewish learning classroom. How much of teachers' time is spent in frontal or mimetic transmission, and how much is spent in guiding more transformative deliberations? In other words, do the teachers consider their job to be more about imparting knowledge of Jewish texts, history, and culture, or do they consider their job to be more about helping learners create meaningful connections to Jewish life and practice? Specifically, we wondered how the teachers negotiated between teaching about Judaism and helping people become more connected or engaged in Jewish life. We wondered whether teachers advocated a particular approach to Jewish life and tradition. We wanted to know how the written materials and the teachers' adaptation of them addressed questions of faith and spiritual development, if at all. We suspected that the answers to these questions would paint a vivid portrait of the Florence Melton Adult Mini-School and also provide a rich context for understanding the core issues and challenges that any adult Jewish educational enterprise must consider as it plans programs and instruction for its learners.

Teaching for Jewish Identity

Another set of questions we posed concerned how the participation in a two-year program of learning affects the learners' sense of themselves as Jews. Does it change how they perceive their Jewish identity or how they tell the "Jewish story" of their lives? Identity is generally understood as one's self-definition, in terms of values, attitudes, interests, behaviors, and self-image. It is how a person defines one's sense of unity, coherence, and purpose (McAdams and de St. Aubin 1998). Identity also is understood to be a social construct, meaning that it cannot be defined outside of the society in which the individual resides. Studies of Jewish identity development have shown that how one defines oneself varies significantly throughout the life span as different priorities, life challenges, needs, and interests take root (Horowitz 2000; Cohen and Eisen 2000).

Jewish identity inextricably blends religious and ethnic components (Glazer 1972). However, as London and Chazan noted, "In most uses of the phrase 'Jewish identity,' the word 'Jewish' does not refer to any agreed-upon or universal set of Jewish beliefs or behaviors, and the phrase does not imply what Jewishness itself means" (1990, 13). Jewish identity education, according to London and Chazan, should promote greater involvement in and commitments to the Jewish community without directing people to one particular set of beliefs and behaviors that constitute the right way to be Jewish.

This approach toward Jewish education appears consonant with the Mini-School's principles of educating in a pluralistic, nonjudgmental environment. We wondered how an educational process that focuses on Jewish literacy would affect how participants would define themselves as Jews. How would it affect their sense of self, their connection to other Jews, their beliefs and their behaviors? Would a deeper understanding of and connection to Jewish texts and traditions inspire ongoing Jewish learning and continued active participation in the Jewish community?

Teaching for Perspective Transformation

A final related set of questions focused on ways in which the learners' experience changed their views and involvement in Judaism. Was their experience indeed one of transformative learning? To find out, we probed learners' background characteristics, such as what they brought with them and what impact their educational experiences had on their preexisting Jewish beliefs, commitments, and practices. We wanted to explore the quality and nature of the changes that took place as a result of their studies. To learn how these adult Jewish learners might change as a result of their learning experience, we needed to understand their points of Jewish and personal origin. With this understanding as a context and backdrop, we asked whether the changes we could discern amounted to what may be called truly "transformational."

A foundational principle underlying adult education is that adult learners (and not their teachers) are the decision makers in their own lives and learning. Effective adult educators work to create learning en-

vironments that empower learners to make more autonomous and informed choices in their lives (Mezirow 1991, 2000). At the same time,
adult educators are almost always involved in facilitating some process
of change, a process that the learners themselves drive. How the learners ultimately interpret the material and, more important, what they do
with it are up to each individual to decide. Jane Vella described this as a
process of educating toward transformation, which she defined as a
deeper self-awareness, "not grasping an external set of information,
knowledge, or skills, but changing into one's self, informed by the new
knowledge and skills" (Vella 2000, 10).

Perspective transformation is not just a matter of changing how one
sees the world, but is a translation of that perspective into how one lives
in the world (Mezirow 2000). It is effectively expressed in the narrative
of one's life story. Jack Mezirow, the originator of the theory of transformational learning, defined this as

> the process of becoming critically aware of how and why our
> assumptions have come to constrain the way we perceive, un-
> derstand, and feel about our world; changing these structures of
> habitual expectation to make a possible a more inclusive, dis-
> criminating, and integrating perspective; and finally, making
> choices or otherwise acting upon these new understandings.
> (Mezirow 1991, 167)

Mezirow argued that the key task in adulthood is the need to make
meaning out of experience. Adults learn when they increase their
knowledge or expand their skills. They are transformed when they focus
not just on *what* they know, but on *how* they know (Kegan 2000). Simply adding compatible ideas to an existing frame of reference, Mezirow
argued, is too narrow a definition of learning. Adults are transformed
only when they critically reflect on the assumptions, values, feelings,
and cultural paradigms that have shaped their worldview. This reflection, generally deepened through dialogue with others, results in a reframing and expansion of meanings. Ultimately, transformative learning
involves "some type of fundamental change in the learners' sense of
themselves, their worldviews, their understandings of their pasts, and
their orientation to the future" (Brooks 2000a, 140).

Transformational learning theory focuses on how people learn to
negotiate and act on their own purposes, meanings, and feelings rather

than those that have been unknowingly absorbed from others. We assumed that finding out how to make Judaism more meaningful in one's life requires going beyond the text to grapple with beliefs, feelings, and assumptions. In our study, we wanted to understand whether and how teachers created a productive tension in the classroom to help their "learners feel safe enough to risk examining assumptions and entertaining some alternate possibilities for ways to do and be" (Vogel 2000, 20).

Throughout our study, we kept asking whether and to what extent these notions of "transformational learning" applied to the adult Jewish education experience. We speculated that at some point during their learning experiences, students would encounter differences between current assumptions, beliefs, behaviors, and values, and what is being suggested or offered by the texts and conversation around them. This could precipitate a process of critical reflection that ultimately leads to a change in perspective or behavior (Brookfield 1995; Mezirow 1990).

In recent years, Mezirow's theory of transformative learning has been criticized for its overemphasis on rational, cognitive thought processes. Ann Brooks wrote, "Any story of transformational learning that grows out of cognitive learning theory is likely to be highly abstract, disengaged, impersonal, technological, and intellectualized" (2000b, 165). What she proposed in contrast is described as a perspective that looks at transformational learning as a narrative process of recasting one's life story. Another alternative to an exclusively rational understanding of transformation can be seen in Boyd and Myers's work (1988), which focuses on how the emotional and spiritual dimensions of learning contribute to transformation. As reported by Dirkx, Boyd and his colleagues have helped broaden the definition of what is transformed: "What matters most in learning is what matters to the deep ground of our being, the psyche or soul" (Dirkx 2000, 2). Rather than an intellectual process of the mind, transformation is seen as a process of the heart, where images "are thought to represent powerful motifs that represent, at an unconscious level, deep-seated emotional or spiritual issues or concerns" (ibid.). Interactions with others or with texts may activate these images. Thus, it appears that "both the rational and the affective play a role in transformative learning" (Imel 1998, 3). We wondered whether the literacy-focused, pluralistic approach advocated by the Mini-School would trigger solely such intellectual and rational change, or whether it could have a more varied impact depending on the personality and motivations of the learners and how they defined themselves Jewishly.

The Study: Personal Interviews, Observation, and a Survey

Late in 1999, a research team assembled to study the impacts on the people who participate in a two-year experience of a systematic study of Judaism in an adult learning setting. This team consisted of four scholars with complementary, but varying expertise: Lisa D. Grant of Hebrew Union College, New York, a specialist in adult Jewish learning; Diane Tickton Schuster, a developmental psychologist who now directs the Institute for Teaching Jewish Adults at Hebrew Union College, Los Angeles; Meredith Woocher, director of the Jewish Educator Recruitment/Retention Initiative (JERRI) at the Covenant Foundation; and Steven M. Cohen of the Hebrew University of Jerusalem, sociologist of the American Jewish community. We worked collaboratively throughout the process, in selecting research methods and developing research protocols, in analyzing data and formulating theories, and through our active advising and editing of one another's individual contributions.

Our analysis drew upon qualitative and quantitative research methods. We conducted formal and informal interviews in person and by telephone, undertook document analysis, performed ethnographic observations of two classrooms over a full year of study, and fielded a self-administered sample survey of graduating students.

We interviewed current and past students, as well as people who did not complete the two years from three Mini-School sites in the United States. The three sites represented some communal, institutional, and geographic diversity: one was located in the Mid-Atlantic region; another was in the Midwest; and a third was in the South. The local Jewish population of these communities ranged from approximately fifty thousand to more than twice that number. In their composition, they are divergent as well. One site has a strong Reform predominance, another is strongly Conservative and Orthodox, and the third has a very low congregational affiliation rate. Institutionally, one Mini-School is sponsored by a central agency of Jewish education, another by a congregation, and a third by the local Jewish Federation. In addition, two of the sites enrolled over a hundred students and sponsored a "graduate" program for alumni; the third site managed to attract only thirty students at the time.

At the same time, all three sites are well established and are characterized by the lead professionals as relatively "successful," with stable enrollments, talented site directors, and veteran faculty. In one instance, the site director selected the interviewees. She remarked that she was trying to find "interesting people who would have a lot to say about the program." Although the interviewees were overwhelmingly positive about the program, they freely shared complaints and concerns as well. The interviews each took forty-five minutes to an hour, and were all quite positive. People were friendly, cooperative, and eager to talk.

As a result of these selection procedures, our results from the qualitative interviews may overstate, to an unknown extent, the extent of impact, although we have no reason to think that they fail to represent the nature of the impact. Indeed, the close correspondence among all our sources of evidence—interviews with learners, staff interviews, observation, and survey—augmented our confidence in our results and commensurately diminished our concerns over bias in site selection.

Beyond the learners, we also interviewed teachers from nine sites and eleven site directors. In addition, we spoke at length with Jonathan Mirvis, international director of the Florence Melton Adult Mini-School Institute; Betsy Katz, North American director; David Harbater, chief curriculum writer; and Florence Melton, now in her nineties, who remains actively involved in the Mini-School. Meredith Woocher undertook ethnographic observations of a class at one site, attending both hours of study for a full year. Lisa Grant conducted interviews with staff in the North American offices and gathered a wide variety of documents, including internal reports, minutes of professional development programs, newsletters, promotional materials, graduating students' testimonials, the operating manual for site directors, and the faculty handbook. She also participated in the February 2001 annual meeting of the Mini-School site directors.

We complemented these qualitative sources with a comprehensive survey of 367 students from the graduating class of 2001, drawn from seventeen sites throughout North America. The questionnaire assessed satisfaction and impact and collected detailed information on socio-demographic characteristics, Jewish education, and socialization, as well as previous and current patterns of Jewish involvement (see Appendix). Site directors managed the distribution and transmittal of the questionnaires. Distribution ranged from asking graduating students to complete the questionnaires before or after class to sending the students home with the questionnaires for their voluntary completion. Cooperation rates by site varied widely.

Overview

This book explores the impact of adult Jewish learning on individual Jewish learners. Focusing first on the experiences of one established adult Jewish learning program, it also moves to a larger discussion about adult Jewish literacy and adult Jewish growth.

We begin in chapter 1 by introducing the Mini-School students— who they are as individuals and as Jews. We discuss the learners, why they enroll, and why they may not enroll. Chapter 2 examines the impacts of the experience on the learners in terms of how they make meaning in Jewish study, their sense of connection to Judaism, and their religious practice. Chapters 3 and 4 provide ethnographic perspectives on an adult Jewish learning classroom over an extended period. Chapter 3 concentrates on the various processes and approaches that learners take in connecting to and making meaning from Jewish tradition. Chapter 4 explores the social dynamics in the classroom that lead to the development of community. Chapter 5 shifts focus to explore how educational philosophy shapes the values, goals, organizational structure, and curriculum. In chapter 6, we analyze how this espoused philosophy is interpreted and enacted by the teachers who function as cultural interpreters in facilitating access to Jewish texts and tradition and helping learners to make meaning from their Jewish study. Chapter 7 examines the essential role that site directors play in creating a positive, supportive, and caring culture for learning.

Finally, chapter 8 returns to consider the initial theoretical questions that we posed about the learning processes and impacts, and explores their implications for adult Jewish learning programs and contemporary American Jewish society.

CHAPTER ONE
Adult Jewish Learners:
Growing as Jews

E very year, almost three thousand new adult Jewish learners begin their studies at sixty-five Florence Melton Adult Mini-Schools. They are by no means a random cross-section of North American Jewry. As a group, they have a number of characteristics in common. At the same time, their differences tend to occupy a range of distinctive points across the Jewish and socio-demographic map.

Taken together, Kim Sherwood, Selma Jones, Daniel Shaber, and Leslie Irwin[1] represent some of the important commonalities and more interesting elements of diversity among Mini-School learners. Their experiences help us to understand the sorts of Jewish adults who seek out intensive adult Jewish learning and the kinds of students the Mini-School site directors no doubt seek to recruit. The backgrounds, timing of enrollment, and learning priorities differ for each of these four, but all of them came hoping to deepen their Jewish knowledge. For them—and for others we will meet later—the pursuit of Jewish literacy may be triggered by a variety of motivations: a search for Jewish identity, a desire to rekindle neglected Jewish connections, a desire for Jewish authenticity, a change in roles in the Jewish community, or any number of other reasons associated with the need to look for meaning in adult Jewish life.

Four Portraits

Kim Sherwood: *Developing a Mature Jewish Identity.* A thirty-eight-year-old mother of two children who attend Jewish day schools, Kim Sherwood signed up for the Mini-School after receiving a flyer in the

---

[1]All names are fictitious.

mail. She needed little convincing to enroll. She told us that day school parents in her midwestern community typically think of adult Jewish learning as a natural extension of their commitment to raising informed Jewish children. In Kim's view, many adults feel incomplete about their own Jewish education and play "catch-up" when their own children begin to become Jewishly literate. When describing her own motivation for studying at the Mini-School, Kim noted: "I wanted my children in a day school because I knew what I didn't get as a child, and I know how important it is to have that kind of base. I needed to push forward and do some learning. I was twelve steps behind where I wanted to be."

When she was growing up in her family's Conservative synagogue, Kim's Jewish education was disrupted when religious school teachers made her feel that, because she was a girl, she was a nonentity. Kim noted that the synagogue "didn't have bat mitzvahs," and she recalled feeling continually frustrated because "I kept asking questions and not getting answers." Years later, when she enrolled in the Mini-School, Kim was intimidated by her lack of knowledge: "It was so over my head. I would walk into class and see if I could just pull out one piece of information that made sense to me. It was overwhelming. I felt like the dumb kid on the block—the silent one in the class."

Selma Jones: Seeking Meaning, Seeking Jewish Meaning. A lifelong learner who has always asked "big questions," Selma Jones anticipated retirement as the right time to study religion in general, and Judaism in particular. When she left the workforce in the mid-1990s at age sixty, Selma, an energetic and purposeful woman, immediately took a Talmud class to explore "what other people thought about the issues of goodness—how to make decisions based on ethical principles." Later, after moving to a new city with her second husband, she shopped for Jewish learning opportunities: "I went to all the synagogues I could see," she recalled. "I drove up and just went in: 'What are you? Are you Reform? Do you have a brochure? What kinds of educational programs do you have?'" When she found out about the Mini-School, she was thrilled: "I said, 'This is for me. This is exactly what I need.'"

As a secular Jew who was raised in "basically a nonreligious Reform household," Selma had long wondered about "God and goodness" and had sought learning opportunities that could help her understand human behavior and choices. She was attracted to the Mini-School because of its program of "formalized, rigorous study." She told us that, like many of her classmates, she is "a book person" who would, if she could, "go to school all the time."

Daniel Shaber: Rekindling Dormant Connections. Although many adults who study at the Melton Mini-Schools are relative newcomers to serious Jewish learning, some are like Daniel Shaber, a fifty-five-year-old university professor who grew up in an Orthodox family, attended a Hebrew high school, mastered the basics of text study early in life, and then left the world of Jewish learning to enter the more secular environment of higher education. Although Daniel never "fled" from his Judaism—indeed, as a choral singer he joined Jewish choirs regularly during early adulthood—he put aside any interest in Jewish learning for many years. He enrolled in the Mini-School several years after his first child's bar mitzvah—an occasion that prompted a significant shift in Daniel's attitude toward his own Jewish growth.

> When Jesse, my older son, became bar mitzvah, the hazan at the synagogue started a program of kids teaching other kids how to read Torah and how to do haftorah. So basically, my wife and I learned how to chant haftorah and read Torah from our kids. Both of us read Torah during the year now, as a result of our kids' Hebrew education.

For Daniel, relearning Hebrew and becoming involved as a Torah reader started him on a course of active Jewish study. A self-described "curious type," Daniel found that once he started taking adult education classes, he wanted to reclaim and revitalize his Jewish knowledge. He realized that he had unanswered questions left over from his early Jewish schooling—questions that he was now eager to answer from an adult perspective. An especially attractive aspect of the Mini-School was its roster of teachers from diverse sectors of the Jewish community. Coming from an Orthodox background, he was eager to learn about Judaism from more than one perspective. Recalling his decision to enroll, Daniel mused, "I knew it was going to be the first opportunity for me in a long time to study text as opposed to listening to somebody lecture on some issue."

Leslie Irwin: From Community Leadership to Jewish Learning. In some instances, adults seek out Jewish study because they did not have the opportunity as children to acquire Jewish literacy or to develop a well-informed understanding of the connection between Judaism and one's life choices. Such was the experience of Leslie Irwin, the incoming president of a Jewish Community Center (JCC) in Florida. Growing up in the 1970s, Leslie followed her parents' model of being "strictly once-a-year Jews" who attended synagogue only on the High Holidays. Her family's minimal Jewish observance meant that even though the family lit candles and exchanged gifts at Hanukkah, they also welcomed "visits from Santa Claus" on Christmas. When Leslie and her Jewish boyfriend decided to get married, they chose to have the ceremony at a Conservative temple "because of the catering." The rabbi who performed the wedding ceremony urged Leslie to make a commitment to give her children a meaningful Jewish education. She later recalled that when she agreed to do so, she realized that she, too, would need to become solidly educated as a Jew. Nevertheless, early in her marriage, Leslie persisted in her highly assimilated lifestyle, annually hanging a picture of Santa on her front door.

After becoming a parent, Leslie realized that she was giving her children the same mixed messages that she had received in childhood. Recalling the rabbi's message, she resolved to involve herself and her children in the Jewish community. She enrolled her daughter in a Jewish preschool and was delighted when almost immediately she was drafted for a leadership role in the school's parent-teacher organization. However, she quickly discovered that her lack of Jewish education put her at risk for embarrassment: "The PTO president told me I was going to be the *tzedakah* chairperson. I came home totally confused. I didn't know what *tzedakah* was. I didn't even know how to spell it!" Later, when she joined various Jewish organizations, she realized that, to be a good leader, she needed to understand Jewish tradition and values on a more sophisticated level. Although her schedule was very full, she determined to make learning a priority in her busy life:

> For five years, I kept saying, "I'm going to do it when I have time." Finally, I decided that I'm just going to make the time. I'm going to do it, and everyone else is going to have to work around me! Now everyone knows that Wednesday mornings

are my time for Jewish study—don't bother me, don't make a meeting.

Commonalities and Differences

Looking across the lives and experiences of Kim, Selma, Daniel, and Leslie, we are struck by what they have in common: a high level of engagement in Jewish life, a willingness to take risks as learners, a desire to find meaning in Jewish texts, and an excitement about "catching up" and becoming more connected to Judaism and Jewish tradition through systematic study. Indeed, as we shall see in the ensuing discussion, most Mini-School learners come to the program after a sustained period of engagement in Jewish communal or intellectual activity. For the majority, this is not their first experience of serious Jewish learning. Most bring a desire to put their Jewish experiences in context and to understand how what they know from the past fits into a larger Jewish picture.

Although they share a thirst for Jewish learning, these learners also are highly individualistic: they all come to the program with a particular set of questions, with different learning or social barriers to overcome, and with anxieties or concerns that stem from their diverse backgrounds. For some (like Kim), developing an authentic Jewish identity is a crucial starting point for gaining a sense of self as a Jewish parent—indeed, as an authentic Jew. For others (like Leslie), becoming Jewishly educated is at the heart of achieving effectiveness as a Jewish communal leader. For people like Selma and Daniel, the "need to know" drives the desire to ask probing questions and to apply what is being learned to real-life situations. For some (like Selma), understanding the relevance of the mitzvot ranks highest among all topics studied; for others (like Daniel), learning about Judaism from multiple vantage points matters most of all.

As we shall see, the stories of these four learners capture many of the common themes and some of the diversity that characterizes the adult Jewish learners in our study. Other students—embodied in the range of the people we interviewed (see Table 1)—give further texture to our discussion of this population.

Name	Age	Jewish Upbringing/ Education	Occupation	Mini-School Status
		Table 1: Mini-School Learners Interviewed		
Judy Abramson	60–69	Secular; no Jewish education	Psychologist	Current
Wanda Benzion	40–49	Conservative; confirmation	Speech pathologist	Graduate
Margaret Berner	40–49	Convert; raised Catholic	Jewish educator	Graduate
Sharon Gottlieb	60–69	Conservative; no Jewish education	Retired teacher	Current
Shelly Herman	40–49	Reform; confirmation	Retired teacher	Current
Leslie Irwin	30–39	Secular; no Jewish education	Former nurse; Jewish Community Center president	Current
Edna Jacobson	60–69	Secular; no Jewish education	Retired	Current
Selma Jones	60–69	Reform; Hebrew school; confirmation	Retired businesswoman	Current
Pamela Kaplan	50–59	Reform	Jewish educator	Current
Debby Kramer	30–39	Secular; no Jewish education	College instructor	Dropout
Mindy Lubin	50–59	Reform	Foundation administrator	Current
Roger Luria	50–59	Conservative; bar mitzvah	Physician	Graduate
Cindy Meyerson	40–49	Conservative; bat mitzvah	Former health-care administrator; home-maker	Current
Marina Perlman	60–69	Orthodox; Hebrew school; confirmation	Retired Jewish social-service worker	Current
Anna Rosenberg	60–69	Secular; no Jewish education	Office manager	Graduate
Linda Rosenblum	30–39	Reform	Former lawyer; home-maker	Dropout
Daniel Shaber	50–59	Orthodox; bar mitzvah; Hebrew high school	College professor	Graduate
Kim Sherwood	30–39	Conservative; supple-mental school	Former small-business owner; now working for Jewish Federation agency	Graduate
Howard Silverman	30–39	Reform; bar mitzvah	Lawyer	Dropout
Seth Steinberger	40–49	Conservative; bar mitzvah, confirmation	Physician	Graduate
Natalie Tecotzky	60–69	Conservative; supple-mental school	Community volunteer; Jewish Federation president	Current
Dana Wasserman	40–49	Reform; summer camp	Human-services trainer	Dropout
Bill Wimmer	70+	Orthodox; bar mitzvah	Retired accountant	Graduate

Who Are the Learners?

Who makes a commitment to a two-year program of adult Jewish learning? The answers to this question may not be as simple as they may initially appear.

From the character and mission of the Mini-School, one might readily make educated guesses as to the character and motivation of its learners. We may take, for example, the fundamental observation that the Mini-School is about Jewish text learning—and thus assume that the program would appeal most to those who traditionally had access to serious text learning: Orthodox men. As logical as this reasoning may appear, it is blatantly faulty. The Mini-School student body comprises hardly any Orthodox learners and is predominantly female. Moreover, the Mini-School experience is not just about traditional text learning. More broadly, it is about Jewish learning and Jewish life. As such, one might expect it to appeal to women more than men. As is found in both Jewish and Christian settings in America, women are notably more active in all sorts of religious activities, be they conducted individually, with family, at the house of worship, or elsewhere in the community (DellaPergola 2001). Accordingly, a disproportionate enrollment of women in the Mini-School is consistent with other types of religion-based programs today.

We might also expect that the program would attract people who are seeking a quick overview of Judaism—the kinds of learners who show up at lectures or short-term "Introduction to Judaism" courses. However, the Mini-School requires learners to participate in systematic and ongoing study of Jewish texts. The Mini-School says, in effect, "You give us just 120 hours (two hours a week for thirty weeks for two years), and we'll give you entry to the entire world of Jewish learning." The introductory nature of this program might suggest a learning constituency of total novices (either those who are newcomers to Jewish learning or those who are newcomers to Jewish life), but as the four vignettes that opened this chapter strikingly demonstrate, these learners are not entirely, or even predominantly, "first timers" in Jewish organizations or classrooms.

Because the Mini-School is a fairly low-cost way[2] to become educated and engage in learning in the company of other Jews, we might

2Tuition varies from site to site but is generally around $500 per year.

expect the program to attract learners across the entire socioeconomic spectrum. Or, because of its close ties to organized Jewish life (Jewish Community Centers, Jewish Federations, synagogues, and so on), we might anticipate a socially upscale clientele. After all, community participation generally rises with affluence, and this observation is particularly applicable to Jewish life. Moreover, adult study generally appeals more to the more highly educated. These findings suggest another reason to anticipate a socially upscale constituency of learners, an expectation that our research indeed does bear out.

In short, different ways of thinking about who attends the Florence Melton Adult Mini-School suggest alternative and competing expectations regarding gender, Jewish engagement, social class, education, and presumably other dimensions as well. The characteristics of the learners tell us inferentially why these Jewish adults enroll and the sorts of expectations, resources, and constraints that they bring to the educational experience. The socio-demographic characteristics of the learners, their current Jewish identity profiles, and their Jewish backgrounds and upbringing combine to paint a detailed portrait of these students.

More Women than Men: A Matter of Time and Timing

Our survey revealed that Mini-School women vastly outnumber men by a margin of four to one (80% versus 20%). The reasons for this discrepancy are instructive.

One explanation entails, quite simply, the matter of flexible time and the closely related issue of orientation to work, career, and profession. Just 37% of students are employed full-time. The rest are almost evenly divided among retirees, part-time employed, and full-time homemakers. The Mini-School demands a weekly commitment of an evening, a morning, or an afternoon (albeit just two hours of class time), spanning a two-year period. Women, more than men, adopt a stance toward their work outside the home that allows time for such sorts of ongoing commitments, be it for learning, volunteering, community activities, or personal pursuits. They are more likely to work part-time rather than full-time, more likely to move in and out of the labor force in ways compatible with the changing needs of their families, and more likely to limit their workweek, even if full-time, to forty hours (Hartman and Hartman 1996). Few women work fifty or sixty hours per week, hours often worked by professionals and entrepreneurs, who make up a large segment of American Jewish men. Noteworthy is that of the male students, 61% are full-time employed, as opposed to just half as many (31%) of the women.

In addition, as noted, American women are more active in religious life of all sorts. Accordingly, American Jewish women, particularly those outside of Orthodoxy, are more active in almost all areas of Jewish life (DellaPergola 2001; Halbertal and Cohen 2002). The few exceptions include serving in governance capacities, taking leadership in liturgical functions, and size of philanthropic gifts. Men, more than women, sit on boards and committees, assume roles in worship services, and report larger donations to charitable causes. Otherwise, in Jewish organizational life, volunteering, child-rearing functions, and holiday celebrations (with the sole exception of erecting—but not decorating—the sukkah), women are more active than men (Cohen and Eisen 2000). Insofar as women participate more in most Jewish arenas, we may also expect them to commit more readily to a long-term program of adult Jewish learning.

One explanation sometimes offered for higher rates of female participation in religious life directly bears on their high participation in a program like the Mini-School. Some researchers (e.g., Jordan et al. 1991; Josselson 1987) note that women make a relatively greater investment than men in interpersonal relationships with family and friends; as such, women attach greater significance to their roles as parent, wife, grandparent, friend, and community member than men do.

Indeed, several comments we heard from the Mini-School women refer to these roles. Some were drawn to adult Jewish learning as a result of their children (or grandchildren) enrolling in Jewish day schools or other educational programs, and some spoke of the reverse effect— how their own Jewish learning affected their thinking about their children's Jewish education. The evidence, while circumstantial, certainly points to the role of children in provoking women's interest in Jewish education.

Debby, a college instructor who was raised with minimal exposure to Jewish education, said that from the "beginning of motherhood," her children's Jewish education was a top priority and led her to pursue both Jewish family education and adult learning activities:

> I believe in learning with my kids. I think they'll get a stronger message if I'm learning with them or if I'm there with them than if I'm dropping them off at the school. It's a great opportunity for me to learn at the same time, when I'm learning with them.

Linda, a lawyer-turned-homemaker, claimed that participating in the Mini-School had raised her consciousness about the importance of her young daughter receiving a solid Jewish education:

> Sara is at Schechter[3] in kindergarten. It grew out of Melton. My daughter knew that we did Friday nights at home and that we had certain things that were called Jewish, but it wasn't until this year that she's actually understood what being Jewish really means. But she's a very spiritual little girl and has always asked me lots of questions: Why are we here? Who made us? Where are we going? I felt Schechter would be wonderful for that.

One other consideration, a feeling of being culturally deprived in Jewish terms, may help explain women's greater participation in adult Jewish learning generally (Cohen and Davidson 2001). Historically, women significantly trail men in the Jewish population in terms of childhood Jewish schooling. Among the learners in our study, more than twice as many (born-Jewish) women as men reported having had no Jewish schooling in their youth (26% versus 12%). Just 3% of the survey respondents (male and female) received a day school education in their youth. Almost half reported Sunday school or other one-day-a-week program as their main form of childhood Jewish education. (Such forms of Jewish schooling constitute the least intensive option for Jewish schooling.) Despite their limited Jewish literacy, Mini-School learners tend to be affiliated with synagogues and exhibit other signs of significant Jewish involvement. Accordingly, many experience a discrepancy between their active Jewish involvement as adults and their poor educational background as children.

Many students seem to be motivated by a drive for Jewish education to compensate for weak educational backgrounds. Edna, a widow in her mid-seventies, reflected this sentiment:

> I had no Jewish education growing up. My father was an immigrant from Poland whose only education was heder. My mother was born in the United States and had a high school education.

---

[3]Solomon Schechter Day School, a network of Jewish day schools affiliated with the Conservative movement of Judaism.

We were a Jewish home in tradition only. I never went to religious school; we celebrated holidays in the most perfunctory way.

Similarly, Sharon, a former teacher in her sixties, recalled:

My brothers were bar mitzvah and that was the end of that. I had no Jewish education whatsoever. I grew up in New York, went to a Conservative synagogue, went to bar mitzvahs, but I never went to Hebrew school or Sunday school. I was the youngest, so I guess they figured they just wouldn't send me.

In like fashion, Debby, the college instructor quoted above, noted:

I basically have very little Jewish background. I have two parents who were Jewish, but we had virtually no Judaism in our home. My father was an agnostic. My mother was frustrated about that. She wanted to save her marriage, so she didn't practice Judaism. Occasionally, she'd sneak us to a temple, but that was about it.

Adults of All Ages: Change, Transitions, and Triggers for New Learning

Adult Jewish education professionals commonly report that their audiences consist heavily of middle-aged and older individuals, largely empty nesters of various sorts. The departure of children from the home provides adults with the inclination to seek out other sorts of activities to engage their interests and relieves them of child-rearing responsibilities that once occupied much of their time. Indeed, nationally, personal enrichment programs generally draw upon individuals largely over age fifty (U.S. Department of Education 2002).

Against this backdrop, the Mini-School clientele appears relatively youthful. As many as 41% of the survey respondents are under the age of fifty, and the median age is about fifty-three. Adults in their fifties and sixties, with larger disposable incomes, constitute a resource backbone for any adult education program. But the presence at the Mini-School of individuals under fifty represents something of a recruiting achievement in expanding the generational reach beyond the traditional middle-aged market.

In part, this age distribution reflects the appeal of the Mini-School to parents of day school children and to parents who are seeking to enhance their ability to serve as educated and educating Jewish parents. Indeed, parents of school-age children are a primary target for the Mini-School. As an early planning document (Melton Centre for Jewish Education 1985), stated:

> Over 80% of the Jewish adults with school-age children are affiliated with Jewish institutions and are good candidates for a relevant Jewish education program. We believe that the time is ripe to organize these parents and attract those adults outside of the institutional frameworks. (2)

Our interviews asked about the timing of the learners' decision to embark on a systematic program of adult Jewish learning. We speculated that these learners would resemble other groups of adults who are changing and growing at midlife and turn to new learning as part of their developmental journey. Studies of adult development show that, rather than retreating from new challenges, contemporary adults anticipate the middle and later adult years as times for forging new identities, exploring new interests, and finding new sources of meaning (Sheehy 1996; Tennant and Pogson 1995). People recognize that because adulthood is not a redundant stretch of "sameness," they likely will take on and give up a variety of roles over time and will have to learn how to adapt to changing lives in changing times. When confronted with change, people typically experience a sense of disorientation as they try to reconcile old belief systems or assumptions with new outlooks or behaviors (Bateson 1989; Bridges 1980; Schlossberg, Waters, and Goodman 1995). Psychologically, they strive to reduce the tension of dissonance between the old and the new. For some people, the adaptive response is to "make new meaning" of past experiences. Others adapt by seeking new experiences that may provide a new sense of purpose or self-worth (Knox 1977; Aslanian and Brickell 1980).

Sudden insights or events may provoke a search for new opportunities to learn or explore parts of oneself, be it through self-help groups, therapy, adult education, or, as in our case, adult Jewish learning. Some life transitions are anticipated, such as relocation when young adult children leave home, or retirement. Some are unanticipated, such as sudden changes in health or downturns in an economic sector that precipitate layoffs. Still others may be "non-events," such as never finding a partner or a promotion that fails to occur. Regardless of the cause of a transition, when people try to adjust to changed circumstances or ways of thinking, they need to engage in a cognitive process of "reframing"— understanding phenomena in new ways (Schlossberg 1999; Watzlawick, Weakland, and Fisch 1974). Diverse trigger events will impel them to seek new definitions of themselves and their experiences. At such times, many turn to educational organizations for support (Aslanian and Brickell 1980; Schlossberg 1999).

Our interviews asked about life changes or significant experiences that might have prompted enrollment. Consistent with the literature on adult growth, a number of people indicated that this experience of in-depth Jewish study offered important support at the time of a major life change. For example, Linda, a former lawyer, described how the Mini-School had helped her adjust when she moved to a new community just prior to having her first child:

> We moved here right after my husband had finished his Ph.D. and I was a few months pregnant. I didn't know anyone in town. I decided that I would stay home with my daughter for a little while. After about a year, I started thinking that I needed to have contact with some part of my new community because I was pretty isolated. I knew it was a big Jewish community, but it was a very scary thought to me to figure out where to jump in. We started exploring places where we might become members. Someone told me that I had to check out Melton. I was really lost as to what my identity was going be. Are we going to be Conservative Jewish? Then I figured out that there was a whole lot of learning that still needed to take place for me to decide.

Like many students, Linda had grown up without much formal Jewish education or Jewish communal experience. She perceived the Mini-School as a supportive organization that could ground her Jewishly as she found her way through a challenging transitional time.

For Debby, the college instructor we met earlier, this Jewish educational experience also provided a secure base at a time of major transition. When she was a child and young adult, Debby's only Jewish role models had been her grandparents, with whom she would occasionally go to shul. Otherwise, she stated, she had "very little Jewish background." After she married a Jewish man, Debby decided that she wanted to "raise my kids Jewish" and enrolled her children in a synagogue preschool; she also became an active volunteer at a Jewish food bank. Nonetheless, in her late thirties, Debby believed that she lacked an authentic Jewish identity. And, as she described it, a major shift in priorities was precipitated by the death of her grandmother. Debby told us that with this loss, she felt an urgency to understand herself and her heritage from a Jewish perspective. For her, the Mini-School became the setting in which to begin to work through her transition to a more meaningful Jewish identity. "I felt grounded by the learning. It was the launching pad to help me figure out where I wanted to go."

Enrolling in the Mini-School during the transition to retirement was a significant experience for several of our older interviewees. Bill, an accountant, said that he had always been interested in learning, but had been too busy with his professional life to do anything but work. When he left his CPA practice, his reaction was, "Well, now is the time to further my education." Bill told us that he and his wife started the Mini-School at that time and, in the eight years since his retirement, they have made Jewish learning the framing activity of their week. His daughters also graduated from the Mini-School, and one of them now joins Bill and his wife at a twice-weekly Talmud class.

Marina, who had a long career in Jewish social-services work, reported that upon retirement she found herself "looking for something more in my life, something to hang my hat on, to give me greater meaning—something a little more satisfying in my life." Marina indicated that initially she had been reluctant to make the two-year commitment. However, once she began, she found that the classes provided her with a structure, as well as a vitally important affiliation in her new life.

In short, trigger events and life transitions can and do occur at every age. The wide age spectrum of the Mini-School student body in part reflects the varied changes in life that motivate younger as well as older Jewish adults to seek new education at times of change.

Married, with Children: Family Members as Triggers and Recruiters

Robert Putnam (2000) observes that Americans who are married and those with children are "much more likely to be involved in religious activities, including church membership, church attendance, and church-related social activities" (278). In like fashion, Jews participate more actively in synagogues, JCCs, and a wide variety of Jewish activities if they are married and if they have, or have had, children living at home (Cohen 1988; Sklare and Greenblum 1979). Parenthood is also associated with increases in ritual practice, organizational belonging, charitable donations, and more. Apparently, these processes operate in terms of participation in Jewish learning as well.

Our survey found that more than three-quarters (77%) of the Mini-School learners are married, and another 3% are "living with someone." These learners are more often married than the American Jewish population at large, and more have children living at home. Our interviews suggested that the presence of family members lends incentive and meaning to Jewish learning. Several of our interviewees spoke about enrolling in the program with a spouse or other family member. For example, Pamela, a public school teacher turned religious-school principal, studied with her husband. She started learning Hebrew as a result of the Mini-School and added, "There are so many positive things that have come out of this for us." Seth, a doctor in his early forties whose previous Jewish education ended with bar mitzvah, said that he heard about the Mini-School from family members—his parents and aunt and uncle were all graduates. Seth reported that when his fiancée, Helen, enrolled in the school after Seth's first year, he decided to repeat the first year, to share the learning experience with her. (Indeed, in many instances, men enroll upon the encouragement of their wives who have taken the courses earlier, or who have decided to enroll and ask their husbands to accompany them.) In other instances, a parent or other relative will enroll simultaneously. Debby, who enrolled with her mother-in-law, enthused: "It was a phenomenal experience for both of us."

Most Not Employed Full-Time: Making Time for Learning

As noted earlier, just 37% of the surveyed students are employed full-time. Clearly, full-time employment—to say nothing of the full-time-plus employment that characterizes the lives of many hardworking, ambitious, and successful Jewish professionals, managers, and entrepreneurs—impedes enrollment in a long-term program of adult Jewish learning. Regular attendance of two hours per week, week in and week out, is essential to the successful operation of the Mini-School. However, this routine requires a commitment that may prove onerous for those with demanding work schedules. Howard, an attorney, told us that he had had to drop out of the program during the second year because of a scheduling conflict: "It was impossible for me to get to class. I had a client who could only meet with me at that time (Wednesday mornings). My leaving the program was job-related, not due to dissatisfaction." Howard's remarks explain why those with full-time, if not overtime, employment are relatively underrepresented in the Mini-Schools.

Highly Educated and Affluent: Attracting an Upscale Clientele

American Jews constitute the most highly educated major ethnic group in the United States, and probably the most highly educated Jewish group in the world. Notably, Mini-School learners report even higher educational levels than American Jewry overall, with as many as 88% having earned a college degree. Perhaps even more impressive, almost half have earned a graduate degree, and fully 15% report some kind of doctoral degree. Interestingly, the learners' spouses (meaning, here, mostly husbands) are even more highly educated. Among the spouses, 56% have a graduate degree, and nearly a third have earned a doctoral degree. These results are truly noteworthy and lead us to ask what might explain these high levels of education. Alternatively, what do the high levels of educational attainment tell us about Mini-School learners? Several features of the Mini-School attract learners with particularly high levels of education. Quite obviously, the school is designed for Jewish adults, and Jews in North America are very highly educated. But more than that obvious fact, our study showed that Mini-School learners are not a simple cross-section of all Jews. Rather, they are institutionally affiliated and involved Jews, and affiliation of all sorts is associated with higher levels of educational attainment (Cohen 1983). Moreover, these are people who are patronizing a cultural program outside the home, an activity associated with education and affluence. Not least, Mini-School learning focuses on text study and intelligent verbal discourse. Predictably, better-educated people feel drawn to such activities and feel more confident about participating in such a setting. Putting all these considerations together, it is no surprise that Mini-School learners are so well educated.

Consistent with their very high levels of education, Mini-School students also reported high levels of income, with most household earnings exceeding $100,000 annually. The median income can be pegged at $115,000, and almost a quarter report that their homes bring in $200,000 or more per year.

The high income levels can be explained in part by the high educational achievement levels, but they also reflect the Mini-School's tendency, especially when becoming established in particular localities, to draw upon the organized Jewish communal leadership for the core of their first classes. In many communities, Federation leadership in particular plays a major role in launching the Mini-School and thereby exerting a collateral effect on the culture and expectations for Jewish learning. At the same time, Federation leaders as a group are far more affluent than American Jews in the aggregate (Cohen and Bubis 1998).

Who Are the Learners as Jews?

Our survey revealed that Mini-School students are highly affiliated Jews. Their Jewish activity levels substantially exceed the American Jewish average and even exceed those of Jews affiliated with congregations. As many as 87% claimed to have been synagogue members before they enrolled. This figure is more than double the national average of 38% in the 2000/01 National Jewish Population Study (NJPS).[4]

That adult Jewish learners should emerge so readily from the congregations is actually quite understandable. Congregational membership is, in all likelihood, the best single dichotomous (yes-no) predictor of Jewish involvement. No other single question on social science surveys so cleanly divides the Jewish population into two segments, with one group (the members) being so much more Jewishly active than the other group (the nonmembers). Consistently, congregational members are more likely to: observe rituals at home; attend worship services; have Jewish spouses, friends, and neighbors; belong to other Jewish institutions (JCCs, organizations); contribute to Jewish charities; visit Israel; and feel connected to Jewish community and peoplehood. Moreover, synagogue membership is associated with larger households (that include spouses, children) whose presence makes Jewish learning more valued and useful. In addition, syn-

---

[4]This and all other references in this chapter to national figures are drawn from calculations performed on the NJPS 2000/01 data set by Steven M. Cohen.

agogue members are somewhat more affluent and more educated than the Jewish population at large. Not least important, synagogue members are visibly Jewish and are engaged in institutionally active Jewish social networks. In all the respects noted immediately above, Mini-School learners tend to surpass congregational members. Just as congregants are more Jewishly active than non-congregants, Mini-School participants are more active than the average congregants.

Not only are Mini-School students overwhelmingly synagogue members; for the most part, they are also ritually active. As many as 86% reported fasting on Yom Kippur, far higher than the national average of just 49% for American Jews. About two-thirds light Shabbat candles, a highly useful barometer of ritual observance, again, significantly higher than the number so reporting (28%) in the 2000/01 NJPS. In this respect, their observance is about triple the national average. About a quarter keep kosher in their homes (according to their own definition of kashrut), and as many as 12% claimed to have kept kosher outside their homes prior to enrolling. This core of kashrut-observant individuals also exceeds national averages.[5]

Indeed, what makes these high levels of affiliation and observance even more impressive is that they derive from a population with very few Orthodox individuals. Just 3% of Mini-School learners identify as Orthodox, well below the 10% who so identify in national surveys of American Jews. From a certain point of view, the near-absence of Orthodox Jews at Mini-Schools is somewhat puzzling. In most arenas of Jewish activity, Orthodox Jews are overrepresented relative to their share of the population, and their overrepresentation is especially pronounced in Jewish learning activities. To take just one indicator, though only 10% of American Jews are Orthodox, Orthodox youngsters constitute the great majority of the day school population in the United States.

Their small number here tells us something about American Orthodoxy today and about the Mini-School. The Mini-School, of course, enrolls learners from all denominations and is avowedly "pluralistic" in its

---

[5]To be clear, we can only infer, albeit with reasonable certainty, that Mini-School learners' kashrut levels exceed national Jewish averages. The data from national and local Jewish population studies use widely varying questions on kashrut, but all point to the inference that fewer than 26% "keep kosher" in their homes, or 12% outside their homes.

philosophy. To be clear, we cannot attribute the lack of a significant Orthodox presence to any explicit design to make them feel less than welcome. After all, the chief professional (Jonathan Mirvis of the Hebrew University) is Orthodox, and the chief curriculum writer for the last five years received Orthodox rabbinic ordination. Moreover, Orthodox Jews are well represented among site directors and teachers.

The Mini-School presents itself as a gateway to Jewish literacy, as denominationally pluralist in composition and in educational philosophy, and as normatively nonjudgmental. These three elements undoubtedly operate to diminish the attractiveness of the Mini-School to potential Orthodox students. Orthodox American Jews, especially in the last few decades, have taken tremendous strides in Jewish education and learning. The proliferation of informal Orthodox study groups and private learning is paralleled by a sharp increase in day school and yeshiva enrollment. Hence, a course of study that promises to open the door to Jewish literacy does not quite suit the needs or self-concept of many Orthodox Jews who see themselves (with legitimacy) as already learned, or deeply involved in regular Jewish learning, or both.

Also, in recent years, reflecting a growing sectarian and segregationist bent, Orthodox Jews have shied away from communal involvement with their non-Orthodox counterparts (Heilman and Cohen 1989; Soloveitchik 1994). Orthodoxy's sectarianism clashes with a key feature of the Mini-Schools' educational philosophy.

Also underrepresented, so to speak, are nondenominational Jews, who represent 11% of the entering student body, just about half the number found in the larger population. Jews who refrain from identifying with a particular denomination tend to score lower on most measures of conventional Jewish engagement, particularly those associated with religious practice and sentiment (Lazerwitz et al. 1998). Here, too, we find a reflection of the Mini-School character in its presentation of being Jewish as a religious (albeit, pluralist) perspective, rather than a more avowedly secular or cultural approach.

The Reform proportion in the student body is comparable to its proportion in the larger Jewish population, while Conservative and Reconstructionist Jews, with almost half the students, are somewhat overrepresented. These distributions reflect a student population that is engaged in Jewish life, congregationally affiliated, pluralist, and nonjudgmental in its orientation. At the same time, they are not so highly educated in Jewish sources as to make the introductory curriculum excessively elementary.

Over half of those surveyed (53%) claimed to have attended synagogue services monthly or more, far in excess of the (also inflated) average of 23% in the 2000/01 NJPS. The Mini-School students' service attendance rates even somewhat exceed rates reported by Conservative synagogue members (Cohen 2000). Hardly any (5%) of these learners go to services just for weddings and bar mitzvahs and not even solely for High Holidays, implying that 95% attend (or said they attend) High Holiday services, a figure that also vastly exceeds the number (52%) reported in the 2000/01 NJPS.

As many as two-thirds reported that most of their closest friends were Jewish, as contrasted with just 33% of Jewish adults who so reported. Thus, the higher than average involvement in Jewish life extends to friendship circles. Not only do these students already have a higher proportion of Jewish friends than most American Jews, but they also appear to want to intensify their Jewish social circle. Socializing with Jewish friends, strengthening ties with Jewish friends, and making new Jewish friends were all mentioned in our personal interviews as some of the benefits of the Mini-School experience.

In addition to their synagogues, learners also are engaged with other major Jewish communal institutions. Prior to enrolling, as many as three-quarters did volunteer work for a Jewish agency. Fully 43% were dues-paying members of Jewish Community Centers (compared with 17% for the national average), and as many as 79% said they had attended a JCC program in the prior year, as against 32% for Jewish adults nationally.

Not surprisingly, these high levels of Jewish institutional engagement are reflected in the learners' attitudes as well as their behavior. (Here the responses refer to the current moment; in part, the answers reflect not only where they were three years ago, but how far they have traveled Jewishly in part because of their learning experience.) When asked about the importance of being Jewish in their life, a remarkable 90% answered "very important," far more than the 52% who so replied in the 2000/01 National Jewish Population Study (NJPS). Similarly, over half (52%) said they felt "very attached" to Israel. This figure, too, is far greater than its 2000/01 NJPS counterpart of 28%. Further testimony of their engagement with Israel is found in the extraordinary number—75%—who have visited Israel. In fact, fully 44% of the learners have been to Israel twice or more. In contrast, just over a third (36%) of American Jews generally have been to Israel, and a mere 16% have been there twice or more. In other words, even before entering the Mini-School, these learners had traveled to Israel more than twice as often as had other adult American Jews.

Adults on a Jewish Learning Journey

To say that Mini-School learners are, on average, significantly engaged in Jewish life is to present only one part of the picture of who they are as Jews. An especially significant feature of their Jewishness is that they are very much engaged in changing, developing, and growing as Jews. In this respect, their experiences are consistent with what has been reported in American religion generally (Wuthnow 1994; Roof 1999) and among Jews in particular (Cohen and Eisen 2000; Horowitz 2000). Seemingly everyone today has embarked upon a personal religious journey. Contemporary Americans conceive of themselves as constantly changing and generally growing, both as human beings and members of their faith. But, as much as this view has become widespread, we suspect that Mini-School students are even more growth-oriented than are most other American Jews. The evidence for this inference comes from several places.

During the five years prior to enrolling, more than a third had studied Hebrew, and as many had participated in an ongoing study group on a Jewish text or theme. Fully 60% had taken a class on a Jewish theme, as contrasted with less than half as many who made a similar claim in a recent national study of American Jews (Cohen and Davidson 2001). Three-quarters or more had read a book on a Jewish theme other than the Torah or the Bible. As many as 82% had attended a Jewish-oriented lecture—again, double the number (41%) nationally (Cohen and Davidson 2001). Within the last year, 71% had turned to the Internet for Jewish-related information, as compared with just 27% among American Jews generally. In short, our survey showed that most Mini-School students come to the program as lifelong learners, veteran learners, or occasional adult Jewish learners.

However, although the majority were active Jewish learners prior to enrolling, the interviews revealed some exceptions. For instance, psychologist Judy Abramson, recently married to a non-Jew, had not participated in any kind of Jewish study during her first marriage (to a Jewish man) but now looked to the Mini-School to "finally gain some knowledge of my background." Likewise, for Kim, the Mini-School provided what was her first adult Jewish text-learning experience, as demonstrated by her reflection on how she was totally unfamiliar with Jewish texts before her Mini-School experience: "When they told us to buy a *Tanakh*, I didn't own one. After I bought it, I didn't know how to look anything up. I had very little knowledge and experience with a lot of that. So it was just that taste, that first step into Jewish learning." Most learners, however, were already on their journey to become more fully educated, understanding, and intellectually probing Jews well before they enrolled. A sizable number of women with whom we spoke reported having previously undertaken an adult bat mitzvah, a ceremony marking a period of study and skill acquisition as an adult.

The length of the journeys in Jewish learning that they have undertaken is also documented by the evidence we have about their childhood Jewish upbringing. As many as 12% converted to Judaism in adulthood, as compared with about 5% among Jewish adults in the 2000/01 NJPS. Significantly, among Mini-School students, just 8% were raised Orthodox, as opposed to 19% of the adult Jews in the 2000/01 NJPS. Taken together, these data point to a relatively large fraction of Mini-School learners who had unusually weak Jewish religious backgrounds in their childhood. The large number of converts to Judaism (still a small fraction overall, but large relative to the pool) points to a particular function of the Mini-School in serving this population segment that, for obvious reasons, is especially interested in fortifying its grasp of Jewish learning. As a group, these learners have moved, in Jewish terms, from lower than average levels of Jewish involvement in their childhood to far higher than average levels as adults. The Mini-School capitalizes and extends this steep Jewish growth trajectory.

Other evidence points in the direction of a population that has grown up with less than average Jewish socialization and education and, as we have seen, has moved to greater than average contemporary Jewish involvement. For example, just 3% attended day school, as compared with 10% of the Jewish population in 2000/01.

For some, the move to greater Jewish intensity likely started in the college years, if not earlier. Fully 25% of the students reported having taken Jewish studies courses during college. This figure may be compared with the 17% who so reported in a Cohen and Davidson (2001) study of Jewish learning. Considering their age distribution, most Mini-School students attended universities when few offered such courses. In fact, upon further inspection by age categories, we find that 46% of those in their forties took Jewish studies courses as undergraduates.

Among those under forty, the figure rises to as high as 63%, suggesting that Jewish learning at an adult level extends, for most of the younger learners, back to their undergraduate years.

Taken together, this evidence points to a lifetime of Jewish growth—indeed, a pattern of involvement in compensatory Jewish education over much of these learners' lives. Participants include converts to Judaism, born-Jews with unusually weak Jewish schooling and socialization in childhood, as well as large numbers of fairly well-educated Jewish adults who seek a more solid and systematic grounding in Judaism to adequately perform their roles as members of Jewish families, synagogues, and organized Jewish life.

Motivations and Longings:
What Adult Jewish Learners Are Seeking

Our interviews provided insight to what Jewish adults who are engaged in a learning journey seek for themselves. Unlike their professional colleagues in the larger community who may look to adult education as a resource for career advancement, most Mini-School participants see adult Jewish learning in terms of personal intellectual enrichment or community building. Four types of motivation were evident in the learners' descriptions of what they were seeking: the need to become more informed, the desire to participate in a Jewish learning community, the quest for intensive Jewish intellectual engagement, and the desire for a substantive intellectual framework.

The Need to Become More Informed

Each of the learners we met at the beginning of this chapter—Kim Sherwood, Daniel Shaber, Selma Jones, and Leslie Irwin—articulated a clear reason for enrolling in the Mini-School. They were motivated by a need to become more Jewishly informed and thus to become more authoritative about Judaism, Jewish tradition, and their own Jewish identity. Studies of adult learner motivation (Boshier 1977; Houle 1961; Johnstone and Rivera 1965; Morstain and Smart 1974) report that most adults who enroll in adult learning programs do so to improve their "status" at work or home—status that has been disrupted because the

individual lacks critical knowledge or education necessary to function
or get ahead. Such adults enroll in learning programs to master a specific competency or achieve a certain goal. For some, participation in
adult learning is associated with the acquisition of credentials that are
prerequisites for advancement. For others, simply becoming "better informed" enables them to feel more competent, which then influences
their perception of themselves and raises their self-esteem.

Many of the people who enroll in the Mini-Schools are, in the language of adult learner motivation expert Cyril Houle (1961), "goal oriented learners" whose ambition is to transform themselves from
uninformed to knowledgeable Jewish adults. A number of individuals
we interviewed were forthright in their recollections of how they had
become aware of their shortcomings in their understanding of Judaism
and Jewish tradition. Sharon, a former teacher who had grown up in an
ostensibly Conservative family, said that, for most of her life, as a syna-
gogue-affiliated Jew, she had never questioned her Jewish identity. Suddenly, at midlife, she felt a pressing need to overcome a strong sense of
Jewish ignorance:

> I didn't get the itch to learn until my sons had their bar mitz-
> vahs, and then something sparked in me. When I went to my
> second son's bar mitzvah, I thought, "I need to find out about
> this. There's something I'm feeling and I don't know what it is."

Prior to her decision to attend the Mini-School, Sharon had never as-
pired to have well-informed views on Jewish issues; typically, she had
deferred to her husband on matters of observance and Jewish thought.
But once she decided to become an educated Jew, she set specific goals
for herself: "This year, we're going to have a seder. And I've been asked
to take part in my niece's bat mitzvah, and I'm going to speak Hebrew
for the first time in front of whoever's out there." Sharon commented
that her determination to become more knowledgeable Jewishly had
been reinforced by her husband's positive reaction to her learning experiences: "Every once in a while, I'll say something I learned at Melton
and he'll say, 'This is so great! I can't wait to come to your
graduation.'" Although Sharon's Jewish "literacy" is minimal, she says
that her study has already motivated her to set new challenges for herself as Jewish adult.

Leslie, the Jewish Community Center leader profiled earlier, said
that her motivation was to "learn the basics" so that she could function

with greater authority in her rapidly diversifying roles in the Jewish community. During her second year in the Mini-School, Leslie was selected for a CLAL development program sponsored by her local Federation. (CLAL, the Center for Learning and Leadership, offers Jewish learning programs for Jewish communal leaders in the United States and Canada.) She was thrilled to discover her increasing confidence as a Jewish adult learner:

> I have been able to apply many things that I have learned in the Mini-School to the discussions we have had in CLAL. When we did role-playing—reactions to the destruction of the Second Temple—we had just learned about the Essenes and the Zealots at the Mini-School. The day after the CLAL session, I told my teacher how great it was that I knew exactly what was happening historically.

Leslie's goal for increased literacy extended to her role as a Jewish parent:

> I could even help my kids, who attend day school, a bit with their homework. I could review their papers and know that they weren't just papers with stuff on them! I understood what was coming home from school. It meant something. For the first time it was meaningful to me, to know that I was learning the same thing that my kids were.

A sense of personal embarrassment about the "holes" in her Jewish knowledge also prompted enrollment by Natalie, a Federation officer who was raised in a Conservative home but had received no formal Jewish education. Natalie said that she had "felt illiterate as far as being a Jew" and was always nervous when she was expected to represent the Jewish community to her Christian neighbors. She recalled how, whenever she was called upon "to speak at a Sunday School class" in her city, she would "cram, read all the books pertaining to the subject." For Natalie, enrolling in the Mini-School provided a chance to develop a sense of Jewish authenticity. She commented, "I cannot tell you how much it has meant to my life as a Jew. I feel as though, for the first time, I'm finding out why I've always done what I did."

In Natalie's view, all Jewish lay leaders should become more fully informed about Judaism. She contrasted her own experience to that of non-Jews ("the Christian people, or a lot of them, are so knowledge-able") and ventured the opinion that "if all the leadership was able to have this background, there would be a lot more understanding about one another and the community." Natalie's goal for her own Jewish literacy has now extended to goals that she is advocating for all Jewish leaders (and Jewish professionals) in her community.

The Desire to Participate in a Jewish Learning Community

A number of the people we interviewed indicated that they enrolled in a program of Jewish learning because of the "social benefits" afforded by the affiliation with a program that they perceived as dynamic and successful. For this group, the Mini-School offered appealing opportunities to interact on a regular basis with like-minded peers and interesting teachers. Initially, they were motivated by what Houle (1961) described as an "activity orientation"—participating in adult learning in order to be part of a particular learning community. Over time, however, some activity learners found that their motivations changed. As these people became part of a learning culture, they intensified their intellectual commitment and became skilled lifelong learners. Adult learning expert K. Patricia Cross (1981) reported that once adults take the risks associated with new learning, they find themselves increasingly motivated to explore further—and better—educational opportunities:

> There is ample research support for [the] position that the more formal education people have, the more they want. . . . The more people know about almost any subject—whether it be antique cars or Greek history—the greater their appreciation of good learning experiences. (143)

Our interviewees included several "activity learners." Anna, a Mini-School graduate (and now a participant in a program for alumni), recalled enrolling with her husband, Sid, in the early 1990s. Anna said she had participated in other Jewish adult learning programs and liked the communal feeling that each had offered. In the interview, her first comment about the experience was, "They were having classes on Wednesday mornings, and Sid had Wednesday mornings off, so Wednesdays became Melton mornings." For Anna, a crucial dimension of the experience was the opportunity to be part of a group in which people cared about one another:

We rush to one another at the coffee break. "What happened to you? Are you OK? How are you?" People share the births of their grandchildren or, a major trip, and then the teacher calls the class to attention and we get down to business. But we are very sociable and interact with people we wouldn't see from one week to the next.

Over the years of a continuing association with the Mini-School community, Anna "institutionalized" her participation and told us that she now feels incomplete when she has to miss a class because of being out of town:

It's part of my life. Wednesday morning is Melton. I hate missing classes. I have all of my missed classes on tape, and we listen to them in the car. I always feel cheated when I get back to class and they say something like, "Well, we finished the *Amidah* last week and we are moving on to something else." I feel a void, a gap. But that's the price you pay when you travel.

For Kim, the day school parent described earlier, participation in the Mini-School enhanced her relationship with other day school parents. She said that the more she learns, the more she wants to continue in Jewish learning activities with other adults:

I'm a sponge: I'm constantly wanting to study and learn more. I do it at shul. Monday mornings I take a class. We study the women in the Torah. We're in our third year, a group of us with the rabbi. I'm doing the *Perek Yomi* [daily text study] program. At the synagogue, once a month, they have little discussion groups. I have friends who are participating in them, so every once in a while we start talking about what we're reading.

Another "activity learner" was Edna, a widow whose daughter attended the Mini-School program in a different city. Edna indicated that when she enrolled, she was "looking for something to do" with her day. After her husband died, Edna attended a daily minyan where she received considerable social support; initially, she saw the Mini-School community as another opportunity for affiliation. However, over time, Edna's motivation to become a serious learner deepened. She commented:

I need to know more, because I've started learning a little about Judaism and I'm not going to stop midstream. Everything you learn raises more questions. I'm really looking forward to next year because there are a lot of ethical things that I need to know.

The Quest for Intensive Jewish Intellectual Engagement

Some adults enroll in adult learning programs to "learn for the sake of learning" (Houle 1961). These individuals typically pursue adult education in a variety of settings and thrive on experiences that feed their ongoing need for intellectual stimulation. In Jewish tradition, such learners have been described as pursuers of *Torah lishmah*: learners who study Jewish texts for the sheer joy and challenge of engaging the wisdom of the tradition.

Our interviews substantiated that some learners are motivated by a thirst for deeper Jewish knowledge. Daniel, the college professor introduced earlier, talked about his desire to revitalize and deepen a long-neglected commitment to Judaism:

> I knew that there were many things that were memories of bits and pieces of my education. I thought this would be a nice opportunity for me to begin to recover some of the things I had lost and put things together in a way that I couldn't have done when I was a teenager.

Wanda, a speech pathologist who had taken many Jewish adult learning classes, indicated that she sought out Jewish learning because it represented an opportunity to encounter intellectual substance:

> I wanted to continue my education. There are a lot of courses here in our community that are offered maybe four weeks in a row, and that's it. It's not enough depth and meat! When I was doing the one-day-a-week course on the Bible and on the Mishnah, I was getting the depth. So I thought it would be nice to be enrolled in a class that had continuity and depth.

Roger, a physician who for several years had pursued a self-study program of Jewish texts, saw the structured, time-bound program of the Mini-School as providing a more "intensive and comprehensive" curriculum than anything he could organize for himself. A voracious reader, Roger welcomed the opportunity to delve deeply into the many levels of text analysis:

> I loved learning Torah, and I loved reading the Sages—the brilliance of it, the intricacy of it, the logic of it. In the rituals course, the teacher would teach us what the ritual was—for example, the lulav and etrog. Then she would give the teaching: that it symbolizes the spine and the heart and the eyes. I found all of that inspiring.

Selma, the retired businesswoman we met at the outset, said that she had "always been interested in pursuing more knowledge of all kinds" and described how much she loved learning: "I felt a gigantic need for information and for an attachment to a body of knowledge." Reflecting on how deeply she and her classmates valued their studies, Selma mused:

> Some people are book people. Maybe Jews are book people. Maybe it's part of some kind of genetic code. But whether it is or it isn't, I know it's true of me. I know it's true of many of us. We're all here because we need to learn. We respect what is written. We read. We remember. We strive to understand the recorded thoughts of ancient peoples and beyond.

Selma was drawn to the "formalized, rigorous study" and the opportunity to engage in intellectual ideas on a regular basis. Eager to learn about Jewish ethics, she was impressed that the program would provide supplemental readings. As a student, she regularly read all outside material and also arranged to take additional Jewish study courses in her community.

The Desire for a Substantive Intellectual Framework

Whether learners came with specific goals, a general curiosity about Judaism, or a social motivation for community building, they also wanted to learn about Judaism in a systematic way. Thus, when we talked with participants about what worked for them, we were not surprised when they said that they liked the rigor of the curriculum and were attracted by the structured opportunities to explore complex texts and issues.

Several learners mentioned that they especially valued the fact that the program provided an intellectual "map" that enabled them to reframe information that they had received elsewhere but had never fully integrated. Margaret's comments were illustrative of these points:

It was very organized. And it's like anything else you study. You can be interested in plants and flowers and not really understand anything if you don't study botany; you get an appreciation but you don't really have an understanding. I could read bits and pieces of Jewish studies here and there and be fascinated. But Melton took it in a sequence and presented it in an organized way.

Seth, who grew up in a Conservative household, reported that the Mini-School enabled him to "relearn things" that he had learned as a child. It enabled him to get more "perspective on certain things than when I learned them as an eight- to fifteen-year-old." He also said that the classes gave him a valuable historical and conceptual overview:

I liked finally getting the timeline of Jewish history organized in my head better than I had in the past. I enjoy history and putting together the pieces, and also understanding questions such as, "What makes Judaism so special? How is it different from other monotheistic religions?" Approaching it at a different time in my life with a different background was good.

Similarly, Daniel, who attended Hebrew high school and grew up with "a firm handle on the ritual," talked about how his learning experience helped him sort out unanswered questions about ritual, "about how it developed, where it came from, how it connected to biblical text—that kind of stuff." He found that the Mini-School enabled him to "recover" some of the ideas he learned as a teenager and to make meaning of these ideas in new, more mature ways.

Adult learners like Daniel, especially if they are seeking to make new meaning of previous experiences, are attracted to learning situations that enable them to "finish unfinished business." Some of the people we interviewed talked about how the learning helped them to fill in blanks from the past and thus become better equipped to explore new ideas. Pamela, a retired teacher who recently had been hired to run the religious school at a Conservative synagogue, said that the curriculum brought back to her many things she once knew but also introduced new concepts that she knew she would need in her new career. Shelly, a former high school history teacher, commented on how excited she felt moving from her earlier understanding of history to a Jewish view of history:

> It's so important to get this foundation. I taught world history. Yet getting this world history from a Jewish perspective is incredible, absolutely incredible! It's as though I didn't know world history at all—because now it's the Jewish perspective.

Marina said that, despite the depth of her earlier Jewish education, the curriculum helped her integrate disparate ideas:

> The Melton curriculum puts all my earlier Jewish learning into perspective. It pulls things together and highlights the things that I've been thinking—what I've lived all my life. It's made it more intense and has made me more aware and tuned in to things.

Why They Leave:
Specific Motivations of the Dropouts

As we can see, the orientation to study and length of commitment of the Mini-School appeals to certain sorts of adults, Jews, and learners. Of those who enroll, some drop out. Insofar as we can understand their motives for doing so, we learn about the specific constellation of motives that bring some learners to the Mini-School, and the outer limits of the constituency to whom the Mini-School appeals.

We interviewed four dropouts. Two or three of them reported that the major reason they discontinued was time: they simply couldn't sustain the demands of a weekly program in the face of their careers, families, travel schedules, or other pressures of modern life. One of these individuals was an attorney named Linda, who had retired from her law practice to be at home with her young children. She said that she had stopped attending because she "couldn't figure out the child-care thing" while she was nursing her second baby. At the time of the interview, she hoped to repeat the first year while simultaneously taking the second-year class. In Linda's view, retaking a year of the Mini-School would only enrich her: "I can't imagine that it would ever be the same twice. There was so much good information. I'd like to immerse myself in it again."

Another attorney, Howard, said he discontinued because he had professional obligations to a client who could only meet with him on the weekday that his class was scheduled. However, Howard stated, to him the important thing was that his limited experience had given him a base of knowledge and had made him "more open to do additional learning." For Howard, one indicator of his "success" was his realization that he didn't have to complete the program just for the sake of it: "Since I was already on my way, I didn't need to go through graduation."

A third dropout, Debby, the college instructor we heard from earlier, said that in her first year of study, she was enriched by the classes and found that the courses "filled an intellectual void" in her life. However, during that same year she developed an independent business that began to consume all her available time and provided alternative intellectual stimulation. Thus, although Debby appreciated how Jewish learning had given her "a better foundation to understand my religion," she seemed to find greater meaning in the opportunities afforded by her new enterprise.

The fourth dropout, Dana, a human-services trainer, had more specific criticisms of the program than the other dropouts, objecting particularly to the tendency of one teacher to encourage *hevruta* learning over frontal presentations. She also was distressed that a favorite teacher would not be continuing on the faculty. However, the real reason for Dana's quitting seemed to be more paradoxical. She said that as she began to become more educated Jewishly, especially about the mitzvot, the more perturbed she became about her own lack of observance:

> It was ironic that I became much more educated but became very frustrated that I couldn't apply what I was learning—because this is not how the people I know live their lives as Conservative Jews. They don't observe the mitzvot that we're supposed to observe.

Dana said that after a year, she felt she couldn't continue:

> I felt like a voyeur, to be sitting in on a class and learning the nuts and bolts of our faith and religion and knowing that I

didn't do 95 percent of it. It made me feel as though there was something wrong here. Why are we sitting in a class learning about Judaism? Why aren't we just being Jews, practicing Judaism?

For Dana, what felt like dissonance between her learning and her real-life experience caused so much stress that she opted to leave formal Jewish learning altogether.

The experience of our limited sample cannot be readily generalized to all dropouts, but our general impression is that few people who enter the program depart because of problems with the content or process. The site directors were forthright in how they market the two-year program and then work closely with learners and teachers to clarify expectations or address concerns. Our findings suggest that learners who leave do so largely for personal or professional reasons, rather than dissatisfaction with content or instruction.

Not for Every Adult Jewish Learner

The Mini-School works well for Jewish adults who are attracted to a structured group learning program that sets no minimum admission requirements, takes an introductory though intellectually challenging approach to text and commentaries, encourages interactive classroom dynamics and intra-group support, and tolerates minimal outside-of-class preparation. However, not all Jewish adults find their learning needs met by the Mini-School's philosophy, goals, or instructional approach. There are individuals and groups that may not find this learning experience particularly appealing. We call attention to some of the "underrepresented" populations and speculate about their low rates of participation.

Practical learners. The literature on adult learning (Apps 1991) describes a type of individual known as a "practical learner." These students like fast-paced teaching that utilizes demonstration and has personal and immediate applicability. They prefer learning through case studies, group projects, demonstrations, and simulations. Typically, they have little patience for "getting acquainted" teaching tools or other activities that foster a sense of community. Practical learners do not place a high value on learning that is centered on dialogue, reflection, or developing multiple approaches for problem solving.

In terms of both structure and content, the Mini-School curriculum does not particularly cater to students with a practical learning style. The Mini-School leadership encourages teachers to engage the learners in discourse. Formally, the curriculum is designed in a sequential fashion, but in reality, the classroom teaching-learning process is more meandering. Mini-School teachers generally refrain from using lecture as the predominant mode of instruction, and often will "go off the page" to respond to students' ideas or raise provocative questions. While the teachers encourage students to consider how the texts apply to their own lives (especially with respect to holidays or life-cycle events), they avoid stressing the practical elements of Jewish observance. In short, the learning is neither straight-line nor particularly practical. For practical learners who want to "get the basics" of Judaism but not engage in critical analysis of Jewish texts with other learners, the Mini-School is not a good fit.

Advanced Jewish learners. The Mini-School curriculum is certainly not designed for "raw beginners" to Jewish learning. As we found in our survey and interviews, few of the students begin their Jewish adult learning journeys in the Mini-School classroom. Nonetheless, the program is also not intended for more advanced and experienced students who are seeking skill mastery or sophisticated text interpretation. Advanced students in Judaica often prefer in-depth text study classes that require proficiency in Hebrew and familiarity with Jewish interpretive sources. Such students may be attracted to the "sequential curriculum" and commitment to group discourse. However, they likely will be impatient with the predominance of novice text students as well as with their need to learn elementary texts and how to engage in textual analysis. In addition, those with more background in the study of Bible, Talmud, and other texts might be more comfortable with ritual observance and ongoing, in-depth Jewish study than current Mini-School students. In these respects, if not others, such individuals would find the Mini-School classroom community possibly less to their liking than would those with characteristics more typical of the current learner population.

Independent learners. Adults begin new, self-directed learning projects all the time (Tough 1979), and many do so without turning to teachers or formal educational programs. These individuals pride themselves on their ability to locate resources, digest alternative perspectives, ferret out problems and contradictions, and arrive at independent conclusions or points of view. If they ever found themselves in a classroom, they might contribute significantly to discourse. However, the independent learner's preferred learning mode is more isolated. The Mini-School structure presumes that learners will participate in group learning activities. Students are not expected to pursue self-selected courses of inquiry. The only independent dimension is through essentially optional reading assignments. Consequently, any structured program of adult Jewish study is unlikely to appeal to learners who prefer a self-determined curriculum or independent learning milieu.

Learners seeking individualized mentoring. Many adult learners prefer educational programs that are tailored to their individual learning needs and have built-in mechanisms for mentoring relationships (Knox 1986; Daloz 1999). Although Mini-School teachers often provide individualized suggestions to address particular student needs and interests, the structure of the program does not afford genuine mentoring for the learners. In this sense, the curriculum is a "one size fits all" model.

People looking for a "rebbe." Although Mini-School teachers are deeply grounded in Jewish history, philosophy, law, and texts, their obligation to the learner is to provide an intellectual framework for understanding Jewish tradition and tools for critical analysis of key texts. The teachers seek neither to guide students through spiritual questioning nor to convey an ideological view about observance. In addition, these teachers avoid even seeming to recruit learners into a particular worship community, or providing religious, pastoral counseling at times of doubt or loss. Thus, even though many of the faculty are ordained as rabbis or are married to rabbis, they are enjoined not to offer their learners counsel or guidance on religious or spiritual matters. Individuals seeking fresh insights about how to lead a Jewish life or how to find deeper connection to Judaism will not find this setting directly responsive to their needs.

People looking for a lecturer. For decades, adult Jewish learning in America has been associated with speaker series, scholar-in-residence programs, and other "frontal" events that draw audiences eager to hear from "an expert" about critical issues in Jewish life. Though potentially stimulating, enriching, and useful for "organizing" ideas, the lecture model does not require the learner to actively engage in discussion about the content or to probe alternative viewpoints. The lecture model, even in a series format, is not intended to build a deliberate community of learning that will continue over an extended period of time. For individuals who prefer the lecture format, the Mini-School's structure and process will leave something to be desired. (This is not to say that some of the Mini-School teachers don't lecture—or don't lecture well. Indeed, some of the teachers are gifted lecturers who skillfully guide their students to debrief frontally presented material in dialogues or other interactive formats.)

"Cultural Jews." Large numbers of American Jews identify with Judaism as a culture and maintain a strong commitment to Jewish values, ethics, and aesthetic pursuits. Often activists in Jewish social or political causes or participants in intellectual discourse, these adults do not look to Jewish text study as an avenue for personal expression or Jewish meaning-making. Their "texts" are more likely to be found in the popular press than in traditional sources, and their sense of Jewish life is centered more in the public arena than in the synagogue or *beit midrash* (house of study).

Men. Only 20% of Mini-School learners are men, and the vast majority of these are over age fifty-five (younger women tend to dominate daytime classes; older men and women of all adult ages attend classes scheduled in the evening hours). The low male participation rate appears to mirror enrollment patterns in all Jewish adult-learning programs throughout the non-Orthodox community, where anecdotal reports suggest that women outnumber men by at least three to one. Some reasons for the low participation of men may simply reflect the general tendencies, and others may apply specifically to the Mini-School.

With respect to the latter, the Mini-School structure and content may lack appeal for many potential male learners. First, few employed men are prepared to commit to a weekly learning program that lasts two years; their careers and lifestyle simply do not support participation in such a time-consuming endeavor. Second, culturally, Jewish men may be less willing than their female counterparts to expose their lack of Jewish literacy. They may feel reluctant to admit their ignorance and to acknowledge publicly their need for compensatory Jewish education. Third, they may feel a cultural press to develop themselves professionally, rather than in more personal ways. As mentioned earlier, responsibility for transmitting Jewish education traditionally rests with mothers; consequently, Jewish men may not perceive any family value in becoming more Jewishly informed. Finally, because the Mini-School is designed to promote interactive learning and to foster a sense of "learning community" among its students, its reputation as a place for dialogue and personal meaning-making may make it somewhat less appealing to men (Hayes 2000).

Solitary types. Large numbers of Jewish adults avoid participation in distinctively Jewish activities or organizations, either because they are not particularly interested in Jewish matters or are not inclined to become involved with any sort of organized activity. As established earlier, the Mini-School tends to attract learners who are already, if not intensively, engaged in Jewish communal life or learning and find social comfort in the Mini-School's learning community. Thus, the Mini-School is not a likely "first address" for Jewish adults who tend to avoid Jewish groups or those who perceive the Mini-School learners as "cliquey."

The young, the poor, the Jewishly alienated. The profile of the typical Mini-School learner does not include unmarried adults under thirty-five or lower- to lower-middle-income individuals who see the Mini-School's tuition as a barrier to participation. Although the Mini-School recently has begun to reach out to underserved populations and to make the program a "safe space" for Jewish adults who do not "fit the mold" of engagement in the Jewish community, the current population remains middle-aged and older, and relatively well-heeled.

Conclusion

The collective picture of participants reveals a diverse population of learners who are seeking Jewish literacy and are attracted to the benefits of a structured, two-year Jewish adult learning program. The commonalities and differences found among these learners showcase several patterns in the motivations and triggers that prompt enrollment and in the socio-demographic characteristics of Mini-School students.

As we have seen, like most settings for adult Jewish learning, the Mini-School population is primarily female. Compared with their male counterparts, Jewish women make more time for Jewish learning—or have more time to do so in the first place. The gender gap likely reflects differences in customary family and community roles, with Jewish women continuing to take the lead responsibility for socialization and ritual functions with children and grandchildren.

Also, although formal Jewish education has become more accessible to younger cohorts of women, many who enroll in Jewish study as adults feel the need to compensate for long-standing gaps in their Jewish knowledge. Our interviews indicated that men who enroll are motivated more for personal intellectual enrichment than for social purposes or to gain enhanced status in the community. Many men attend at the behest of their wives or as a response to retirement.

Since its inception, the Mini-School has succeeded in attracting a clientele across the adult age span, achieving a participant age median that is relatively youthful for adult education programs. The special appeal to Jewish day school and preschool parents leads to a significant proportion of students under age fifty. The wide age range of learners overall supports the observation that critical developmental changes occur throughout adulthood and that enrolling in an adult Jewish learning program is a viable response to diverse turning points in the life cycle.

While some learners enroll in response to life transitions, others are motivated by family members' participation or by the desire to be educated while their children are learning about Judaism. Most of the people we interviewed reported that they were on some kind of a Jewish journey in which their Jewish learning constituted a vital part of their overall Jewish growth. Whether focused on a particular learning goal or on the positive social engagement, most people who attend the Mini-School view it as a place for serious learning by dedicated learners.

Mini-School students are socially upscale. They are advanced in terms of education and income. These characteristics may well reflect the Mini-School's long-standing strategy of recruiting affiliated Jews and Jewish communal leaders into learning experiences that demand confidence in study and talking about written texts. More pointedly, when compared with most American Jews, Mini-School learners are more ritually observant, more highly affiliated, and more involved in Jewish communal activities. Their higher rates of engagement in Jewish life even exceed those of people affiliated with synagogues. Thus, they come to the Mini-School with a strong commitment to Jewish life and, in many instances, are veteran adult Jewish learners. These learners are drawn to the opportunity for systematic Jewish text study and the chance to learn about Judaism from multiple perspectives. The religiously pluralist emphasis of the Mini-School is particularly attractive to the learners, although this emphasis may also serve to discourage Orthodox adults from enrolling in the program.

Although a primary appeal is the curriculum for Jewish literacy, the social dimensions and connections to the larger Jewish community also play a crucial role in attracting enrollments. In chapters 3 and 4, we shall see how the social and educational processes combine to foster change and adult Jewish growth.

Not all types of learners are attracted to the learning environment typical of the Mini-School. Underrepresented groups include independent learners who prefer to learn in more isolated settings; and students who have little patience for the dialogue and extensive classroom participation that characterize this type of adult learning experience. Also, the Mini-School is not primarily designed for advanced students of Jewish texts who may well have already encountered many of the texts, ideas, and skills offered in the two-year cycle. Nor will we likely find people seeking highly individualized, self-paced instruction and mentoring, those who prefer lectures, or those who might be looking for a Jewish guru (or rebbe) who will definitively guide them in a particular direction. "Cultural Jews" and men also are absent from Mini-School rosters, perhaps because of the focus on text study and the expectation for an ongoing commitment to Jewish learning.

CHAPTER TWO
The Impact of Jewish Learning and Its Impact on Jewish Identity

How does an intensive experience of adult Jewish learning affect the hearts and minds of its students? To what extent and in what ways does this learning experience deepen and enrich their Jewish identities? How are they different, as Jews, than when they started this learning process two or more years prior to our survey and interviews?

These questions go to the very heart of this study. As seen by its founders, leaders, and supporters, the mission of the Mini-School is to provide thousands of Jews worldwide with access to comprehensive Jewish literacy through the study of classic Jewish texts. They tacitly assume that through study, students will grapple with the meaning of being Jewish.

As we shall see, the evidence—from the in-person interviews, the survey responses, and the answers to the open-end survey questions—points to diverse areas of change, varying in terms of nature, extent, and pace. Sociological investigations of religious commitment often distinguish three dimensions: belief, behavior, and belonging. The adult Jewish learning experience apparently engenders effects that cut across these dimensions, even if it may do little to effect profound change in religious beliefs, or large modifications of behavior, or significant expansion of ties to Jewish community, both organized and informal. Rather, as we shall demonstrate, learning at the Mini-School appears to influence beliefs about behavior, that is, the meaning that learners attach to their ritual practice, prayer, and learning, as well as the Jewish lens through which they view their everyday life. Additionally, learners come to a new understanding of their relationship with other Jews—whether family members, friends, classmates, Jewish organizations (including synagogues), or the broader Jewish community. Thus, it is not beliefs alone, or behavior alone, or belonging alone that undergoes change. Rather, it is in the nexus of all three.

In this chapter, we review seven dimensions of impact reported in varying degrees by the Mini-School learners we surveyed and interviewed:

1. Making new meaning of preexisting Jewish activity
2. Expanding involvement and interest in Jewish learning
3. Connecting ethics and everyday life
4. Developing appreciation for "traditional" Judaism
5. Encountering God and spirituality
6. Transmitting meaning to others
7. Building belonging through Jewish networks and community involvement.

Later we will review some less evident patterns of behavioral change, the challenges inherent in measuring such change, and the social constraints that may inhibit how contemporary Jewish adults manifest changes in their "practice." We also consider the kinds of impacts that may occur subtly, over time—changes that sometimes are more immediately evident to teachers than learners or changes in perspective that learners note only gradually as their lives take new turns. Finally, we explore how the experience of making new meaning and forming new connections through learning at the Mini-School appears to strengthen adult Jewish identity.

1. Making New Meaning
of Preexisting Jewish Activity

As we noted in the introduction, many American Jews, like other Americans, have embarked upon a search for enhanced meaning in their lives. Contemporary adults feel freer to choose their religious denomination, their level of involvement, and the nature of their involvement. Jews have been feeling and behaving in similar fashion. As "sovereign selves" who pick and choose their religious options and practices rather than accommodate to conventional patterns of observance and affiliation, they seek to understand in highly personal ways whatever religious traditions they pursue.

Hence, it follows that the core impact of the Mini-School upon learners' Jewish identities centers on "meaning-making," the enhanced ability to derive sense and purpose from one's everyday Jewish activities (activities already existing in one's life). We believe that here, the main story of the impact is to be told. As we shall see, while the extent to which Mini-School learners reported changes in behavior were relatively limited, the extent to which they indicated the acquisition of a more meaningful understanding of their Jewish practices was widespread and significant.

Therefore, even when these adults reported little or no change in practice or communal involvement, they expressed pleasure in how their learning provided them with greater understanding and meaning connected with their preexisting Jewish activities. For example, Sharon, a homemaker and budding artist, commented on the greater meaningfulness of lighting Sabbath candles, which, we have every reason to suspect, was something she had been doing well before enrolling in the two-year program of study:

> The practical suddenly has more emotion to it. There are more feelings with it. Lighting the candles like that is not as routine as, "Oh, I know why I do it. I know why I cover my eyes. I know why I cover my head and sing." Knowing enhances the practical application, and I think it facilitates it, too.

For Sharon, her studies probably made little difference with respect to the likelihood of her lighting Sabbath candles (according to our survey, 67% of the sample lit Shabbat candles before attending the Mini-School, and just 6% more did so when they were graduating). But the experience was important for enhancing her appreciation of a preexisting and continuing ritual practice.

In like fashion, Marina, a retired Jewish communal worker raised in an Orthodox home, only hinted at more attendance at religious services; but she was very explicit in crediting the Mini-School with enhancing the meaningfulness of her experience with services: "I'm a Shabbes shulgoer. I get so much more out of the service because of Melton. Everything has so much more meaning."

Leslie, the Jewish community leader we met in chapter 1, was clearer about attending synagogue more often, and was also quite explicit about the benefit of obtaining more meaning from her service attendance:

Everything seemed much more meaningful. Melton helped me get over that feeling of inferiority I had when I spoke with my rabbi sixteen years ago. We as a family go to synagogue much more often now. Certainly there are things that still interfere with going—baseball games, and so on—but I really enjoy going now. I participate in synagogue services much more—I don't daydream through the service any more. I used to be one of those people who would be too busy people-watching and not connecting. But part of what happened is that we finally found a synagogue that met our needs. My husband could go to any synagogue. But when I would go to a Conservative service for a bar mitzvah or something, I had no clue of what was going on! But now, at our Reform synagogue, I feel I can participate and know what is going on.

In these comments, Leslie also intertwined references about how learning had affected her beliefs, her sense of belonging, and her behaviors:

I am involved in many Jewish organizations. It used to be so meaningless for me to sit in so many meetings and listen to a *dvar Torah*. It was meaningless because I didn't make a connection. Why were we doing this? Why did we have to start every meeting with fifteen minutes of this? I was always thinking, "Come on, hurry up, we have things to do." Melton pulls so much of it together. There is so much more to learn, but now I have pieces of understanding. I can participate in many more conversations. I can celebrate with my family. I really feel a connection.

2. Expanding Involvement and Interest in Jewish Learning

Although conventional wisdom about adult learners posits that "the more adults learn, the more they want to learn," to date there have been no empirical studies about Jewish adult learners that could fully confirm such an assertion. The one relevant piece of evidence comes in a recent national survey on Jewish learning that documented the small number of Jewish learning "junkies," who participate in a large number of Jewish learning experiences (Cohen and Davidson 2001). Our interviews revealed that participation in adult Jewish learning has the potential to tap into—and build on—a deep longing for sustained Jewish knowledge among contemporary Jewish adults. Sharon, for example, testified to the process of becoming increasingly enmeshed in Jewish learning: "One thing affects the other. Touch one little thing and you're inspired to go on and on and on. It's like a constant domino thing, except you go up, instead of falling down!"

Leslie attested to a heightened interest in Torah and Talmud, two of the mainstays of her adult Jewish learning experience:

> I really want to learn more about the Torah, especially now that my daughter is approaching bat mitzvah. I'm not interested in what happened in 822 B.C.E.; that doesn't mean anything to me. But I love the Talmud—how everyone has taken the pieces and interpreted them differently. Really fascinating!

Equally enthusiastic remarks from Bill, a retired accountant, added the dimension of the impact on family members who participate in Jewish learning. In fact, the strong family-centeredness of Jewish life in general may well extend to learning, such that spouses and children function as inspirations for or impediments to Jewish learning. Bill reflected: "My wife is really into this, too. We've both gotten involved. Once you start, it's pretty hard to stop. We love it. I wish I had more time to study."

Shelly's comments pointed to the "discovery" process inherent in Jewish text study, in which one insight can lead to multiple levels of inquiry or understanding. Coming from a limited Jewish intellectual background, Shelly commented that her studies alerted her to the vast extent of Jewish textual materials: "I once thought that Melton was going to quench my thirst for Jewish knowledge. And I was attending because I was learning all this. All of a sudden, I realized that, no, it's just whetting my appetite, because there's so much more that I want to know."

Even Howard, an attorney who had dropped out of the Mini-School because of scheduling problems, nonetheless connected his classroom learning experience to a newfound interest in Jewish books:

> Melton gave me a foundation and made me more open to do additional learning. During Jewish Book Month at the JCC, I was more interested in learning about new Jewish authors and Jewish-related books. As an intelligent person, I can feel com-

fortable in lots of realms in the secular world, but I felt inadequate in the Jewish world. Once I obtained a certain baseline, I wasn't intimidated any more.

These learners were highly energized by their studies. They reported that they often found themselves wanting to spend every spare moment deepening their Jewish knowledge. They asked their teachers for additional time, explored courses on the Internet, attended summer study programs, read independently, traveled to Israel on Melton study tours, and regularly looked for additional study opportunities. Many urged the Mini-School to create a third year (and beyond) program; some asked if they could take the two years over again. Their passion for learning is palpable, and even though not all of the people we interviewed displayed such a thirst for knowledge, the "infectious" nature of Jewish learning was evident in the majority of our interviews.

The teachers' perspectives on what happens supported what the learners themselves said about their intellectual development. Arnie Roth described how his students develop a basic vocabulary, a sense of the sequence and structure of Jewish history, names of key people, and an understanding of basic Jewish concepts:

> What I tell them is: "You can go to a bookstore or library after or during Melton, reach up and take any book on any aspect of Judaism and feel comfortable reading it." It opens a door for continual lifelong learning. Before Melton, people don't know what Sanhedrin is, or what a Sage is, so they close the book because they don't know what is being talked about. They go through the program and that becomes something familiar and they are able to go on. So this is not the end, but rather the beginning.

Several teachers observed that students grow intellectually more sophisticated even after one year in the program. It appears that the learners become more discerning and are equipped with a new language of Jewish discourse. Frieda Gottlieb, who teaches Dramas of Jewish Living (a second-year course), noted that by the time students get to her, they have learned how to ask questions. For her, this is a sign of their growth, "because asking questions is more important than my answering, and how they think is more important than what they know."

Ted Butler, another Dramas teacher, said that his students acquire a Jewish vocabulary in the first year that prepares them for grappling with more complex issues in the second. He observed that Mini-School teachers all endeavor to get the learners "in the habit of thinking Jewishly about historical problems, thinking Jewishly about the ethical problems."

Our survey results further reinforced the views expressed by the individuals we interviewed. In fact, the most frequently documented impact emerging from our study was the development of an enhanced appreciation and passion for Jewish learning. As can be seen in Table 2, we asked the respondents, "Listed below are several possible outcomes of studying at the Mini-School. To what extent would you say that you have been affected, if at all, in each of the following ways?" By far, the most popular answer was, "I have become more comfortable studying Jewish texts (in English)," with 49% answering, "to a great extent."

The Mini-School seems to demystify Jewish learning as well as enlarge learners' appreciation for the volume of material that they have yet to master. Personal Jewish intellectual engagement seems to have substantially increased during the years of study. For example, from their recollection of "three years ago" to their reports about "this year," the number of survey respondents who read a Jewish periodical leapt twelve percentage points. In like fashion, the number who had read a Jewish book climbed nine percentage points. Interest in taking a class next year on a Jewish theme rose fourteen percentage points. Even more striking is the growth of twenty-two percentage points in interest in participating in an ongoing study group on a Jewish text or theme. Just 35% had done so five years before enrolling, while 57% claimed interest in doing so the year after they graduate. Likewise, the study of texts outpaced all other potential changes in beliefs and behaviors, with 23% saying that they are "much more active now" than they were earlier (see Table 3). Internet use for Jewish-related information also soared (from 35% to 71%), but a large part of this particular growth can be attributed simply to the widening use of the Internet over the last three years.

The brief comments in the optional, handwritten portion of our survey affirm this increased interest in Jewish learning. A selection of illustrative remarks follows, in response to the question: "In your own words, how has the Florence Melton Adult Mini-School affected you?"

Table 2: Effects of Studying at the Mini-School*			
	Not at all	Somewhat	To a great great extent
I have become more comfortable studying Jewish texts (in English)	8	43	49
I have become a more committed advocate of community support for Jewish education	22	38	40
I have developed a greater appreciation for Jews who are more observant than I	24	41	35
I more often see ethical implications in a lot of my ordinary activities	11	57	33
I have undertaken more Jewish learning on my own	20	48	32
I have become more attached to the Jewish people	30	39	31
I have become more active in my family as a Jewish resource	21	51	29
I have become more attached to the Jewish community	23	49	28
I see myself more as a Jewish role model for my family or friends	24	49	27
I have become more spiritual	32	43	25
I have become more in favor of Jewish day school education	40	36	23
I have developed a new set of friends	24	53	23
I have acquired new networks of people in the Jewish community	23	54	23
I have deepened my faith in God	37	41	22
I find prayer more meaningful than before	36	42	22
I have become more of a Jewish "pluralist"	34	45	21
I have developed a greater appreciation for Jews who are less traditional than I	39	45	17
I celebrate Shabbat more than I used to	55	30	16
I have become more active in my community as a Jewish resource	42	44	15
I now take on more roles in synagogue worship services	59	27	14
I feel more strongly than before that there is a right way to be Jewish	68	20	12
I have become more observant	51	37	12
I know more Hebrew than I did before	57	32	11
I contribute more than before to Jewish charities	48	41	11
I have became more active in a synagogue	60	29	11
I have become more observant of kashrut	71	18	11
*Totals are averages and may not total 100%.			

Table 3: Changes in Jewish Practice as Compared with Three to Four Years Ago*			
	About the same	Somewhat more active now	Much more active now
Studying Jewish texts	31	45	23
Teaching family members about being Jewish	41	43	14
Celebrating Jewish holidays	50	34	15
Celebrating Shabbat	58	25	14
Attending synagogue services	59	23	13
Contributing to *tzedakah*	63	27	8
Other synagogue activities	67	19	8
Observing kashrut	74	13	8
Working on committees, boards of Jewish organizations	72	14	7
Working on committees, board of a synagogue	71	13	7
Engaging in social action	72	22	4

*This table does not report those who answered that they were less active in various areas of Jewish life. Typically, they amount to no more than 9%.

It's made me want to keep learning about Judaism, which I had taken for granted. I now realize that in my lifetime I couldn't learn enough.

* * *

When I first started, I felt as if I were fairly knowledgeable. Now I know that I know very little and have much to learn. I'm excited about the possibility of continuing in "graduate" school.

* * *

It has sparked my curiosity not only about our present way of observance, but the observance of the Jewish people through the years.

* * *

I will continue with my Jewish education but will really miss this group.

* * *

It has given me a background that I lacked for further study.

3. Connecting Ethics and Everyday Life

Significantly, for Mini-School students, the value of adult Jewish learning appears to extend beyond the domains of ritual observance, synagogue services, and Jewish communal activity, and to embrace everyday life. When asked about the impact of their learning, 33% of the sample said that, to a great extent, "I more often see ethical implications in a lot of my ordinary activities." Of the list of twenty-six possible sorts of impact, this item ranked fourth-highest with respect to the frequency with which respondents assented. Margaret, a convert from Catholicism (who completed her conversion process six months after enrolling), cited specific examples from lessons that apparently affected her behavior and certainly lent an ethical lens to her everyday experience:

> When I studied the ethics, they were applicable to everything. It fascinated me that you don't tell a sick person that he or she is going to die. And you try not to embarrass people when you give them charity or *tzedakah;* giving *tzedakah* is just what you do. You don't do it to feel better. This was a whole new concept for me, so it changed my behavior. When somebody on the street—and I live in the city, so I see a lot of people—gets money from me, even if it's only a dollar or fifty cents, now it's a ritual. It's a part of my life. I'm obligated, because I'm Jewish, to give them something.

Anna, a business owner long active in B'nai B'rith, was able to cite a specific incident where what she learned influenced her ethical behavior. Moreover, she acted with a strong sense of consciousness of Jewish ethics, or, more precisely, of what she believed that Jewish ethics demanded:

> We had a situation where we had a bad falling-out with an employee. We had made her a promise, and a promise is a promise.

So I went back to my thoughts on what I had studied at Melton, and said that we would conduct this in a Jewish ethical way because this is how Jews live. She got her compensation and so forth, so I can say that in some aspects, the way I think and live has been modified, has been enhanced, or has made me think about how I am dealing with a particular issue.

She also said that learning about mitzvot affected her behavior in other ways:

How I treat my fellow man, how I treat other Jews: there were things that affected my ethics—specifically, lashon hara [gossip]—that will stay with me forever. Having it explained in the way it was explained, and knowing what terrible damage is done with the tongue, I have become very aware of that aspect. Another thing would be the honest and ethical Jewish way in which we treat our workers.

Arnie Roth, a teacher at one of the sites, made this general observation about the changes he perceived among students who have studied with him:

The most amazing change is that students, after about six months or so of class, give up lashon hara. They become very sensitive to the way they talk. It comes out in the Ethics class, but it comes out in Purposes, too. It comes out in everything we teach. That is the one thing I notice that is almost universal. If you ask my students what they have learned over the years, they will say that they don't like gossip any more.

4. Developing Appreciation for "Traditional" Judaism

The majority of American Jews have little patience for traditional concepts of norms, obligation, and commandment. Their strong sense of voluntarism, autonomy, and religious individualism militates against the traditional Jewish notion of a divinely ordained legal system, interpreted by rabbis, and subject to social and communal sanctions (Liebman and

Cohen 1990; Cohen and Eisen 2000). The Orthodox, whose rabbinate and rank and file seem most committed to this view, are especially subject to disdain by most American Jews, who are, obviously, non-Orthodox. Mini-School teachers and the school leadership not only spoke favorably of all major Jewish denominations, but appeared to remain neutral and nonjudgmental with regard to students' individual choices in terms of religious beliefs, belonging, and behavior. At the same time, the curriculum and teachers attempted to provide the rationale of ancient Jewish concepts of commandment, religious law, and observance.

The emphasis on pluralism and its sympathetic treatment of a normative approach to Jewish life worked to reduce alienation from and antagonism toward Orthodox Jewry. As a consequence, learners became more accepting of and appreciative of Jews whose approach to being Jewish differs from their own. However, the growth in tolerance was not entirely balanced. Specifically, more reported a growth in appreciation for more traditional Jews than for less traditional Jews. To a great extent, 35% said that they "have developed a greater appreciation for Jews who are more observant than I." Marina, the retired Jewish communal worker we heard from above, reflected this change in perspective in the following remarks about Orthodox Jews: "I think of them differently because I now know what they believe. If you really believe what they believe, you have to live a certain way. And, for them, there are not a lot of choices. That fact has made me have a greater respect for them."

With respect to those Jews whom students perceived to be less observant than themselves, tolerant feelings also increased, but at a much lower rate. In contrast with the 35% who said that they felt more tolerant toward those who are more observant, only about half as many (17%) said, in response to the statement, "I have developed a greater appreciation for Jews who are less traditional than I." Although teachers did not appear to dictate normative practice, the students' understanding and acceptance of normative Judaism did seem to grow. Pertinent here are these remarks by Dana, a human-services trainer, and from Cindy, a former health-care administrator:

Dana: Why is it that the rabbis don't get on us for not doing what we're supposed to do and pretend that we're doing everything we're supposed to do, when we're not?

Cindy: I don't observe Shabbat as I should. I do not keep kosher, as I should. I keep kosher-style so that I'm working toward the ideal. Taking a course like this reminds me of where I should be. Even though I may not be there, I'm not forgetting where I should be, and I have something to work toward.

In both cases, we may note the way in which these women related positively to "what we're supposed to do" and to the synonymous "shoulds" of Jewish life, that is, what Jews should do. Clearly, this sort of language runs counter to a complete rejection of the very notion of norms, or the related concept of the "good" Jew. (Many American Jews deny that one can even speak of a "good Jew.") At minimum, these students acknowledged the norms as a legitimate part of Judaism, even if they don't ascribe to them personally. As we saw in chapter 1, for Dana, the gap between her level of observance and what she perceived she ought to be doing unsettled her enough to precipitate her withdrawal from the Mini-School.

To further illustrate this point, Leslie below reflected a newly acquired understanding for kashrut, emblematic of a greater appreciation for ritual and observance. Perhaps for her and others, kashrut specifically, and the system of commandments more generally, symbolize tradition and authenticity. Through this process, learners may have sensed that, for the first time in their Jewish lives, they are encountering the "real thing," the traditional system of norms and obligations. "I used to be a once-a-year Jew, but now I see Judaism much more holistically. I understand kashrut a lot better and am much more tolerant of it. It wasn't that I was intolerant; I just never understood why people chose to do it."

5. Encountering God and Spirituality

Thus far, we have seen evidence of learners experiencing greater Jewish meaning and connection in the worlds of texts and ethics. Another significant remaining sphere is the theological or spiritual. What sorts of change occurred with respect to God and spirituality? Although the vast majority of American Jews say that they believe in God, a focus upon God actually plays a small role in their consciousness. American Jews are not especially sophisticated in thinking about or talking about God. They tend to reject or be ignorant of conceptions of God that are distinctively Jewish, even expressing discomfort with the traditional view that God bears a special relationship with God's Chosen People. Perhaps the most distinctive feature of the Jewish notion of God is that it lacks any connection to Jesus (Cohen and Eisen 2000).

At the same time, as reported by 62% in a recent survey (Halbertal and Cohen 2002), most Jews also claim to be "spiritual." Indeed, Americans generally are found to be more enamored of describing themselves as spiritual than as fond of organized religion (Roof 1999). "I'm spiritual, but not religious," is the watchword of a major segment of the American population, and one that seems to hold sway over a good many American Jews.

With this said, the testimony of some survey respondents suggested that their learning seems to have exerted a positive influence on their feelings for God and for spirituality. As a result, 22% said that to a great extent, "I have deepened my faith in God." A slightly larger minority (25%) answered in like fashion with respect to, "I have become more spiritual."

Also, the classroom conversations about God were important to a number of people we interviewed. Natalie, the Federation officer, pointed out how unusual it was to be in a group that supported spiritual discussion: "I like it when we talk about God because that doesn't happen in a group very often in your life. For some reason, people are a bit private about their interpretation of God. Yet it's interesting to be able to share those thoughts and feelings."

Bill said that discussions of God naturally and appropriately emerged from the texts that they studied in various classes: "In 'normal' activities, a lot of people don't even think about God. But because of the material we're studying, we have to think about God." Sharon spoke about how thinking of God became a more frequent occurrence for her:

I think about God all the time, and I didn't used to. In my day-to-day life, if I'm feeling really good about something; or, for example, that plane crash you saw on TV. It's all over the news this morning. They showed this plane—a mess—but no one was hurt. And I said to myself, "That's how you know there's a God up there." I'll find myself saying a lot of things like that. If I'm taking a drive and it's gorgeous, I'll say, "Boy, God really—look what he did!" I never used to be that way.

Shelly, a former high school history teacher, to take another instance, attributed a better understanding of God to her classroom learning: "People question God and then you begin questioning, well, why does this happen? I think Melton gives you a greater understanding of God and God's role in your life." She attained what must be seen as a greater sense of purpose, if not transcendence. In short, Shelly found meaning in a spiritual fashion.

> It has changed my whole way of thinking. It has made me a better person. It may sound silly, but I look at life in a whole different way. There's a reason we're put here on this earth. We don't want to mess it up. It's the only shot we have. You have to try to do the right thing for yourself, the people around you, and your family.

Marina, the retired communal service worker, gave voice to a spiritual consciousness as well: "The wonderment of the world: Melton has added that for me. I appreciate nature a lot more than I did."

In the context of very little discussion about God and theology among American Jews, even among those who are frequent worshipers, learning at the Mini-School represented something of an innovation. It offered Jewish adults rarely experienced opportunities to seriously encounter Jewish theological teachings and their own feelings about God and spirituality. Apparently, a significant minority was moved by these learning experiences, and report some measure of increased interest in matters of faith and the divine.

6. Transmitting Meaning to Others

The practice of Judaism is more home-based than the church-based practice of Christianity, especially its Protestant variant. Accordingly, between Judaism and Christianity, the relative importance of service attendance differs sharply. Simply put, American Christians attend services at houses of worship far more than Jews do. In contrast, Jews celebrate many of their holidays at home, with significant home observances attached to the Sabbath, Passover, Hanukkah, and other widely celebrated holidays. In recent years, American Jews' energies have focused even more decidedly upon the home (Cohen and Eisen 2000). The greater enthusiasm for the personal, or the private aspect of being Jewish, undoubtedly contributes to the enlarged importance of the home and nuclear family as venues for the expression of Jewish commitment and passion.

Consistent with Judaism's emphasis on the home as a key arena for Jewish expression, a large body of research documents the importance of parenting for prompting involvement in religious life. In other words, many Mini-School participants were not only pursuing learning for personal meaning-making but also for enhancing their position as Jewish role models and teachers in their families. As we saw in the previous chapter, some respondents decided to engage in Jewish learning in direct connection with their changing roles as parents. For Debby, a part-time college instructor, parenting—specifically, her relationship with her third daughter—sparked a greater involvement with Judaism generally: "I'm more involved in Judaism than I used to be because of my third daughter. She questions everything and is very spiritual. So I think that pushed me to learn more because this little kid was asking me all these questions."

Indeed, comments such as these are consistent with the repeated social scientific evidence that parenting elevates Jewish involvement (Cohen 1983; Sklare and Greenblum 1979). But the claim here goes beyond that generalization. Mini-School learners attach significant importance to their roles as parents, spouses, and grandparents. We saw considerable evidence that they felt increasingly competent and capable of transmitting their enhanced Jewish knowledge to other family members.

When asked on the survey about eleven ways they may have become more Jewishly active, "teaching Jewish family members about being Jewish," ranked second (57% answered "somewhat" or "much more active now"), just behind studying Jewish texts. As many as 29% said that to a great extent, "I have become more active in my family as a Jewish resource," almost twice as many who answered in like fashion for their role "in the community." Almost as many (27%) answered likewise with respect to "I see myself more as a Jewish role model for my family or friends."

Various interviewees cited their roles as informal Jewish teachers in their families. For example, Shelly, a former high school history teacher, spoke of teaching her daughter, son-in-law, and grandchildren: "Whenever we get a chance, I will bring up something and say, 'Oh, do you remember this from your classes?' so that my daughter, my son-in-law, and I could discuss it. Sometimes I'll share information with my grandchildren." Shelly also waxed enthusiastically about teaching her children and grandchildren. For her progeny's Jewish development, the teaching-in-a-family interactions she described are, in all likelihood, not particularly valuable for the "information" being transmitted from older to younger generations. More critically, the interactions offer the grandmother the chance to express her enthusiasm and passion for Judaism and Jewish learning:

> I bring specific information from that week to my family. With my kids for dinner, I'll say, "You know what we did in class this week?" They'll say, "Oh, God!" roll their eyes, and say, "We'll hear about Melton again?" I tell my children and grandchildren about what I'm learning. For example, that we're a holy people and because we're a holy people we have certain things that we have to do that are different from the rest of the world. We can't do what the rest of the world does.

Cindy's newly acquired mastery of Jewish knowledge emerged in conversations with her husband, often provoked by ongoing learning at her synagogue. In other words, her formal studies, along with family and community interactions, combined to make possible her displays of Judaic efficacy, providing pleasurable Jewish educational moments in her everyday life:

> Often something comes up either in discussion with my husband or at a synagogue-related event, and I am able to remember something that I've learned. Each year, we have a different topic; this year's was *Pirkei Avot* (The Teaching of the Sages). Someone's facilitating the session, we're doing one of the chapters, and there is something from *Pirkei Avot* that I've done in class. And I was able to say, "Well, in Melton we learned that," and to explain what we had discussed in the class.

The learners above spoke about their functioning as explicit teachers, albeit informal, of their family members. They initiated conversations and offered observations informed by their classroom experience. Others spoke of instances where they functioned more passively, as a Jewish-education role model. Leslie's remarks revealed the impact of her learning on her son and her husband:

My older son saw me studying Hebrew and came in and started reading it with me. I was flabbergasted. I said, "Michael, this is so much fun. I can't believe you're doing this with me."

For the first ten years or so of our marriage, my husband didn't care if we had a Passover seder. It didn't make any difference to him. As he sees that I'm evolving as a Jew, he encourages me and participates in Jewish life much more. We didn't belong to a synagogue until two and a half years ago, and I pushed us to join. But now he encourages us to go there more. Recently, we were talking with someone about going to services. The other person was complaining about how boring it is, and my husband said, "We love it!"

Not at all coincidentally, Leslie referred to growth in Jewish involvement that began well before this current learning experience, that continued during her years of study, and that presumably will continue beyond. Significantly, all these steps were tied to her family involvement, be it the seder (a quintessentially family experience) or synagogue membership and attendance.

If family teacher may be distinguished from family role model, both may be distinguished from nurturer, a third informal Jewish educational function that was provoked or enriched by two years of adult Jewish study. As parents, Mini-School learners have numerous opportunities to more enthusiastically and knowledgeably nurture and encourage their children's Jewish growth. Pamela, a retired teacher, cited an occasion where she explicitly demonstrated a tolerant and pluralistic approach to Judaism and Jewish learning:

We have a very Reform daughter who says, "I am happy as a Reform Jew. I am happy in how we live. I am happy in my temple. I will not be a Conservative Jew." I said, "I didn't ask you to be. You are who you are and I'm proud of you. All I ask is that you're always knowledgeable about what you do. And when you make a choice, you make a choice. Just understand it."

Perhaps ironically, Pamela echoed a distinctive stance of Reform Judaism, one embodied in the slogan, "informed choice," even as she distinguished her own Conservative affiliation with the "very Reform" stance adopted by her daughter. (In this context, "very Reform" may either mean strongly attached to Reform Judaism or, as sometimes colloquially used, equivalent to not being strongly attached to Judaism.)

The ties between religion and family are well known and documented. Parenthood brings people in general (and Jews as well) to their houses of worship. Religiosity is associated with marital stability and more conventional family norms. Here we have uncovered one other connection between religion and family. These adult Jewish learners, more enthusiastic, confident, and knowledgeable about their religious identities, understandably became more active models, teachers, and nurturers for their children, spouses, and grandchildren. Presumably, then, the impact extends beyond the learners themselves, touching those near and dear to the learners themselves.

7. Building Belonging through Jewish Networks and Community Involvement

Not only did the learners bring their experiences to bear upon their family relationships; they also became more embedded in Jewish social networks. Learners reported a number of changes, large and small, in terms of their sense of connection to the Jewish community. Learners reported feeling an increased attachment to the Jewish people in general, to Jews in their community, and to those in their own immediate social circle. On the survey, almost one-third (31% answering "a great extent") reported having "become more attached to the Jewish people." Slightly fewer (28%) reported having "become more attached to the Jewish community." Just under a quarter (23%) noted a change in their own personal lives, responding that since enrolling, "to a great extent" they have "have developed a new set of friends."

In chapter 4, we look more closely at the strong social bonds and sense of community that were developed and nurtured in these adult Jewish learning classrooms. Here we read an illustration of how those social networks of new friends function and how lessons learned in the classroom were applied to a real-life situation. As Leslie, the Jewish Community Center leader, related:

We were learning about death rituals in class when Laura lost her father. We learned all about shiva. Many of us were in

shock when we learned about this. Many of us—myself included—were under the impression that shiva was a time of entertaining! Along with my friends, we would go to make a shiva
call—and it was always around mealtime—and we thought we
were supposed to eat the food that they had so that they
wouldn't be left with food. The discussion in class helped us to
understand what shiva is really about.

Anna, the business owner, reflected on the networks that emerged
from the experience of learning. Those networks, in turn, facilitated the
application, expression, and deepening of Jewish learning in the classroom. She remarked, "Overall, it has been a phenomenal experience—
social and learning. I call it my *havurah*. We all care about one another."
    The social significance of formal adult Jewish learning is apparently
felt in even wider circles, among those who are Jewishly engaged in the
organized community. Cindy, the former health-care administrator, reported feeling that students enjoy a fellowship with other students and
alumni, as well as a prestigious place in certain precincts: "It's an honor
to go through this program. I know that sounds strange. You meet great
people and you're known as a Melton student. That is an honor. I'm
very proud."
    Kim, the day school parent in our opening portrait, reported an-
other aspect of the nexus between adult Jewish learning and social networks of religiously engaged Jews—in this case, parents of Conservative
day school youngsters. Apparently, in her area, enrollment in the Mini-
School has taken on a near-normative quality in these communally active circles.
    The prestigious and normative features of Mini-School participation
in highly involved Jewish social networks have a notable historical
precedent. For centuries, engagement and excellence in Jewish learning
brought with it a measure of social prestige and even social advancement (Katz 1961). In premodern Eastern Europe, if not in other times
and places, boys from poor, low-status families could win the hand of
brides from affluent, high-status families by virtue of brilliance in the
study of traditional rabbinic texts. In recent years, organized Jewish
communal life, even outside the bounds of Orthodoxy, has begun to accord prestige to those who appear more learned and those who seem to
make an effort to learn. More pointedly, many site directors, especially
in the early years of their institutions, have recruited their students heavily among the local philanthropic leadership. By involving those at the

summit of the social hierarchy, these site directors have turned Mini-School participation specifically, and Jewish learning generally, into a matter of recognition and social prestige in organized Jewish life.

We also find evidence of other consequences for the organized community. Of the twenty-six possible sorts of change we listed in the survey questionnaire, ranking second in popularity was, "I have become a more committed advocate of community support for Jewish education," for which 40% answered, "to a great extent." On a personal level, 23% said that to a great extent they "have become more in favor of Jewish day school education." For example, Bill, a retired accountant, remarked, "It strengthened how I feel about Jewish education. I'm always an advocate for more education, particularly adult education."

Natalie, the past president of her local Jewish Federation, echoed a theme that is consistent with, if not possibly strengthened by, her learning experiences:

> It is so valuable to have professionals with a good Jewish background. When we hire people, we are very aware of their Jewish background. We have great professionals in Federation. As president, I worked very closely with our executive director. There were so many times that his education was called upon. It's so important to be knowledgeable.

Teachers and site directors also noted an increased involvement in Jewish communal activities among many students, either as Jewish educators themselves or as more involved lay leaders. Frieda Gottlieb mentioned that three of her former students became board members of the Jewish Federation. Ellen Rosen, a director at a large site, said: "I don't know exactly how many, but there are a number who have become Sunday school teachers. They now feel that they want to give back some of the things that they've learned."

In some cases, the Mini-School appeared to function as a catalyst to creating a higher communal value on adult Jewish learning. At a synagogue-based site, Marcia Jacobsen, the director, noted that this program has become the centerpiece of a learning congregation: "Learning—adult, children, whatever—is the core of existence at our congregation. That's not to say it displaces worship—absolutely not. But worship is a kind of learning as well. You have to learn in order to participate meaningfully."

Elsewhere, participation of community leadership appears to give adult Jewish learning greater visibility and respect in the Jewish community at large. Louise Milstein, a director at an established site, noted that the Jewish Federation in her community tries not to schedule programs on the evening that the Mini-School takes place. She said, "I hear regularly from leaders in Jewish Federation about how they want to be a part of this. I hear all the time, especially from Women's Division, that they won't schedule on Melton night." Similarly, another director said that an increased enrollment of communal leaders has raised its visibility and prestige: "It's known now in the community and it's looked upon as a respectable and significant step that the community has taken in bringing Melton here. I think it's a respected educational program for adults."

Thus, the Mini-School strengthens the ties of the learners with other Jews, be they in their immediate circle of friends and fellow learners, or the more abstract notions of Jewish community and peoplehood.

Smaller Changes: "Before" and "Now" in Selected Behaviors

Even though "behavior change" is not the primary focus of the Mini-School experience, our inquiry revealed that small numbers of students did alter their ritual observance and religious service attendance. At the same time, our key finding of stability in observance cannot be ignored. In our interviews, we occasionally heard allusions to strong changes in attitudes but only modest changes in practice.

In our survey, we asked learners to report relevant behaviors at the time of the survey (the end of the two-year learning cycle) and to reflect back on their behavior three or five years earlier. While the results we report below were themselves significant and revealing, so, too, were the unexpected responses that we encountered in this part of the survey. Upon receipt of the questionnaire, a few site directors and some respondents vigorously expressed their resentment over the inclusion of ritual and other behavioral items in our questionnaire. Although we, as researchers, could be conceived of and presented ourselves as independent from the leadership and staff, we were subject to the expectations applicable to the Mini-School's lead professionals. Apparently, our questionnaire violated implicit promises of the Mini-School, that is, never to appear to judge learners' level of ritual observance and never to challenge their patterns of practice. Both the curriculum and the teacher-training documents emphasized a commitment to avoid seeming criticism of these adult Jewish learners' choices in the area of observance and religiosity. In any event, behavioral change was not an explicit goal of the Mini-School, and, as we shall see, the evidence suggests only rather modest changes in behavior, at least those that we could easily measure on a questionnaire.

Gail Silver, a teacher, captured the spirit of this philosophy when she noted her own priorities and preferences for what an adult Jewish learning experience should be:

> I've seen students become more observant in terms of kashrut, Shabbat, and so on. But the fact that people are thinking in a different way, rather than a big life transformation, is what's more significant. They are taking their lives as Jews—things that they've done by rote all these years—and seeing things in a new way with an expanded perspective.

As noted earlier, we asked respondents to report on several Jewish identity measures that they exhibited as of three years ago, and for "this year," the year of the survey. We found a consistent pattern: very small increases across all measures. Thus the small margin of just one to six percentage points separated the reports for the two points in time with respect to a wide variety of measures: synagogue membership, fasting on Yom Kippur, lighting Sabbath candles, keeping kosher at home, keeping kosher outside the home, attending services monthly, and having mostly Jewish friends.

In broad terms, notwithstanding the strong evidence of impact in such areas as meaning-making and text study, these results also point to a rather limited effect upon certain behaviors, particularly ritual practice and involvement in the synagogue or Jewish organizations. When asked about areas where they may have changed over the last few years, relatively few indicated Shabbat observance, community involvement, synagogue involvement, observance generally, and kashrut observance.

At the same time, we certainly heard some people speak of increased activities in all these areas. One handwritten comment addressed the process of gradual change in behavior that was accompanied, it seems, by both reflection and passionate enthusiasm:

> I have become much more observant. Although I do not (yet) keep kosher, I can no longer bring myself to eat *treyf*. I am more

grateful that all my kids are married to Jews. All belong to synagogues and are giving their kids a better Jewish education than
we gave them. I love, love, love being Jewish!

Denominational affiliation also shifted slightly over the two to three
years, uniformly in the more traditional direction. Thus, the generally
under-engaged "just Jewish" category declined slightly, as did the percentage of Reform Jews (two percentage points in each case). The Reconstructionist and secular responses held steady. Conservative affiliation
increased by one percentage point, and the percentage calling themselves
Orthodox increased by three points. The proportion volunteering in the
Jewish community increased by seven percentage points, while JCC involvement climbed by just two to three points.

To examine change more comprehensively, we constructed an eleven-
point index including the items mentioned above at both points in time.
By subtracting the "this year's" score (of zero to eleven) from the comparable score for three years ago, we can learn how many respondents reported an increase, decrease, or stability in their overall levels of Jewish
involvement as measured by several indicators at two points in time.

Fully 54% remained stable on the index, reporting no change from
three years ago. At the same time, just over one-third (34%) increased
their involvement, and 12% decreased. Moreover, of those increasing,
more reported fairly sizable increases than the comparable number reporting sizable decreases.

Although the overall tendency pointed to more growth than decline
in the index of Jewish involvement, these results point primarily to stability in Jewish identity behavior: a vast majority (81%) either changed
not at all (54%), or changed minimally (by one unit) in both directions
(27%). In other words, more than four in five hardly budged with respect to religious practice and affiliation.

How do we explain this relative stability over time? One possibility
entails obstacles to change posed by life circumstances, social environment, and the readiness to change (or the lack thereof). Learners may
have vastly enhanced their appreciation for things Jewish, but they remain at approximately the same stage of life, with the same family and
the same friends. Moreover, they came to the Mini-School with no
commitment to change, or even, as we learned, brought a resistance to
reexamining their patterns of religious practice. Indeed, the Mini-
School's ethos militates against pressing learners to change their religious behavior.

Even when the learning affected people's beliefs and attitudes, change in behavior was another matter, as one of our handwritten survey comments suggested:

> I have always had a strong commitment to the Jewish community and to Judaism. The Mini-School has given me a more solid basis for my beliefs. I was never very observant, and at seventy it felt silly to change. If I were younger, I believe I would be more observant.

Two other handwritten comments from the survey suggested limited behavioral change as well, notwithstanding a high level of satisfaction with the learning experience:

> I was active and committed before I signed up. I enjoyed studying and discussing Judaism. However, I do not feel that I was affected by the Mini-School at all. My level of observance and commitment already was and is high.

* * *

> It was a rewarding and wonderful learning experience. However, it did not change my personal involvement in Jewish life. I have taken courses throughout my life. I am active in my synagogue. I have supported Jewish education. I contribute very generously to Jewish charities and organizations.

One reason that our survey may not have uncovered changes in practice is that such changes may occur in highly idiosyncratic ways that no survey could anticipate and detect. As an example, we may take Wanda, a Conservative Jew who was involved in Jewish learning for several years prior to starting the Mini-School. For Wanda, Shabbat took on new meaning after her participation in the program, accompanied by changes in practice:

> I'm more aware of Shabbes, but I don't know if that's from my studies. I used to think nothing of cleaning the house on Saturday. Now I don't do it. Maybe it's an excuse not to clean, I don't know. I also started to make yarmulkes for women. I did that when I was a teenager for the guys. When I became bat mitzvah as an adult, I started doing it for the Melton class. It's

become a little business. I've become more aware that you don't do that on Shabbes. We did learn what was appropriate on Shabbes and what wasn't—so that did change, yes.

In another example, Howard, an attorney, remarked, "I am more serious about my Judaism—not necessarily more religious. I have done further study." Cindy, the former health-care administrator, reported stability in ritual practices alongside the emergence of some very positive feelings about Jewish learning:

> I don't think the program has enhanced or changed my ritual life. I just feel much better knowing that I'm learning. Even though I believe you never learn everything—you can do this until the day you die—I feel as though I'm accomplishing something. I'm in the room, I'm listening, I'm enjoying it. Just to do that is something. What I do in terms of my practice is probably now because of my congregation and the people I associate with. I don't think that Melton necessarily changed that.

Social Constraints:
Why Behavior May Not Change

The evidence above points to two factors that help explain the rather small number of learners who reported significant change in their religious behavior. For some, advanced stage in life may undercut the possibility of making dramatic changes in practice. Perhaps for even more, their initial expectations included a readiness to learn and rethink, but not a readiness to modify patterns of observance they had observed for years. In essence, the Mini-School experience encouraged engagement in the first part of a transformative learning process, whereby learners questioned old ways of understanding and knowing and broadened their perspectives, but few translated this reassessment into distinct behavioral change.

In addition to individual reluctance to change, another inhibiting factor is the power of social constraints, the limits set by one's family and community. An intensive experience in adult Jewish learning may well change one's perspective, but it is unlikely to instigate a change of one's social circles (new spouse, children, friends, or synagogue). Without a social support system, the process of transformation becomes all the more challenging.

One set of especially poignant comments made by Dana, the human-services trainer who ultimately dropped out of the Mini-School, demonstrated the difficulty in undertaking change in practice without the support of one's significant others:

> I made efforts to put into practice some of the things that I've learned. I was doing it myself, and as a family we were doing a little bit. But there's only so much you can do when you're already in a family unit. I didn't want to know any more about Jewish observance, because the more I knew, the more I felt I wasn't doing. It gave me the feeling of being an observer and not a participant.

Site director Marcia Jacobsen also reflected on the tension between the potential changes that studying may spark, and the realities of people's lives:

> Sometimes we create conflicts that we aren't equipped to handle. Those come from situations in which students are learning about a particular ritual in Jewish life, and through their learning, they consider taking on a mitzvah that affects not only them, but their spouse or children. For example, making the house kosher or going to the *mikveh*. Of course, we say, that's great! They're becoming more observant. But not so fast: it can result in turmoil in a home where the house is not supportive of this. These issues can be unsettling, and I don't think we're good yet at knowing how to deal with them.

Although most of the people we interviewed said that their learning experiences had a positive impact on their families, a few noted that their involvement had actually caused tensions or discord. Wanda, an active Jewish community volunteer, reported that she had experienced "some conflicts because I want to change my way of life and my husband is not into it yet." Bill, a retired accountant, said that he wanted to keep kosher, but getting to the kosher butcher was inconvenient for his wife and, since the family had only one dishwasher, sometimes Bill's requests "seem like *mishegoss* [craziness]" to his wife.

The Subtle Nature of Change

To say that few learners changed their Jewish behavior leaves much of the story of impact untold. Change did occur. Of course, not all learners changed in the same ways or at the same pace. Indeed, in many cases, changes were quite subtle, in ways that would not necessarily manifest themselves in obvious behaviors.

The teachers' insights on the qualities of the type of student who is most likely to be changed by their experience are helpful to note. Consistent with adult learning theory (Mezirow 1991; Brookfield 1986; Vella 1994), Ellen Rosen described learners who were most open to new ideas as the ones most profoundly affected: "I would say that the students who come in knowing that they don't know a lot and really want to learn a lot are the ones most influenced by their experiences." Later, when reflecting on the type of student who continues after completing the two years of prescribed study, she said: "If you look at the graduates who keep coming back, it's people who are open to the idea of learning, open to the idea that there is so much to learn and that they need to keep going on, no matter what age they are." Gail Silver also commented on how those students who are most open to learning are the ones most affected:

> The know-it-alls never get transformed—well, rarely, anyway. People who are open and people who are at a crossroads in their lives are most likely to change. People who are open to looking at things with a different perspective, who don't come in with an agenda, and who come regularly—they are most likely to change.

Many of the learners we interviewed reflected this openness that the teachers described. They said that their participation led them to "new ways of seeing" and to "become more aware." More often, this awareness developed over time. Wanda, a community volunteer, described her own evolution:

> It has been a gradual journey of awareness. I came from a home where we knew we were Jewish, but my parents were never educated in the details. When you learn the details, things become more sharply focused. I remember when I first started studying:

the teacher was talking of seeing things through Jewish eyes. And I do have Jewish eyes now—whereas I don't think I did ten years ago.

For Selma Jones and Daniel Shaber, both profiled in chapter 1, their studies helped them to clarify and contextualize old beliefs and also to take steps toward specific changes in behavior or outlook. Unusual for their intellectual vibrancy, both were able to "move off the page" and interpret text at several levels. They were able to fully engage in "transformational learning," a process that involves deliberate reflecting on past experiences, questioning old assumptions, exploring options for new ways of behaving, and acquiring information that will support functioning (or thinking) in new ways (Mezirow 1991). For Selma, learning about traditional mitzvot prompted her to think anew about her values:

What we learned was definite: "Do not do these things." First of all, I got the idea that these are sacrificial or ritual commandments that we cannot follow today since we have no temple. So, okay, put those aside. But those mitzvot that relate to how you live your life—I was impressed with the ones that deal with how you treat your fellow man. If you have wages that are due an individual, don't hold them overnight because the man may be too poor.

Like Selma, Daniel also showed signs of having engaged in a transformative learning process. He reported that his studies made him think more deliberately about how he translated what he was learning into how he led his life as a Jew:

We begin with a question, and then we have an opportunity to discuss what we think the answers might be, and then we get a little education, and then we hear from the teacher what the real content issues are. The final piece, which is what a lot of the experience is for me, is to take that knowledge and apply it to our own individual lives and consider what it means for us as individual Jews to deal with.

More than grappling with texts, however, Daniel said that he found that learning caused him to reflect on aspects of his Orthodox upbringing, to rethink old assumptions about what constitutes being "authentic" as a Jew, and gradually to develop new ways to understand his Jewish identity. His comments about his emerging sense of self provided insight into how transformed Daniel felt as a learner:

> I have a lot of old friends in the Orthodox community whom I can have discussions with now, whom I never felt comfortable having discussions with before—because I felt inadequate. A lot of that was presumptuousness on my part: just because they were Orthodox doesn't necessarily mean that they got the same kind of learning experience that I had. But Melton gave me an opportunity to discuss issues of historical and spiritual content with people whom I probably wouldn't have before.

For many students, the Jewish growth experience neither starts nor stops with two years of study, as Kim, the day school parent we met earlier, made clear:

> Gradually climbing up that ladder, I guess, is the best way to put it. Constantly pushing forward. I think the more knowledge I have, the more observant I become. Ten years ago, we started having Friday night dinner at home. Friday night dinner meant that we lit candles, we said motzei, we said the short kiddush, and I brought in dinner. We were going to shul at that time. But Shabbat basically ended Saturday morning when shul was over.

Of course, some respondents seem to have gone through some dramatic changes in practice. These take place even without the total compliance of their family members, yet sometimes with their support. Kim portrayed such a development in her home:

> I think my observance is getting stronger and stronger. I don't watch TV anymore on Shabbat, although if it's on in the family room and my kids are in there, I'm not going to run into another room. I was sitting with my daughter a couple of weeks ago on Shabbat. She had the TV on and was getting up to go into the other room. She said, "Would you like me to turn the TV off?" So she understands that I would prefer it not being on. But there's got to be that *shalom bayit* [domestic harmony] in the house. That's more important, as far as I'm concerned.

These respondents shared with many others fairly high initial levels of involvement in Jewish life. On some level, their studies answered their needs. Otherwise they would not have continued attending classes week in and week out for two years. At the same time, their high starting levels of engagement, as well as the Mini-School educational philosophy that abjures explicit emphasis on behavioral change, militated against their testifying to significant changes in their Jewish-oriented activities.

Stronger Jewish Identities: More Meaning, More Connection

Taken together, the results presented above point to changes in learners' understanding of Judaism and in their personal Jewish identities. The enhanced meaning for the Jewish lives they were already living, combined with the enriched connections to other Jews (be they family members, friends, acquaintances, fellow congregants, or community members) served to strengthen a commitment to and appreciation for what may be called "the real Jewish me." The emerging Jewish self, at the end of the two years of study, was considered by the learners continuous with the developing, dynamic Jewish self who entered the Mini-School. But the feelings about that self deepened and broadened. Judy, a clinical psychologist, spoke to this process:

> It's a part of knowing who I am. I've been trying to understand who I am, forever, in all kinds of ways: who I am in relation to my family and my patients and my husband, and who I am in terms of my Jewishness and the fact that everybody has been Jewish all the way back to God. It's my history. And it didn't seem right for me not to have more information about that.

Even Margaret, a convert to Judaism, saw her Jewish identity as a fundamental and inalienable part of her. Adult Jewish learning helped Margaret learn more and understand more about being Jewish. In a way, the learning experience was therapeutic. Her studies were not about some unconnected tenet or disembodied concept but rather entailed learning more about herself as a Jew and herself in relation to some significant Jewish others: "My learning is like my family tree. It's like my base. It's where I come from. And Melton anchors me and gives me a bit of an identity. I guess that's why, especially being a Jew by choice, you can flounder out there and not know what's going on."

The experience of Debby, the college instructor, reinforces several of these themes. Debby's Jewish journey goes back many years before her Mini-School experience. But while Debby's approach may have changed, the essential connection to being Jewish was an inalienable and central part of her identity:

> I would say that fifteen years ago, if you asked me who I was I would have said that I am an American woman. Now I would say that I'm a Jewish woman. It's a part of me culturally, it's a part of me spiritually. It's my fiber. I didn't grow up with any of this, but it was always there.

Once again, the learners' views were supported by the Mini-School teachers, who uniformly reported that the Jewish identity of virtually all their students was strengthened through their learning experiences. However, as might be expected among a group of adult learners who come with varied backgrounds and goals, this intensification was expressed in a wide variety of ways. Each teacher cited a few cases where students' experiences led to changes in level or style of Jewish practice. More often, however, they observed students becoming more confident as Jewish learners and about themselves as Jews. Frieda Gottlieb's students seemed to be reading more books with Jewish content, and they wanted to share that information with her: "I don't think a day has gone by when I haven't gotten a book to read from one of the students at both sites."

Marci Newhouse provided a specific example of this kind of expanded perspective. She described a student who became more confident in her ability to participate in text study outside of the classroom. Here the behavioral change related to her increased knowledge base, but did not necessarily affect her level of observance:

> A woman recently told me that she goes to Shabbat services at her synagogue every week, and the rabbi does a Torah dialogue with the congregation. She stood up a couple of weeks ago and answered something he asked, and he was so impressed that he approached her after shul, congratulated her, and said that it must have been Melton! And she said yes, she was taking Melton.

So did these learners change? In certain ways, as we have noted, no change took place; in other ways, change certainly loomed large. In any event, the impact cannot be measured in its entirety at a point close to completion of two years of study. Rather, as Selma and Cindy made clear in separate comments, the impact may well unfold as the Jewish persona unfolds over the years:

Selma: Certainly I will not become a religious person because of what I've learned here. But I feel that I have much more of a foundation as a Jew.

Cindy: I have now been exposed to readings, texts, and opinions that have enhanced and enriched me. So yes, I think that has changed me. I am using the information and am really happy about that. I'm very proud that I can do it.

Conclusion

The core impact of Jewish study upon learners' Jewish identities centered on meaning-making, the enhanced ability to derive sense and purpose from everyday Jewish activities, be they specifically Jewish practices, or everyday activities that may have ethical import.

Beyond these matters, learners became more accepting and appreciative of Jews whose approach to being Jewish differs from their own, particularly the more traditional. Accordingly, they seem to become more understanding of normative Judaism, also accompanied, for some, by more positive feelings for God and spirituality.

These changes in learners' attitudes and beliefs found expression in aspects of their Jewish belonging. Within their families, many reported enhanced roles as explicit informal Jewish teachers, or as Jewish-education role models. More widely, they expressed increased attachment to Jews in their immediate social circles, their Jewish communities, and to the Jewish people in general.

At the same time, the learning experience exerted rather limited impact upon certain bellwether behaviors, particularly ritual practice and involvement in the synagogue or Jewish organizations. The vast majority reported little or no change in the total number of rites and practices that they were performing regularly. The one major behavioral change (accompanied by new attitudes and abilities) occurred in relation to Jewish learning generally and text study specifically. Here, learners seem to have taken on new interest, confidence, understanding, competence, and activity.

In sum, learners came to a new commitment to and appreciation for what may be called "the real Jewish me." They discovered and enlarged upon the authentic Jew inside each of them.

Educational researchers observe that the impact of particular programs can be difficult to observe, demonstrate, or assess. We may well have overlooked some sorts of impact, or imputed impact where none or little really occurred, or misconstrued the evidence of impact we encountered. All of that is possible. Yet the consistency of evidence here does encourage confidence in our findings. As we have noted, the quantitative survey and qualitative interview evidence reinforced each other. The consistency of the evidence was matched by the consistency in the initial orientations of the learners (as we understood them) and the intentions of the faculty and Mini-School leadership. Learners and educators were generally in tacit, if not explicit, agreement on educational goals and methods. They agreed that the experience should be about deepening understanding and widening appreciation of Judaism generally, and texts specifically. They agreed that personal engagement, discussion, socializing, and community building should be part and parcel of life inside and around the classroom. As we documented in the previous chapter, these learners, like many other adults, came for intellectual stimulation, companionship, and some degree of social prestige in a community that increasingly values their learning activity. And learners and staff agreed that, in this age of denominational pluralism and non-judgmentalism, learners are insulated from even the subtlest pressure to change their practice.

All these elements worked to heighten the learners' sense of belonging, be it to the classroom community, the local Jewish community, or the community of Jews throughout time and space. As we shall see presently, in chapters 3 and 4, the Mini-School draws upon and strengthens the links of these Jewish learners with one another, their Jewish "significant others," and the Jewish people throughout history and the world.

CHAPTER THREE
Creating Torah and Making Meaning
in the Classroom

All that a seasoned student will one day innovate in his learning was said to Moshe at Sinai. (Vayikra Rabbah 13:3)

The Rabbis wrote these words to emphasize the continuity and unity of Torah. In the rabbinic worldview, all commentary and interpretation of the Torah, no matter when it is actually written, was foretold at the original revelation at Sinai. Today we might extend this teaching to say that the words uttered by students in the course of learning Torah are themselves a form of Torah, and thus adult Jewish learners are not merely passive recipients of a corpus of Jewish texts and teachings, but also active creators of "Torah" through their readings and interpretations of the tradition. As one teacher astutely observed, the students are the "living texts" of Judaism who come to learning to encounter the "written texts" of the tradition. Their questions, interpretations, and conclusions thus constitute a set of "oral texts," through which they develop and express the meanings that they give to Jewish belief and practice.

While these interpretations may not hold the same communally normative force as the interpretations in centuries past, on a personal level they similarly enable students to take ownership of the Jewish textual canon and forge new links on the chain of Jewish tradition. Adult Jewish learning becomes, in sociologist Samuel Heilman's words, "sentimental education," in which learners "rediscover and express the fundamental character or spirit of their culture along with their responses to it. In the process, they define their picture of the world or make sense of the events through which they and their forebears have lived" (Heilman 1983, 109). This interplay of tradition and individual, text and response, is what makes adult Jewish learning more than the acquisition of knowledge. Students find themselves having intellectual as well as emotional reactions to Jewish texts as they recognize that the ideas within them have real and profound implications for the ways in which they define and live their Jewish lives.

This chapter will explore some of the ways in which adult Jewish learners respond intellectually and emotionally to Jewish texts and ideas, and thus make sense of and contribute to the body of Jewish tradition. The range of responses is, of course, nearly as vast and varied as the number of students. Nevertheless, close observation within the classroom reveals certain themes and frameworks that shaped many of the classroom discussions and interactions. Using the imagery offered by the Torah, one could say that these students not only study, but often follow the paths of their biblical ancestors. Like Isaac, who redug and refilled his father's wells, students renew the "wells" of their ancestors by finding new meaning and relevance in traditional teachings. Like Jacob, who wrestled with a divine/human figure, students wrestle with difficult and troubling teachings of the tradition, as well as their own human reactions. Like Sarah, who laughed when faced with the doubtful prophecy of her impending maternity, students use humor to reinforce shared cultural meanings as well as to express resistance to certain Jewish laws and traditions. And like the women of Israel, who followed Miriam in her dance of victory, students look to their teachers to provide the models of Jewish life and set the boundaries of acceptable interpretation.

Research Methodology

This chapter and the next one provide a panoramic glimpse into the Mini-School classrooms by means of ethnographic research conducted at one site.[1] For the length of the academic year, I became a participant-observer at this site, attending four one-hour classes a week (first- and second-year courses). Most of the time, I assumed the role of a silent observer, speaking only when directly addressed, as happened occasionally. While there is always the danger that the mere presence of a re-

[1]The research for this and the following chapter was done by Dr. Meredith Woocher, henceforth "I."

searcher will change the course of events, the nature of the discussions that took place around me led me to believe that I did largely succeed in becoming a "fly on the wall" and that students did not censor their questions or comments because of my presence.

These classroom observations provide an important dimension to this study. While much can be gleaned about the experiences of adult Jewish learners though the reflections of students and teachers, such as are included throughout this volume, many dimensions can only be absorbed through the direct and sustained observation possible though ethnographic study. Ethnography allows the researcher to take an insider's or emic perspective, as she or he becomes a fellow traveler with those being studied, and thus privy to insights and experiences that can only be fully grasped from within. It is one thing to hear a student describe a joke told during a class, or a moment of disagreement between students; it is quite another to experience the sense of connection that comes from shared laughter, or a palpable tension that a teacher must skillfully negotiate and defuse. Ethnography also captures the details that are often lost in the filter of memory. The overall theme of a classroom discussion may be recalled, but rarely the actual exchange of ideas, the ways in which one student's words build upon, or challenge, another's. These unique perspectives offered by ethnography allow for a detailed portrait of community building and learning as it occurs in the adult Jewish learning classroom.

In addition to observing students and teachers in the classroom, I also engaged with them though informal conversations before and after classes, and formal, semi-structured interviews in person and by telephone. Approximately eighty students were enrolled in the classes I observed, ranging in age from their late twenties to early eighties (with the majority in their fifties and sixties). Consistent with the overall gender mix at Mini-Schools across North American, as reported in chapter 1, nearly all the students in these classes were women. The classes that met during the day typically had only one to three men in each class; the evening courses contained more men (usually five to ten per class) and had slightly younger students on average.

Finally, through observation and interviews, I became well acquainted with the three instructors whose classrooms I entered, and their personalities and perspectives will emerge through this ethnographic portrait. The teachers profiled here are Marc Salzman, a young and "hip" (yet traditional) Conservative rabbi who was as likely to quote the Grateful Dead as the Talmud; Frieda Gottlieb, a Reform rebbitzen who had recently moved from the Midwest, where she was a longtime Melton teacher and former site director; and Hadassah Stein, an Orthodox child of Holocaust survivors, a graduate of Stern College at Yeshiva University and former lawyer who switched careers to reengage with her true love, teaching Jewish texts.

My ethnographic analysis is organized into two chapters. Here, we will investigate how the sense of community and trust created in the classroom enables Jewish learners to delve deeply into Jewish texts, together exploring how these texts reflect and shape their lives as Jews. In chapter 4, the focus will shift to describing the social dynamics within the classroom that lead to building community and fellowship among the learners.

Drawing from the Wells: Finding Meaning and Relevance in the Text

Isaac dug anew the wells that had been dug in the days of his father, Abraham, and that the Philistines had stopped up after Abraham's death, and he gave them the same names that his father had given them. (Gen. 26:18)

Much of the Torah that is created in the classroom answers the questions that many students bring with them about the role of Jewish tradition in their lives: What meaning do Jewish texts have for contemporary Jewish society? How can we interpret the words of the Rabbis or the Torah so that they are most relevant today? What place does Jewish tradition ultimately have in the modern world? In interviews, a number of students remarked on how much they enjoyed being able to see links between the ideas and texts of the tradition and the modern realities of the world around them, describing such lessons as "relevant," "contemporary," and "valid." Some students, even nonobservant ones, found that the ritual dimensions of Judaism particularly resonated with them. As Joanne, a second-year student, explained, "I do not keep a kosher home, but I learned a lot about kashrut that I did not know. What's so interesting sometimes is that things that are in the *Tanakh* and in the Torah are so relevant in today's world." Her classmate Tammy was pleasantly surprised to find how contemporary many of the ethical teachings of the Talmud seemed: "One thing I was surprised by was, especially with these ethics issues, how contemporary the texts are. You read them and you think, 'Oh my gosh, did they write this yesterday?' I think that's neat." Sandra, a Mini-School graduate, agreed that the moral precepts of the Bible and Talmud seemed to her to be especially salient for today, providing a firm foundation that she found personally very valuable:

> The whole business about halakhah—specifically, mitzvot—was extremely helpful. The particular ones I was impressed with were how you treat your fellow man. For example: if you have wages that are due an individual, don't hold them overnight because the man may be too poor; and every seven years you forgive a debt. All kinds of things like that have been enormously instructive. It helps you visualize sayings that were written thousands of years ago that are valid today. If we live like that, we will survive as human beings.

As Tammy's and Sandra's remarks suggest, students often found particular meaning and relevance in texts that addressed thorny ethical issues. In one example, during an Ethics lesson on approaches to euthanasia, the class studied a talmudic text in which the martyr Rabbi Hananiah, sentenced to being burned alive by the Roman authorities, is implored to take actions to hasten his tortuous death. The text reads:

> Rabbi . . . open your mouth that the fire may enter [and you will die]. He said to them, "It is better that He who gave my soul should take it and let no one harm himself." The executioner asked him, "Rabbi, if I intensify the fire and remove the mats from your body, will you bring me into the World to Come?" He said, "Yes.". . . [The executioner] immediately removed the mats and increased the flames. [Hananiah's] soul speedily departed. Then [the executioner] leaped up and fell into the fire. A *bat kol* [heavenly voice] went out and proclaimed, "R. Hananiah and the executioner are prepared for the Life to Come." (Avodah Zarah 8a)

After the class read and pondered the text, Michelle, one of the students, voiced her puzzlement with it, and was answered by Marc, the teacher:

> *Michelle:* I don't understand this text. Why is the rabbi giving the executioner permission to remove the wet wool any different from him opening his mouth and inhal-

ing the smoke to hasten his death? Both cases involve doing something to bring about death more quickly.

Marc: It does seem to be a gray area, but I think that the text is pointing out the difference between active and passive actions.

Leah: What I find so interesting is that we're still having these same debates today about active and passive medical actions. This is still so relevant.

Marc: Yes, although it's even more complicated today, because we have technologies that let us extend life in ways that the Rabbis couldn't even have imagined. With modern technology come great blessings but also great challenges.

Rebecca: So how would you match up Jewish tradition with all this new technology? It seems almost impossible!

Marc: Well, it happens gradually, by looking for analogies with what we have in our sources.

Michelle: So then, this text might tell us that we can remove an impediment to death, like a life-support system, but we can't give someone something that would bring on their death, such as drugs.

Michelle's opening question focused on the facts of the text, as she sought to understand the basis on which the Rabbis distinguished one death-hastening act from another. However, once Marc answered by pointing out that the text divides these acts into broader categories, active and passive, the students quickly began to recognize their contemporary relevance. This led one student to raise what is, in effect, the central question driving the Mini-School's Ethics curriculum—how can we apply traditional Jewish teachings to contemporary situations unimaginable when these texts were written? By the end of the discussion, Michelle was able to answer both her original question—What is the difference between these two actions that serve to hasten death?—and the broader underlying question—How can we see links between the distinctions made by the Rabbis and contemporary realities? In doing so, she forged an important link between the world of the Rabbis on the page and the world of modern medicine.

At other times, students applied principles gleaned from the tradition to contemporary cultural or political events, enabling them to apply a Jewish lens to familiar incidents or icons and thus understand them in new ways. In another Ethics lesson, one such discussion was inspired by studying Maimonides' dictate on *lashon hara* (evil speech, i.e., gossip): "Even though it be true, the person [who gossips] destroys the world" (*Mishneh Torah*, Laws of Human Character, 7:3). In the conversation that followed, students were quickly able to see how the realities that Maimonides described were still very evident in modern life:

Marc:	Notice that Maimonides says that gossip "destroys the world" even if it's true.
Evelyn:	I think it's a matter of privacy. Your privacy is invaded when someone tells things about you, even when they're true.
Marc:	Yes, we're very aware of this today in society because of how the media act.
Susan:	Look at things like Princess Di, or O.J., or Clinton and Monica Lewinsky.
Robin:	Is there a difference between gossip and news?
Marc:	That's a very interesting question. What do you think?
Evelyn:	I think that the Clinton story was gossip and not news. That was no one's business except Clinton's, Monica's, and Hillary's.
Roberta:	You could say that Linda Tripp's whole motive was destroying the world, because she was trying to bring down the president, which could have destroyed the country.
Marc:	Here, you could say that Linda Tripp was the *rechila*, the one who gossips, and then Ken Starr and the Republicans used the information for disparaging purposes, which is how Maimonides defines *lashon hara*.

The scandal surrounding Bill Clinton and Monica Lewinsky, perhaps because of its recent occurrence and inherent drama, was often discussed through the framework of Jewish teachings. Upon learning from Hadassah, the Purposes instructor, that the *yetzer hara* is not necessarily an "evil" inclination but may be understood as a libidinous force that can produce both positive and negative results (and hence the talmudic principle, "the greater the man, the greater the *yetzer*"), a student immediately deduced, "Bill Clinton should have used that as his defense!" During an Ethics lesson that included the biblical story in which Natan the prophet chastises King David for his adulterous dalliance with Batsheva, a student announced, "He's Joe Lieberman to David's Clinton." In both cases, linking the contemporary event with the traditional principle seemed to help students gain new insights into each. Facets of life that might have seemed far from the religious sphere, such as the media or politics, were suddenly drawn into their Jewish worlds. Doris, a first-year student, reflected on how her learning had given her a new perspective on the presidential election of 2000:

> I began to think of the election in light of what I've learned about Judaism. I started to think about the conflict between brothers and relate that to the text of the Bible, and the laws regarding governance and Judaism, and what you look for in a leader. I started connecting things and seeing how relevant a lot of what was written in the Bible was.

Karen, a Mini-School graduate, saw an even broader relevance to the Jewish texts she had studied. Her learning, she reported in an interview, "enabled me to see that all of life can be seen through a Jewish lens. It's a way of looking at the world."

In the scenes described above, students used traditional texts and teachings as lenses to gain new perspectives on contemporary life.[2] At other times, students engaged in a reverse process: by examining texts through the lens of their own experience, they discovered new contexts for historical ideas or events that had deep personal meaning and relevance. This occurred, for instance, during a Jewish history class on Zionism, when students were given the space and time to shift a histori-

---

[2]Samuel Heilman identified this process among Orthodox adult Talmud students as "contemporization." The opposite process, in which students enter the world of the text to the extent that they seem to lose sight of the contemporary world, he termed "traditioning" (Heilman, 1983, 62–63). For further discussion of the significance of Heilman's theoretical formulations for contemporary non-Orthodox adult Jewish education, see Burton I. Cohen, "An Accidental Teacher Researcher Looks at a Synagogue Talmud Study Circle," in *Essays in Education in Honor of Joseph S. Lukinsky,* ed. Burton I. Cohen and Adina Ofek (New York: Jewish Theological Seminary, 2002).

cal lesson to an intimate level. After Frieda, the instructor, began the class with an overview of the early years of the Zionist movement and its core ideologies, Libby directed the conversation to more immediate personal concerns:

Libby: I think that the generation before us, who remember when there was no Israel, felt much more Zionistic. It's very different today among our generation.

Susan: But we do still have a lot of Zionistic feeling. Will our kids be Zionists? That's the question. My kids, who are in their twenties and thirties, don't understand when I say that we need Israel for Jewish survival. They're Americans first and Jews second.

Amy: I hate to say it, but it makes me think that if it weren't for anti-Semitism we probably wouldn't have had Israel at all. It's weird to say that there's something good about anti-Semitism, but I think we wouldn't be so bonded together otherwise. I'm the same age as your kids, Susan, and I have to say that growing up here, where it was so easy to be Jewish, I really did take Judaism for granted.

Pam: For my son, it took going to college in Denver to realize how important Judaism was to him. He thought I was crazy when he was applying to college and I pulled out the Hillel books,[3] but then he got there and realized how much it mattered to have other Jews around.

Leah: My daughter, who is twenty-seven, sees anti-Semitism as just part of the hatred that's in the world, not something directed specifically at Jews. She and her friends don't relate to the Holocaust like we did. It's just distant history to them.

Roberta: Even with all the Zionist ideology, I agree with Amy that if it weren't for the Holocaust, I don't think there would be an Israel. It was the world's guilt that they let this happen that paved the way.

[3]Pam is referring to *The Guide to Jewish Life on Campus,* published by Hillel: The Foundation for Jewish Campus Life.

Throughout the discussion, Frieda withheld comment and allowed the students to direct the flow of the conversation. As they did, they wove together their personal and communal concerns: fears about the future of Zionism in America, questions about the relationship between the Holocaust and the creation of the State of Israel, and revelations about how parents try to keep their children connected to Judaism (and, in Amy's case, her own admission that at one point in her life, she had taken her Jewishness for granted). The intermingling of the personal, the communal, and the historical seemed to give each dimension a new framework of meaning. Susan's, Pam's, and Leah's struggles to instill a sense of Jewish identity in their children, which might have before seemed to them to be isolated familial challenges, were placed in the context of the struggles of world Jewry for Jewish survival. On the flip side, grand and overwhelming historical dramas such as the Holocaust and the founding of Israel were examined through the lens of immediate, personal events.

Even the most distant points in Jewish mythic history, such as the events in the lives of the biblical patriarchs and matriarchs, became more real for students when they could see a personal connection. Karen described in an interview how her learning made these figures real, and personally relevant, to her: "I felt the whole generational link, going back to Abraham, Sarah, Rebecca, Isaac, and Jacob—feeling part of our people and feeling actually linked through the generations, as opposed to feeling that this is just history and doesn't relate to me." Hadassah helped students in her Purposes class come to a similar insight, commenting on the description of the Torah's complexity in *Pirkei Avot:* "Turn it and turn it and turn it, for everything is in it" (*Pirkei Avot* 5:22). Her explanation of this dictum helped students see the ways in which the characters and events of the Torah could be related to immediate and personal concerns:

> *Hadassah:* Torah changes not only through the generations, but it changes with you throughout all the phases of your life. It will mean something new each time. If you read the story of Joseph and his brothers as a child, it's just a story. Then you read it as an adult, and think, I could never sell my brother into slavery. How could they do that?
>
> *Joan:* Or maybe you think that you could!

Ronnie: I've just now realized the purpose of this course more clearly than ever. It's such an enlightening experience to read these stories as an adult, and compare it with what I thought as a child. Now, when I read about Sarah or Hannah, I think about all the women I know who have had fertility problems. Or, as you said, you read about all the problems between brothers, and I find myself thinking about my own sons. It adds many dimensions and makes it meaningful for me.

As students were exposed to figures of the Jewish past, literary and historical, they found more avenues of connection between themselves and the texts in the curriculum. Frieda, the instructor of Jewish history, encouraged her students to imagine themselves living out the dramas of Jewish history, facing the choices and struggles of previous generations. Her lessons always included the requisite historical dates, people, and places, but, as Frieda repeatedly told her students, the transmission and absorption of these factual details were not her primary goal: "It's important that you know that this isn't really a history course. I don't care if you remember names or dates; I care that you have a sense of the big ideas that I want you to concentrate on. My goal in every class is to try to put you back into the historical context of the lesson." While this approach to the course sometimes left students a bit confused as they sped through hundreds of years of history in an hour, it did encourage imaginative—and, at times, impassioned—discussions of the Jewish past and the complex choices and struggles that Jews faced throughout the centuries.

During the year, Frieda asked her students to place themselves in the minds of the zealots at Masada as they contemplated suicide, of Spanish Jews facing expulsion or forced conversion, and of medieval Jews pondering whether to sell all their possessions and throw themselves into the messianic fervor surrounding Shabbetai Zvi. One of the greater imaginative challenges for the class came when they tried to absorb the meaning of the Holocaust by putting themselves not in the place of victims or resisters, but of the Judenrat, the Jewish councils that served as the intermediaries between the Nazis and the ghetto dwellers. After reading a selection from the records of the Bialystok Judenrat, Frieda asked the students for their reactions:

Michelle: It seems as though they thought that they could protect the ghetto by their actions.

Helen: But there was corruption among them, too. There are
stories of how the wealthy could pay them to make
sure that their kids weren't selected first.

Leah: Middle management is always vilified, and that's
what they were. They had no choice. They had to
carry out the orders of the Nazis. If they resisted,
everyone in the ghetto would have been killed, anyway. They thought that they could hold that off for
as long as possible.

Roberta: But we always condemn the Nazis, who say they
were just following orders, and so were the Judenrat.
They made a choice. I'm not sure, though, if any of
us would have made a different or better choice.

Wendy: Did the members of the Judenrat think that they were
doing the right thing?

Frieda: It's hard to know. I always want to see the best in people, so I see this as them doing what they had to do.

Helen: The fear tactics that the Nazis used can't be underes-
timated. Try to imagine yourself living in those situations, with that horror and fear every minute, and
you can't escape it. Your mind would start to see
even terrible things as normal, just so you could cope.

As this discussion suggests, connecting to Jewish history in all its dimensions can be emotionally challenging. Here, the students seemed to vacil-
late between wanting to identify with and distance themselves from the
moral dilemmas of the Judenrat. The ways in which they discussed these
historical figures—particularly their choice of pronouns—showed how
the connection developed during the course of the discussion. At the beginning of the conversation, although students sought to find justification
for the Judenrat's actions ("They thought they could protect the ghetto";
"They were just following orders"), the Judenrat was still a distant
"they," an external and remote entity. Roberta was the first to frame the
issue in personal terms, speculating on whether "any of us" would have
made different choices in the same situation. Rather than immediately following this train of thought, the discussion then moved back to distancing

the Judenrat, as Wendy asked if "they" thought that they were doing the right thing. Finally, Helen explicitly challenged her classmates to put themselves back in time and history: "Try to imagine yourself living in those situations: your mind would start to see even terrible things as normal." The distancing "they" had become the intimate "you," bridging the gap between the comfortable lives of the students and the horrible conditions faced by their fellow Jews half a century before. By engaging in this connection—transforming "they" into "we" and "you"—students declared themselves to be linked to all actors in Jewish history.

A number of students reflected upon how the act of linking themselves with Jewish history had added personal meaning and relevance to their learning. Sam found that as the Dilemmas[4] course followed the Jews from ancient Babylonia through nineteenth-century Russia and Eastern Europe, he was able to see himself as a product of this historical progression:

It helped give me a sense of my people that was not the religious sense I had before—what we would read from the Torah and so on. It helped give me a sense of the journey taken, which has helped me in trying to further an identity for myself—to figure out, Where do I fit in? Where do I want to be?

Amy, a classmate of Sam's, similarly felt a sense of personal connection to the story of Solomon Maimon, an eighteenth-century student who left the yeshivot of Poland for the philosophic academies in Berlin, straddling the worlds of tradition and modernity and finding himself at home in neither. Amy saw in Maimon's willingness to transcend boundaries a model for Jews who feel a similar sense of dislocation as well as a reminder of the historical precedents of seemingly contemporary dilemmas:

He was like all of us. You feel as though you don't fit here and you don't fit there. He wasn't accepted by his community because he cared about secular culture. But he wasn't accepted by the secular culture; they laughed at him. I'm drawn to so many

---

[4]The course currently called "The Dramas of Jewish Living" was previously entitled "The Dilemmas of Jewish Living" and had a slightly different curriculum. As this was the course title used during the time when the data were collected for chapters 3 and 4, it is referred to as such herein.

different kinds of Jews and people who put themselves out on a
limb. We think that today is different; but as they say, there is
nothing new under the sun.

Both Amy and Sam found models from Jewish history to help them
make sense of very contemporary and personal questions: Where do I fit
in? How do I find my place both within the Jewish story and modern
society? Amy's discovery that "nothing is new under the sun" (which
she did not seem to realize was from yet another Jewish source, Eccles.
1:9) was not a source of discouragement, but comfort. Finding a connection to the words and experiences of an ancestor (spiritual if not lit-
eral) who had struggled to find his place in Jewish society helped Amy
feel that her own searches and questions were not only an acceptable response to being Jewish, but an authentic and meaningful one.

Wrestling with the Divine: The Challenge of Difficult Texts

*And the man said to Jacob: "Your name shall no longer
be Jacob, but Israel, for you have wrestled with beings
divine and human, and have prevailed." (Gen. 32:29)*

While students found that many of the texts that they studied offered
new and meaningful connections with the tradition, other texts turned
out to be difficult and disturbing, confronting students with aspects of
Judaism that they might rather not face. Wrestling with these difficult
texts, however, could prove to be just as valuable an experience, bringing students' own values, ideas, and interpretations into sharper focus.
Their resistance to certain concepts within the tradition—such as images
of a punitive God, or limitations on the roles of women—became another way to create Torah in the classroom, as they worked to formu-
late new images and ideas to replace the old. Whether these students,
like Jacob, "prevailed" in their struggles with the texts, depended on
whether they, too, emerged from the confrontation with new insights
into the tradition or their own Jewish identities.

One student's struggle with what was, for her, a difficult text occurred during an Ethics lesson on "Imitation of God," exploring how
God's benevolent actions offer a model of morality for humans to fol-

low. As the lesson began, the students read a talmudic passage that cautioned against taking too literally the idea of following God, explaining that God is a "consuming fire." Rather, as the Rabbis explained, one should strive to imitate God's compassionate actions:

> The Holy One, blessed be He, visited the sick—as it is written, "The Lord appeared to [Avraham] at the Oaks of Mamre" (Gen. 18:1)—so you should visit the sick. . . . The Holy One, blessed be He, buried the dead—as it is written, "He buried [Moshe] in the valley" (Deut. 34:6)—so you should bury the dead. (Sotah 14a)

After reading the text, Marc, the teacher, led the students in unpacking and interpreting the nuances of the passage, pushing them to think about the implications of trying to "follow" God:

Marc:	The question in the text is, "Can a person follow after the divine presence?" What is the problem here?
Sam:	As a human, how can we be Godlike?
Marc:	And why can't we?
Sam:	Well, we can't perform miracles.
Marc:	Think about this phrase, "consuming fire." What happens when you get too close to fire?
Students:	You get burned!
Laurie:	Maybe it means that you should never get to the point where you think you are God. Not that you'll be consumed by God, but that you should never think that you are God.
Marc:	That's a nice interpretation. If we take it more literally, can you think of a passage from the Torah that relates to this idea? One you read in synagogue just recently?
Robin:	Aaron's sons.
Marc:	Yes, what was that about?
Robin:	His sons were killed because they came too near to the tent.
Marc:	In fact, what does it say they were killed by?
Robin:	Strange fire.

As the class pondered this idea, Michelle, who had been looking increasingly disturbed and puzzled, spoke up:

> *Michelle:* I thought that last year in class, we learned that our God doesn't rule with the power of fear, but with love. I don't think fear should be a part of how we view God!

Marc took a moment to think, and then began to answer slowly.

> *Marc:* Well, I don't really agree with the idea that God isn't to be feared. I think that to our ancestors, fear was an important part of worship. Again, think about the Yom Kippur service, and the passage we read about when the high priest would approach the Holy of Holies and pronounce God's name, which of course we can't pronounce any more. The whole people fell on their faces and were terrified because they knew that they were being judged at that moment. We've lost that sense of fear today, especially in the liberal denominations. But my father told me that he can remember, when he was growing up, the sense that people really were afraid of judgment on Yom Kippur, and that he would walk around afraid all day.
>
> *Susan:* I think that even today during *Ne'ila,* there is that sense of the closing gates—and will our prayers make it in?
>
> *Michelle:* That bothers me. I'm not sure I want to believe in that kind of God.

Marc's explanation did not end Michelle's need to wrestle with the idea of a God who inspires fear as well as love. Though not willing to accept it, she seemingly also could not dismiss the idea as irrelevant to her personal belief or God image. After Michelle declared her doubts and resistance, the issue was put aside and the lesson returned to its main focus. The following week, however, she raised the issue again in Frieda's class, seeking reassurance that her interpretations of God also had their basis in the tradition: "Last week in the Ethics class, Marc left me thinking that I was supposed to be fearful of God, but I thought we learned last year that God is loving and merciful, a renewal kind of God." Frieda, perhaps unwilling to contradict another instructor, did not answer Michelle's concern directly, but instead encouraged her to bring the debate back to the Ethics class: "I think that you should keep struggling with this and with the Ethics instructor. Get your hand up! Ask questions!"

In Frieda's eyes, the fact that Michelle was wrestling with Judaism was itself a sign of success, as it meant that she was truly engaging with difficult texts and concepts, and perhaps on the path to genuine Jewish growth and learning. However, Michelle never did raise the issue again in the Ethics course, nor did she speak about that moment in class during later interviews, except to say that because she was so focused on learning the basics of Jewish practice, she wasn't paying that much attention to "all that God stuff" at that time in her life. While Michelle seemed to have put aside her theological wrestling for the time being, one imagines that her questions—which neither of her teachers seemed fully able to answer to her satisfaction—will linger, and likely erupt again in new moments of struggle, confusion, and, perhaps, insight.

Another student, wrestling with the role of women in Jewish tradition, had a very different reaction to her struggle with the texts. In a Purposes lesson on mitzvot, the class read a Torah passage laying out the procedures for divorce: "A man takes a wife and possesses her. She fails to please him because he finds something obnoxious about her, and he writes her a bill of divorcement, hands it to her, and sends her away from his house" (Deut. 24:1). The teacher, Hadassah, an Orthodox woman, explained to the students that although the laws of the Torah give greater weight and authority to men in matters of marriage and divorce, women have recourse in later laws created by the Rabbis. For Robin, however, later rabbinic emendations did nothing to erase the power and sting of the Torah's words and their implications, as she vehemently expressed to the class.

Hadassah: Divorce is given by the husband, and we can't do anything about that right now. But under rabbinic law, a woman can go to the *beit din* if her husband refuses to give her a *get.*

Robin: Is this translated in an Orthodox or a Conservative light? Would a Reform Bible have this in it?

Hadassah: They wouldn't change the Bible, but they might change the application of the law—although in the case of Reform, they don't really require religious divorce, anyway. But, as I said, the Rabbis tried to find ways to put pressure on a husband to give a *get* if he wouldn't do it voluntarily.

Robin: I would think that they would change this, because it's so offensive! I don't understand why it's the man who gives the *get!*

Hadassah: Well, it's also the man who gives the *ketubah* and the ring.

Anne: No, they both give each other rings.

Hadassah: That's something modern. Traditionally, only the man gives the woman a ring, not the other way round.

Robin: So does that mean we're property? Because I know the *ketubah* is all about property. Am I the only one who's disturbed by this?

Students: No! Not at all.

Hadassah: Well, in many ways the *ketubah* was to protect women, because it obligates the husband to give her a divorce settlement. It's something that he gives to her—it's hers.

Robin: I still think the whole idea behind it needs to be changed, as the Reform movement has done.

Reading the Torah's rules for divorce crystallized for Robin her difficulties with and objections to certain traditions regarding women's roles in Judaism. Though Hadassah tried to defend the traditional position—explaining why such Jewish creations as the *ketubah* were actually advancements for women—Robin continued to struggle with the message of the laws and teachings about women that, to her, seemed limiting or degrading. Ultimately, as she explained in a later interview, her ability to freely question this and other dimensions of traditional Judaism led Robin to a greater appreciation of her own, more liberal, branch of Judaism:

The most important thing that the class has done for me, which I never expected, is to make me a Reform Jew by choice. Hearing all the Orthodox viewpoints has made me delighted that I am Reform. I appreciate the thought and the evolution of Reform Judaism. I want to get more information on Reform Judaism in order to be the advocate for Reform in the class. The class made me become Reform not because my parents were, but because I believe that's what I want to be.

Another student who shared Robin's beliefs might have been reluctant to voice them in class, especially if taught by Hadassah, Robin's dynamic Orthodox teacher. For Robin, however, it was precisely the confrontations with both teacher and text that gave this experience with Jewish learning its power. Although her views remained seemingly unchanged, Robin was indeed "transformed" by her wrestling with tradition, evolving from a Reform Jew by rote to a "Reform Jew by choice." Had she not been confronted with dimensions of Jewish law and life that were disturbing or unacceptable to her, she would likely never have embraced so strongly the branch of Judaism that shared and celebrated her liberal ideals.

And Sarah Laughed:
The Role of Humor in the Classroom

And Sarah laughed to herself, saying, "Now that I am withered, am I to have enjoyment—with my husband so old?" Then the Lord said to Abraham, "Why did Sarah laugh, saying, 'Shall I in truth bear a child, old as I am?' ". . . Sarah lied, saying, "I did not laugh," for she was frightened. But He replied, "You did laugh." (Gen. 18:12–15)

Not all the scenes in Mini-School classes were as serious as the ones described in the sections above. The lessons were also full of lighthearted and humorous moments, with frequent joking and teasing among students and teachers. Even these lighter moments, however, often became a form of "Torah," serving as subtle but revealing commentary on the experience of learning and the relationship to the texts. Some jokes highlighted and reinforced the shared cultural frameworks—language, experiences, and assumptions—that existed among the students. At other times, humor allowed students to express discomfort with or uncertainty about aspects of Jewish tradition. Unlike Sarah's laughter, which draws rebuke from God, humor in the classroom was nearly always welcomed and encouraged by teachers and students alike.

Many jokes were used to demonstrate the shared knowledge and experience of the classroom, as when students humorously referenced something that had been learned earlier in the lesson or on a previous day. Students might cite a previously learned law or ritual in an unusual and humorous context, thus demonstrating their understanding of the nuances of that tradition. A Rhythms lesson about Shabbat, filled as it was with numerous rules for observance, provided fertile ground for this sort of humor. To Frieda's query of her students, "Why do you think that the Rabbis said that the Messiah would not come on Shabbat?" Maxine quickly answered, "Because you can't travel on Shabbat!" Later in the lesson, the discussion turned to Shabbat traditionally being a time to enjoy sexual activity. "You just have to do it differently," joked Naomi, referring to the law that certain actions can be performed on Shabbat if they are done in an unusual manner. In both cases, the laughter that filled the classroom after these quips showed that the students enjoyed a shared knowledge about these particular rituals.

Humor about Jewish observance also served to acknowledge that certain ritual laws are not universally observed, thus highlighting another shared, if less overt, experience among students. Often, these jokes centered on kashrut. For example, during one Purposes class, the issue of *shatnes*, the prohibition against mixing linen and wool, was raised. Hadassah, the teacher, explained that Judaism has a great concern with boundaries between species, and therefore one is not allowed to mix humans and animals, animals with other animals, or plants with other plants. "However," she concluded, "if a mixed species has already been created, then we are allowed to use it." "Really? There has to be a way to tie that in with lobster somehow," Joan responded, to the laughter of the class and the Orthodox teacher. In a Dilemmas lesson on the American Jewish experience, Frieda provided the students with a menu from the infamous "*treyfe* banquet" at Hebrew Union College, and explained its role in creating the Conservative movement in America.[5] "This looks

---

[5]At Hebrew Union College, the rabbinical training institution of the Reform movement, shellfish was served at the first graduation banquet, in 1883. This sparked great protest within the traditional wing of the movement, and eventually played a role in the establishment and growth of the Conservative movement in America.

like a great dinner!" exclaimed Evelyn, a student. As the class laughed, another student noted that not only did it include a preponderance of shellfish, but also dairy served after the meat courses. "But if you stuck to the seafood menu," Evelyn responded, "then you could have the cheese and ice cream!" Frieda, the instructor, chuckled, "Evelyn, you have the answer for everything!" In her answer, Evelyn incorporated both dimensions of observance-related humor—demonstrating a familiarity with the laws of kashrut along with a willingness to twist and subvert them. Both Joan and Evelyn seemed to be using humor to proclaim at least a desire to break with Jewish tradition, but in a way that would not threaten perceived norms of the classroom. In both cases, therefore, the instructors could laugh along with the class, apparently appreciating the humor without worrying about the message.

A third dimension of humor contrasted Jewish life and tradition with the contemporary world outside the classroom. Students recognized that there is often a discrepancy between these worlds, and they used humor to acknowledge and define it. During a discussion in a Rhythms class on the customs of naming, a student mused, "It's going to sound so funny when some of our children become grandparents someday—'Bubbe Ashley' and 'Zayde Todd.' " Embedded in the quip is a recognition that the names of the younger generation of Jews are thoroughly Americanized, but also the optimistic hope that these children will someday have grandchildren who would call them Bubbe and Zayde. Other humor pointed to the changes that have occurred in social mores since the time of the Rabbis. In a lesson on marriage, Frieda asked the class to speculate on why a groom would be exempt from reciting the Sh'ma until the marriage is consummated: "Imagine a man who is twenty-four and he's a virgin. . . ." "What, in these times?" Maxine interjected. Laughing, Frieda acknowledged that such a scenario would be unlikely today. Finally, in a humorous exchange between a student and an instructor, both gently mocked the tendency of modern Jewish institutions to occasionally exaggerate their importance. When Marc asked his Ethics class, "Where does the phrase tikkun olam come from?" a student responded, "the Federation."[6] "Yes," Marc rejoined. "In fact, if you read the Creation story very closely, you'll see that the Federation is actually mentioned." The class erupted in laugh-

---

[6]Federation, the organization that coordinates many Jewish philanthropic efforts, is often framed in the context of tikkun olam, "repair of the world."

ter, seeming to enjoy the opportunity to poke fun at an esteemed communal institution and at the same time reassure themselves that there was indeed Jewish life before the American Jewish Federation system.

Dancing with Miriam:
Teachers as Cultural Models

Then Miriam the prophetess, Aaron's sister, took a timbrel in her hand, and all the women went out after her in dance with timbrels. (Exod. 15:20)

Although this chapter has until now focused on the ways in which learners interact with texts and create new interpretations and meaning from them, students are, of course, but one dimension of the dynamic interactions between teachers, curriculum, and students that take place in Mini-School classrooms. As will be described more fully in chapter 6, students' relationships to the text are shaped and inspired not only by the curriculum materials themselves, but by the interpretations given to these materials by the instructors. The teachers function as both transmitters and living examples of what they teach. Through their public engagement with and analysis of the material, the teachers create the contextual lenses through which these texts are viewed, setting the boundaries of acceptable discussion and interpretation.

In order to serve as cultural interpreters and models, the teachers I observed had first to demonstrate their authority as authentic interpreters of texts and repositories of Jewish knowledge. Some had the advantage of title. Marc, as a Conservative rabbi, could be expected to have a great deal of familiarity with Jewish law and tradition. He generally lived up to this expectation, often supplementing the Mini-School curriculum with texts, stories, and interpretations that displayed the breadth of his Judaic knowledge. Whereas other teachers were always referred to by their first names only, Marc was occasionally addressed as "Rabbi," particularly by the older students who seemed less comfortable addressing religious leaders informally. As an observant Jew, Hadassah carried the authority of her personal commitment to live by halakhic standards. As such, her words held weight and authenticity, particularly because she provided an accessible window into a mode of

Jewish life different from that of virtually all her students. As Doris commented, "When Hadassah brings in teachings from the Orthodox movement, we understand why this group of people, this sector of religion behaves the way they do. She demystifies it."

Frieda, neither a rabbi (though married to one) nor an Orthodox Jew, nevertheless seemed to be accorded the same level of authority as the other teachers. This was perhaps due to her engaging personality and rapport with her students, which led them to hang on to her words. In a lesson on the Babylonian exile, after the students located three cities on a map, Frieda asked them, "If I told you that Nehardea, Sura, and Pumbedita, three places you've never heard of, were the most important Jewish places at that time after Jerusalem, would you believe me?" "Of course we would," Linda immediately replied. "We believe everything you tell us!" Though this comment was made lightheartedly, it was rooted in truth. Joy, another of Frieda's students, explained how her teacher's words legitimized beliefs that she might otherwise have thought transgressive: "To me, the Bible is stories, probably written by many different people. And before, even to say that would have made me think, 'Oh my God, am I going to be struck down?' But now I know it's okay to say that because Frieda said it."

Whether consciously or not, teachers constantly model cultural beliefs and assumptions by their words in the classroom, letting their students know what is, as Joy put it, "okay to say"—what the boundaries are of acceptable and reasonable behavior, belief, and discourse. Marc, for instance, often expressed to his students the view that Jewish law is not the only moral standard, but could and should be judged against other ethical principles. When teaching about Jewish views on homosexuality, he opened the class by strongly expressing his disapproval of the Conservative movement's policy of refusing ordination to openly gay and lesbian Jews. In another class, Marc offered his opinion on the increasingly strict adherence to kashrut in some Orthodox communities: "Some people in *frum*[7] communities today won't even eat at one another's houses because they don't trust one another's kashrut. This is a definite example, for me at least, of taking the law too far." On the other hand, Marc emphasized that there are elements of tradition that should be preserved and valued, even if they contradict a modern or hu-

---

[7]*Frum,* a Yiddish term for an observant Jew.

manistic ethos. For example, during a discussion of marriage in the Jewish tradition, he explained to the class that he valued the historical significance of using a traditionally worded *ketubah* in weddings instead of more egalitarian variations: "I prefer the traditional because I like the idea of using something that Jews have used for centuries—the text is right in the Talmud. It connects Jews across time and space." By articulating his preferences, Marc modeled for his students a path for negotiating the tensions between tradition and modernity frequently faced by modern American Jews.

Hadassah, though more traditionally observant than Marc, also seemed to be modeling a path for her students balancing the importance of traditional beliefs and practices with the need for individual choice and expression. During one discussion about whether souls are reincarnated in new bodies, a student expressed her doubts about the concept: "I'm not sure I can believe that we all have someone else's soul." In her response, Hadassah emphasized that there is a diversity of belief among Jews and that in certain instances, individuals can and should choose whether a particular tradition "works" for them: "That's okay. This is not something that you have to believe in to be a good Jew. It's not one of the big thirteen. If it works for you, great. If not, that's fine. It's good to have a whole bunch of ideas in the back of your mind, and then you can see which ones work for you in different situations." In a class on prayer, Hadassah suggested to the students that they might find the act of praying more meaningful if, for some of the service, they put aside the traditional liturgy and instead tried a meditative exercise:

> You don't have to use these particular words. The point is to make you think about God. Prayer can even be a guided imagery, without words. For example, in the first paragraph of the *Amidah*, where it says that God is huge and awesome and powerful, you picture three things that are huge and awesome and powerful—I picture the universe, the ocean, and the sun—and then remember that God is bigger, more awesome, and more powerful than all of them. Or you can pray in the English only, if the Hebrew doesn't mean anything to you. You should pray so that it works for you.

This use of language emphasizing individuality—doing what "works for you"—was especially striking coming from a strictly Orthodox teacher. It offered a powerful model to students that for this teacher, individual expression and Jewish tradition are not incompatible. Of course, there were definite limits to Hadassah's messages about individuality. She never suggested that when it came to practices or beliefs more central to Jewish observance—such as Shabbat, kashrut, or the divine authorship of the Torah—students should base their decisions on "what works for them." During most lessons, in fact, the cultural model that Hadassah presented was indeed one of strict adherence to tradition. However, her espousal of traditional observance was always done within a context of respect for more liberal Jewish movements, leading many of her students to praise her as a model of both observance and tolerance. Robin, perhaps the leading advocate among the students for liberal Jewish viewpoints, was particularly moved by this: "What I love about Hadassah is that she can always see the other side and is not condescending. She is not critical of our levels of observance. And whether she thinks I'm a heathen or not, she certainly doesn't give that attitude."

The ability to, as Robin said, "see the other side," was a critical part of cultural modeling, and integral to the Mini-School philosophy of teaching. To retain students' confidence in them as authority figures, teachers had to be careful not to give the appearance of bias and to keep personal opinion separate from objective teaching as much as possible. Another instructor, Rina, though highly praised as a knowledgeable and skilled teacher, drew criticism from some students for inserting personal opinions about certain Jewish movements into her teaching. One student, Sandra, was particularly disturbed upon hearing Rina refer to some ultra-Orthodox Jewish sects as *meshuganas*:

> It's not that I disagree with her point of view, but how could she say that? She should just say that there is a group of ultra-Orthodox Jews who believe this. We can all figure out what we think about them without her opinion. She could say that people who go to the *mikveh* are *meshugana*. That's not the way it should be. This is what they do, this is why they do it, and you can figure out for yourself what you think about it.

Naomi was also disturbed when Rina presented her personal opinions as facts, even when the statements were more complimentary:

> I remember Rina saying something about how Orthodox boys make the best soldiers. Who did the study that came to this conclusion? When I'm told that the Bible says such and such and

then we read it, I may not agree, but I can see that it's there in the text. But where does this other information come from, and why is it in this class?

These students were concerned not so much by the opinions being expressed, but by the blurring of the line between fact and opinion, the creation of absolutes where there were none.[8] It may be that students were particularly attuned to this issue because many are themselves torn between their need to explore choices in Jewish belief and practice, and their desire, at times, for definitive answers. Perhaps because they were aware of this tension, teachers often explicitly encouraged students to ask questions, express doubts, and offer dissenting opinions. In one of the first classes of the year, Hadassah surprised her students by interrupting her lesson to ask: "You know, one question you've never asked me is, 'Am I supposed to really believe all this stuff?' Isn't anyone here concerned with that?" When the students hesitantly agreed that they were, she chided them, "You should remember that you can ask me anything. That's what this class is all about!" In a later class, Hadassah offered herself as a model for questioning and doubt. When a student asked whether Adam and Eve had sinned by questioning God's commandment, she replied, "Well, I don't want you to think that questioning is a sin. I question everything, every day. If I didn't, I wouldn't have anything to teach you! I think that's the most Jewish thing there is—questioning and trying to understand." In this way, Hadassah impressed upon the class that questioning is central not only to Jewish learning, but to Judaism itself.

Frieda also emphasized the importance of questions and reassured her students that if they were struggling with uncertainties, it meant that they were on the right path. Recall Michelle's discomfort over the idea proposed in the Ethics course that God could be a source of fear as well as love. Rather than answering Michelle's concerns about God directly, Frieda encouraged her to keep thinking about her questions and to raise them with her teachers: "I think that you should keep struggling with this and with the Ethics instructor. Get your hand up! Ask questions! I

[8]This likely explains why students did not seem bothered when Marc expressed his preference for using a traditional *ketubah* in wedding ceremonies. Traditional beliefs and concepts were acceptable to students as long as they were presented as opinions and preferences, rather than as objective facts.

know that a lot of what you learn in Melton is complicated and mind-boggling, but you'll get it if you ask the right questions. If you're feeling a little lost, then you're in just the right place." On the path of learning, according to Frieda, getting "a little lost" is not only acceptable, but inevitable. If the path were straightforward and easy to navigate, she implied, the journey would be far less worthwhile. Marc, in his address at the graduation ceremony for second-year students in 2001, also encouraged students to keep "wrestling and questioning and learning" as part of a journey that is both circuitous and endless:

> [One of] the most interesting things about [the Torah] is that it is a book with no end. If you think about it, when we reach the end of the cycle of reading, the Israelites are still outside of the land, and then we go right back to the beginning. . . . And [this] teaches us that it is all about the journey. Torah is not about reaching a specific place, but about the process, about the wrestling and questioning and learning, and that's what you've been doing for these two years in the Melton Mini-School.

Conclusion

During their two-year journey through Jewish learning, Mini-School students entered into a dialogue between their own "living texts" and Judaism's canon of "written texts," creating new interpretative texts in the process. Some students found that traditional ideas provided new frameworks for looking at contemporary ethical dilemmas—such as euthanasia and other medical quandaries—and current events, such as the all-too-human foibles of political and cultural leaders. Others discovered that events or figures from the Jewish past could offer insights into personal religious quests and questions. Recall Sam and Amy, who found meaning in the realization that many Jews before them had also struggled to find a place in the larger world and to find a balance between tradition and modernity. Wrestling with difficult texts and ideas helped some students, such as Robin, identify their own beliefs more clearly, as she found that her conflicts with Orthodoxy drew her closer to the Reform movement. Laughing together enabled students to express and reinforce shared knowledge and cultural meanings, or a shared resistance to traditional rules and norms. And at every stage of connection and discussion, the teachers offered models for approaching Jewish texts and created boundaries of as well as space for acceptable interpretation.

Of course, not all students in these classrooms experienced a deep and powerful connection to Jewish texts or found that their learning dramatically increased Jewish meaning. Some approached their learning as a purely intellectual exercise, or one that added just a few nuances to an already satisfying religious life. Those who did enter into emotional engagement with learning, however, often emerged with a deepened sense of ownership of Jewish tradition and real changes to their worldview or self-identity. Some, like Karen, began seeing the world through a "Jewish lens." Others, like Robin, began to identify themselves as a "Jew by choice," rather than by accident of birth. There are important questions still to be answered about the process of making meaning and creating Torah within the adult Jewish learning classroom: What leads some students to enter into deeper engagements with texts than others? Is this a process that reflects only the first flush of excitement with learning, or does it continue, and possibly grow, as more and more time is spent with Jewish texts and ideas? This brief glimpse into the adult Jewish learning classroom reveals that many adult Jews are eager and able to add their voices to the ongoing conversation of Jewish tradition.

CHAPTER FOUR
Social Dynamics in the Classroom:
Creating a Community of Learners

When ten people sit together studying Torah, the divine presence resides in their midst, as it is written, "God stands in the edah [assembly of ten people] of the Lord." (Pirkei Avot 3:6)

As this rabbinic text teaches, the idea that Torah study is ideally done in the context of a community is a concept that stretches back at least to the days of the Mishnah. It is also an ideal that shapes the programmatic goals of the Florence Melton Adult Mini-School. Indeed, the text above is used as one of the concluding teachings of the Mini-School's "Purposes of Jewish Living" course, offering an apt summation of learners' experience as they approach the end of their first year of study. In commenting on this text, the teacher's guide even more directly underscores the link between the ancient wisdom of the Rabbis and the realities that are enacted in adult Jewish learning classrooms:

> Much of the knowledge and understanding of the ideas presented in this course were hopefully gained not merely by the reading of the text but by the reactions of the students to the text as well as their interactions with one another. The impact of Talmud Torah in the privacy of one's home would likely pale in comparison to the experience of learning in a group setting. (Harbater 2000, 6)

As we heard in many of the students' quotes in the previous chapters, most adult learners likely would agree with the assertion that their interactions with their fellow students played an integral role in their experience of Jewish learning. Even those who may have begun their learning with little thought as to who might be sitting in the seats next to them often find, by the end of their two years, that the collection of individuals who entered the classroom has been transformed into a true learning community. Sociologist Samuel Heilman notes this phenomenon in his classic study of traditional Talmud *lerners* (Yiddish term for learners engaged specifically in text study). In *The People of the Book,* he writes: "Simply put, people get together ostensibly to *lern,* but their common activity makes them care more about getting together and about one another than they did at the beginning" (Heilman 1983, 204). Heilman describes the sense of deep fellowship and friendship among the *lerners* studied, who, after years of learning together, "feel as if they have no choice but to be close to one another, as if they are one family" (204).

Most contemporary learners usually do not spend years studying together, as Heilman's *lerners* did. So we would not expect them to achieve this same level of bonding with their fellow students. However, learning together as a community can indeed be transformative for individuals as well as institutions. Isa Aron (2000) has written extensively on the impact of Jewish learning within a synagogue community. Similar to Heilman's findings about Orthodox male learners, Aron found that learners of all backgrounds often form close ties to one another, which take the experience of Torah study far beyond the intellectual:

> All Jewish learning, whether it is devoted to a study of sacred texts, Jewish thought, or Jewish history, enables learners to connect their personal struggles to larger social and ethical ideals. When a group of learners engages in this type of discussion over an extended period of time, the bonds that form among the participants are strong and durable. Though the participants' original purpose in joining the group may have been intellectual stimulation, the solace they find in the text and the emotional and social connections they form with fellow learners are what keep them coming back. (Aron 2000, 24)

Ideally, Aron explains, learning "grows out of the life of the community" and in turn "strengthens the community" (28). Thus, Torah learning and community building function together as a mutually enhancing and self-sustaining process. When this learning takes place, as it often does, within a communal setting such as a synagogue, the results can be transformative not only for the individual learners, but for the entire surrounding institution and community: "The congregation of learners is both a means to an end and an end in itself; it is an instrument for en-culturating individual members into active participation in Jewish life, and it is also a model for Jewish community" (28).

Even when learning takes place outside of the synagogue context, it still can become a model for Jewish communal engagement. Student reports and classroom observations suggest that fellowship and community play a central role in the adult Jewish learning experience, creating the foundation for intimate and intensive learning. This chapter details some of the social dynamics in the classroom that seem to encourage and create community and fellowship among students, including friendships and cliques, "shmoozing," personal sharing, gender dynamics, the role of the teachers, reactions to disruptive students, and the strength of group ties.

The Classroom Setting

Even before students exchanged a word with one another, the physical setting of their classrooms seemed designed to foster a sense of collegiality. Students sat facing one another during the lesson, at tables covered with white cloths placed in a U- or E-shaped formation (depending on the size of the class), rather than in rows facing the instructor. Each student was given a name card at the beginning of the year. In theory, these cards were to sit before the student during every lesson, so that students (as well as the teachers) could address one another by name. In reality, the display of cards varied in inverse proportion to the students' familiarity with one another: nearly universal display of cards at the beginning of the year in the first-year class, fewer than half of the cards displayed by the end of the year in that class, and almost no cards displayed in the second-year classes.

Students grew quite attached to the physical setting of the classroom and their place within it. Although the seating arrangement was completely open, students quickly fell into a pattern after the first or second class, and rarely varied their seating during the rest of the year. Occasionally, the pattern was disrupted, either because a visitor had joined the class, or because a daring student decided to change location, "just to get a different point of view," as one explained. When this happened, people quickly acquiesced to the new arrangement, but with much joking about their "assigned seats" being usurped.

A more serious disruption to their sense of place that was not met with such good humor occurred one morning when a class arrived to find their tables in a new arrangement. With one table missing, about five students would have had to find room for themselves at the other tables. While there was physically enough space for this to be accomplished without much problem, the missing table obviously unsettled many of the students. Nearly everyone commented upon it as he or she entered the classroom; complaints were made to the teacher, and finally the coordinator was called in to observe the problem. About ten minutes later, a maintenance worker arrived with the missing table. As he quickly set it up in its proper place and covered it with the requisite white tablecloth, the students spontaneously burst into applause. Although in reality only a few students would have been displaced by the missing table, the class reacted as a whole, all sharing equally in the anxiety over the change to their communal setting. Having the same seating arrangement each time, with the same familiar faces adjacent and across, seemed to give students a critical sense of grounding and continuity.

The other significant community-building feature of the physical classroom setting was the food and drink offered at every lesson. Not only did the snack table provide a place for students to gather and chat before class and during the break, the food itself often fostered social interaction. Some students routinely brought extra food back to the study table with them so that they could sociably offer their neighbors some pretzels or crackers. Many of the female students would simultaneously nibble at their cookies while bemoaning to their friends how they shouldn't be indulging, giving the other women the chance to commiserate over how hard it is to stay trim. While the snacks usually stayed the same from week to week, there were the occasional surprise treats, such as doughnuts. These breaks in the routine, like the missing table, provoked comments from nearly every student and a palpable change in the tenor of the classroom. These, however, were positive remarks, with the atmosphere in the room festive rather than frustrated. "What's the occasion?" many asked delightedly, upon spotting the glistening pile of glazed doughnuts. When no explanation was given, some students jokingly proclaimed that it must be a reward to them for being the best class. While they likely suspected, as was indeed the case, that every class received the same goodies that day, they did not let that knowledge interfere with an occasion for forging group ties over food—a time-honored Jewish tradition.

Friendships and Cliques

One reason that students in this particular site seemed to project such a sense of warmth and collegiality toward one another may be that many of them come into the class with at least one friend by their side. Almost all were acquainted with a number of their classmates from the larger community. Some friends signed up for the course together, requesting that they be placed in the same classroom (most of these requests are honored, space permitting). Stacy, for instance, was part of a group of women who had been studying together weekly at her synagogue. When that group ended, Stacy took the lead in encouraging her classmates to continue learning together. She "contacted the other women in the group and said, 'Let's go learn together in the Melton program,' and four out of five of us did. So that's where we are now, and we all sit together in class, and often go out for lunch together afterward." Others strike out into the world of adult Jewish learning on their own, only to find that in their class might be two other parents they know from the local Jewish day school, a neighbor from down the block, or even, given the deep roots of many residents in the community, a childhood Hebrew-school classmate. Libby, a community native in her sixties, could trace her life history in the faces of her classmates. "Let's see," she mused one morning, "Gil I've known since we were kids, Nancy and I sat next to each other in college, and Ann and I have been friends since our kids were in nursery school together!"

Given the social networks that many students brought with them into the classroom, it was not surprising to find a certain amount of "cliquishness." Students tended to sit and chat with those they already knew. Particularly in the second-year class, which had a wide age range, the territories were clearly delineated: the older generation (mostly longtime community residents and *machers* in local Jewish institutions) on the left side of the room; and "youngsters" (mothers in their thirties, many of them more recent transplants to the community) on the right. As the year progressed, however, the social boundaries seemed to become more fluid, as more conversations occurred between people who, based on the questions they asked each other, did not know each other outside of the classroom. In the second-year class, students occasionally made use of their age differences, with older women offering motherly advice to their younger counterparts on child rearing or navigating the region and community. Many students acknowledged that certain groups of students tended to stick together, but did not seem to find this a disturbing exclusivity.

Shmoozing

Although students might enter the class with one or two close friends, these groupings were made less apparent by the comfort that most students showed with almost all their classmates, as demonstrated by the lively talking that filled all classrooms. The downtime surrounding the classes—before, after, and during breaks—provided ample opportunity for community building through shmoozing (truly the best term to describe this interaction). The topics of student conversations reflected the dimensions of their outside lives that they felt most comfortable bringing with them into the classroom and that promoted social bonding with their classmates. A typical morning might find Ronnie showing pictures of her newest grandchild to Claire; Doris, a social worker, advising Kay on how to cope with an aging mother; and Margot and Lynne debating where to find the best window treatments in town.

Each of these conversations fulfilled a different social function. On the less weighty end of the spectrum were chats about material goods and lifestyle events: shopping, vacations, restaurants, and so on—easy conversations for people who might not know one another all that well. In addition to providing an accessible entry point for social interaction, these discussions suggested, at least to an outside observer, that most students in the class shared a fairly similar socioeconomic background and a familiarity with the same cultural touchstones of upper-middle-class society—including trips to exotic locales abroad, lavish celebrations of milestone events, and regular visits to manicurists, hairdressers, and other personal-care professionals. The high socioeconomic class of most students was also suggested visually, by the frequent (though by no means ubiquitous) display of expensive jewelry and clothing in the classroom and the prevalence of luxury vehicles in the parking lot outside.

A step up in seriousness and in personal revelation were discussions about books and literature. Reading appeared to be a fairly common leisure-time activity for these students, whether on their own or as part of book groups, and they often enthusiastically shared with one another information about books they had enjoyed. Often, though not always, the books discussed had a Jewish theme, such as Milton Steinberg's *As a Driven Leaf*, Naomi Ragen's *Sotah*, Noah Gordon's *The Last Jew*, and Myla Goldberg's *Bee Season*. The last—a complex and somewhat disturbing book about a troubled Jewish family that deals with kabbalah, Hari Krishnas, and mental illness—inspired a particularly animated discussion among three students after class. One had the book with her, the others had just finished it, and all wanted to hear what the others had made of the strange and enigmatic tale. They agreed that the book had sparked their interest in kabbalah and particularly the writings of Abulafia, which figure prominently in the book's plot. Finally, they pondered whether the Hari Krishna group that recruits one family member is more disturbing and cultish than the father's mystical obsessions, or Hasidic sects within the Jewish community. "I once heard that forty percent of Hari Krishnas are Jewish and another forty are Catholic," one student observed. "Well," replied another, "the *ba'ale teshuvas* aren't that different from a cult. My niece became ultra-Orthodox, and now she has to ask her rebbe about every detail of her personal life." "That sounds like a cult to me!" proclaimed the third.

As this discussion suggests, no matter where a student conversation began, the realm of family was never far off. Most of the shmoozing between students did indeed revolve around their families and family celebrations: children, grandchildren, weddings and b'nai mitzvah celebrations, and occasionally, funerals. These conversations were lively and touching, and often supplemented with photographs. Occasionally, conversations about family moved beyond sharing wedding portraits and school pictures, and allowed students to reveal more intimate details about their lives and seek advice and support from others. In one class, a student mentioned that her daughter had recently given birth to her first child by cesarean section and was a bit troubled that she was not able to have a vaginal delivery. Immediately, other students jumped in to say that either they or their daughters had had cesarean sections, that it was much more common than people think, and that her daughter should not feel bad in any way. In another class, Doris, a psychotherapist, often spent the moments before class "counseling" other students who shared their stories of aging parents, difficult children, or newly retired husbands. Though hardly offering the privacy of a therapist's office, the classroom nevertheless seemed to be a "safe space" for these students, where they could vent their worries and frustrations about their families to Doris and anyone else within earshot.

Personal Sharing

The openness with which students discussed their lives with one another during moments of downtime extended to the more formal lesson time as well, when they often interwove personal stories and details with the textual discussions. As Robert Wuthnow described in his study of the support-group movement, the act of sharing stories is key to the development of community within a group, as members offer up details of their personal histories as texts for examination and response: "Through storytelling individuals turn their own experiences into a collective event. They preserve their individuality but at the same time find community in the similarities between their stories and those told by others in their group" (Wuthnow 1994, 302). Patty, a first-year student, thought that this process of sharing was a positive one that helped forge bonds among the class members: "I think that the sharing is wonderful. People make comments in class about their past, their children, or whatever. They start to talk and confide in one another, which they wouldn't do with anyone else. But we have a bond where we can say things like that."

As Patty suggests, family and life-cycle events were particularly common subjects for personal sharing in the classroom. Nothing seemed to create and reinforce bonds among students as readily as an announcement of the birth of a grandchild, which occurred at least three times during the year. In each case, the announcement was made at the beginning of the lesson, rather than before class or during the break, and was greeted with great joy by the students and teachers. Students immediately gathered around the new *bubbe*, photos were produced, and statistics of birth weight and time in labor proudly shared. In one case, the announcement turned into an impromptu lesson on Jewish traditions surrounding birth, when a student asked why the new grandmother was sharing these details, but not announcing the baby's name. Sherry, the teacher, explained that it is a custom not to announce the name until the *brit milah* or *simchat bat,* at which point the grandmother interjected that she wished she could invite the whole class to the bris, "but my daughter would kill me!"

At the other extreme of the life cycle, experiences with death proved to be another trigger for personal sharing. One topic covered in the second-year "Ethics of Jewish Living" curriculum was euthanasia, concluding a three-lesson segment on the value of life. Marc, the instructor, began that class by inviting students to share their own experiences with the topic. The outpouring that followed lasted nearly half the class period. One after another, students recounted times when they had been faced with difficult end-of-life decisions about parents or siblings, some growing visibly upset as they shared difficult memories. Diane, a student in her late forties, recalled, "I remember when my mother was dying, and she begged us to help her out of her suffering. She likened it to that movie *They Shoot Horses, Don't They?* She couldn't understand why no one could help her." Helen, a social worker, tried to offer Diane some comfort: "It's hard for us who are still young and healthy to understand, but death is a real option for people when they reach that time in their lives." As the discussion continued, Marc held back from interrupting or directing it in any way, and did not express or show any impatience to begin the formal lesson. Only once it had run its course did he suggest turning to the sources to explore the rabbinical view, and the students, having had the chance to release some of their emotions, readily agreed. As with the announcements of a birth, sharing stories of death had the power to stop class for a period of time, as if everyone in the classroom understood that allowing the discussion to occur was more important than pushing ahead with the textual material. More than any other classroom moments, these discussions seemed to draw the class together, creating a community that celebrated and grieved together.

In the sharing of stories of birth and death, the students remained within dimensions of life that were socially common and acceptable and even, in the case of welcoming grandchildren, lauded. There were also times, however, when students revealed details about their lives and families that might have been viewed as outside the realm of normative Jewish experience, especially in a relatively conservative Jewish community. During another Ethics lesson on Jewish views of homosexuality, Libby, an older woman and community *macher*, explained that she had direct experience with the topic at hand:

My daughter is a lesbian, and about seven years ago she had a commitment ceremony with her partner, who she's been with for fourteen years. I've always been supportive of her, but I had said that I didn't think she should have a Jewish ceremony. But when her siblings were planning the ceremony, they turned the tree into a *huppah,* and used a havdalah candle to talk about two lives being braided together, so it was Jewish, anyway. Now she and her partner are going to have a baby (her partner is pregnant), and we've asked them to have a bris for the child if it's a boy.

In a lesson on conversion during the Rhythms course, the instructor, Sherry, asked if any students had been to a conversion ceremony. Joyce immediately answered, "My grandson was converted because my daughter-in-law isn't Jewish." This prompted a number of other students to share stories of grandchildren who were converted as infants, leading to a broader discussion of the practice of converting those who are too young to choose.

In both cases, these students readily shared details about their children that, in a previous era, might have been considered shameful and kept carefully hidden. This openness could be interpreted as a sign that homosexuality and intermarriage have now become more widely accepted in the Jewish community, such that these students feel no differently about revealing their children to be gay or intermarried as they might about revealing them to be lawyers. However, while there is today greater acceptance of these once "deviant" lifestyles within the Jewish community, they are not so normative that they would be introduced into the classroom discussions without a second thought. Rather, these instances of personal sharing about family members suggest that these students probably felt fairly confident that they were in an environment in which they would not be judged or suffer social penalties for their willingness to discuss these details. Indeed, Joyce's description of her grandchild's conversion seemed to release an outpouring of sharing, as if students were relieved to be bringing these stories out into the open. It may be that the dynamic in these situations is similar to what Wuthnow described, in which the sharing of stories helps individual students define their identities even as they are contributing to the building of community: "Feeling comfortable in a group comes about as a result of developing a socio-biography that reflects both the member's own and the group's input. What a person chooses to share in a group becomes ever more important to that person's identity. The group's affirmation of this identity reinforces and legitimates it" (Wuthnow 1994, 302).

Diverse Perspectives

Although most of the sharing and group dynamics focused on creating a sense of social comfort in the classroom, at times the deliberate creation of discomfort actually became another means to enhance and strengthen the classroom community. When students who felt outside of the mainstream of their classmates purposefully challenged cultural or social assumptions that they did not share, they often ended up broadening discussions and bringing new perspectives to the table. During a discussion of intermarriage (a subject that often brings up strong emotions) in one Dilemmas lesson, a number of students expressed their feelings that intermarriage was a negative factor in American Jewish life, and bemoaned the rise of intermarriage among "the children" today. Implicit in the discussion was the assumption that intermarriage is both a definite route to assimilation and decreased Jewish involvement, and mostly a problem in a younger, more disaffected generation. Both of these assumptions were immediately challenged when Leah, a woman in her fifties and one of the most knowledgeable and enthusiastic members of the class, revealed that she herself was married to a non-Jew. Without responding directly to her classmates' previous comments, Leah challenged the class to think about how intermarried couples are treated by the Jewish community, and the effect that might have on their involvement or disaffiliation. After the visible ripple of surprised reaction had passed ("Did she say what I thought she said?" one woman whispered to her neighbor), the tone of the conversation began to change. While students still openly expressed their preference for in-marriage, they no longer used "othering" language to describe the mixed married. Leah had successfully challenged their cultural assumption that no one who had chosen to marry outside the faith would then choose to engage in Jewish learning.

Another, more subtle, example arose during a Rhythms class on *Yom Ha'atzma'ut* (Israel Independence Day). Frieda had her students read and study selections from Israel's Declaration of Independence. As they discussed the text, the students focused on the historical milestones of this event and the implications for the Jewish people that they finally had a political homeland. Then they reached a line that stated, "The State of Israel . . . will ensure complete equality of social and political rights to all its inhabitants irrespective of religion, race or sex; it will guarantee freedom of religion, conscience, language, education and culture." Naomi, normally a very enthusiastic member of the class who had been unusually quiet, immediately raised her hand. "This is an amazing statement! Do they really mean all inhabitants? Even the Arabs?" "Yes, I think so," said Frieda. "That seems to be what it says." "Then this was a great beginning!" Naomi exclaimed happily. "Do the people there, the kids, study this so that they know the principles that the state was founded on?" "I'm sure they do." Frieda replied. "Then maybe there is hope for this terrible conflict," Naomi concluded, "if this is what Israel was founded on."

Although in this case, the other students did not seem to react to Naomi's statements, she nevertheless introduced an entirely new element into the conversation. Neither the Palestinian-Israeli conflict, nor the contrast between the triumph of Israel's founding and the current political situation, had been raised in class before. The class had seemed to be operating on an implicit assumption of a morally uncomplicated Israel, and the complete absence of non-Jewish citizens within its borders. By focusing on those few lines within the document, Naomi challenged those assumptions and brought a new dimension to the discussion. In a later interview, she explained how that moment during the lesson had changed her own assumptions about Jewish history as well as her role in the classroom:

I'm very angry. I'm ashamed of Israel. I'm ashamed that people who have been persecuted all the time have now created a country where they are persecuting another people, where they engage in torture, where they plow down farms and houses. I certainly didn't want to have anything to do with celebrating the anniversary of that kind of country. But then, we read the Declaration of Independence, which said that there will be no discrimination and everyone will be treated equally regardless of race or religion. That was a wonderful thing to read. I never would have known that. I never would have read the Declaration of Independence of Israel. I was so glad that I was there, so that I could read that and bring other people's attention to it.

Because of this classroom moment, Naomi went from feeling out of step with her classmates, to recognizing that her perspective was not only valuable in its own right, but added a crucial element to the classroom discussion.

Gender

Many of the female students reported during conversations and formal interviews that the predominance of women in their classes, although not something that they had initially sought out, was a positive factor, creating a sense of openness and comfort in the classroom. Cindy, a recent graduate whose class was entirely women, felt that this helped facilitate the kind of personal sharing described above: "We're all women, so we can say whatever we want! I think that it has made it much easier to talk about our feelings or personal topics. We talk about sex, we talk marriage. It's a lot easier to say whatever it is you want to say and not have to think, how I can say this with a man in the room?" While none of the classes I observed were devoid of male students, the absence of the sole man during one particular lesson seemed to bring out the dynamic that Cindy described. The instructor, Frieda, discussing rabbinic views of marriage and sexuality, at one point referred to the rabbinic authors as "horny little men." As the class burst into laughter, Frieda, laughing herself, said, "I can say that because it's just us women here today." Patty, a student in this class, agreed that women learning together feel more freedom to speak, but attributed this to dynamics of dominance and intimidation, rather than embarrassment: "I think that if men were in the class evenly, the men would tend to dominate the discussion more than the women. I think that if women are in the class alone, they're not intimidated by the men. We can say things because we don't feel that some guy is going to pounce on us." Sandra, a second-year student, noted this same phenomenon of openness among women, crediting it to innate differences in communication styles:

> I believe that the male mentality and the female mentality are completely different, not one better than the other by any means. But without any scientific research, there's a way of looking at things, a way of interacting, a way of communicating that's essentially female. I think women communicate more fully than men do. I think women have had to communicate better to survive. I think women listen better. It's possible to talk about anything with women.

The gender imbalance also held meaning for some students because it reflected upon other dimensions of their individual or communal lives.

Naomi explained that being in a community of women gave her learning a sense of familiarity and connection to other experiences that she had had: "It's real nice being in an all-women group. There are not too many places in my life now where I'm in all-female environments. I used to consciously look for those much more. I used to be part of an all-women's circle here that was really kind of a Wicca [earth-based pagan religion] circle. So it feels very natural." Learning with women allowed Naomi to find the kind of female-centered environment that previously she had only experienced outside of the Jewish community, perhaps helping to further her return to Judaism from other religious traditions. For her classmate Paula, the excitement of being in a classroom of women was in entering a realm of learning that had long been exclusively male: "It's been fun studying when I think about how men have always studied, religious men, studying piece by piece and phrase by phrase. So this is fun to see a bunch of women studying this way."

While one might expect more students to comment upon this dimension of women's learning, Paula was alone in this observation. The fact that more students did not mention or reflect upon the relatively recent opportunity for women to engage in Torah study suggests that women's learning has indeed become normative in their eyes. Thus, while they appreciated the role of gender in encouraging openness and bonding among students, they did not seem to see themselves as taking on historically or socially groundbreaking roles.

The Teacher in the Community

As much as the interactions between students fostered a sense of community in the classroom, their teachers were equally, if not more, important in creating an atmosphere of warmth and openness. The shmoozing and sharing that went on among students often included the teachers as well. Before many classes, certain teachers would circle the room asking about people's families, upcoming or past vacations, or books they were reading. Just as students did, they often wove personal stories into the discussion of the lesson, giving students glimpses into their lives outside of the classroom. Especially when the teacher's background was quite different from that of the students, their stories provided important teaching moments, as well as a means of personal connection. When

Hadassah, a traditional Orthodox woman, described preparing her home for Shabbat and holidays, the learning she and her husband did with their *rav* (rabbi), or hearing her son *layn Torah* (chant the Torah portion) for the first time, her students vicariously experienced the tenor and texture of her Orthodox world. Frieda, the wife of a Reform rabbi, was in a unique position to offer glimpses of different Jewish lifestyles: those of her own family, her Lubavitch brother, and her mostly secular in-laws. In one class, she shared the "Tale of Two Family Bat Mitzvahs": one a glitzy affair at a country club, where dinner included lobster and shrimp; the other a small, women-only ceremony held in her brother's living room. The point of her tale was not to praise one approach and disparage the other, but to emphasize that both extremes represent expressions of Judaism and that they can coexist in one family. Marc, by sharing a detail of his own background, challenged some students' expectations and assumptions about committed Jews. He revealed that in addition to being a Conservative rabbi, he was a devoted "Dead-Head" who has seen the rock group the Grateful Dead perform hundreds of times. Most of the class first looked shocked, and then broke into broad grins upon hearing this news, a few whispering to one another comments along the lines of, "Maybe there's hope for my son!"

Some teachers also opened themselves to their students by sharing their personal difficulties with certain aspects of Jewish tradition, which both humanized them and validated their students' struggles and concerns. Marc, in particular, often illuminated the issues that arose in his Ethics class with his own experiences. When discussing how to balance the need to take care of other people with the obligation to serve God, Marc described how difficult it is for him to devote himself to his morning prayers when he knows that his children need his attention. "Usually," he said, "I'll be standing in the middle of my living room with a siddur in one hand and holding the baby with the other, rushing through my davening as fast as possible so that I can change or feed her." Besides endearing himself to all the mothers in the class, Marc's comment let his students know that even rabbis, living as they do in the real world, cannot achieve perfect piety. At other times, Marc openly discussed his difficulties with certain tenets of the Conservative movement and conflicts that they had caused in his life. In the lesson dealing with homosexuality, he admitted that he did not support the Jewish Theological Seminary's position of refusing ordination to openly gay and lesbian Jews. A discussion in another session about whether an ab-

solute truth can be imposed upon others led to a dual revelation about
Marc's sister's intermarriage and how he dealt with the situation:

> *Wendy:* I'm wondering how this idea would translate to par-
> ents and children. For instance, if your child were
> going to intermarry and you were opposed to it—
> would that be imposing one's beliefs?
>
> *Marc:* That's a very tricky issue, how to balance family with
> beliefs. I was in just that situation when my sister mar-
> ried someone who isn't Jewish. The Rabbinical Assem-
> bly of the Conservative movement has a ruling that
> rabbis and rabbinical students cannot attend an inter-
> marriage.
>
> *Joe:* You mean perform one?
>
> *Marc:* No, even attend. But of course I did—I wouldn't have
> not gone to my sister's wedding. And I was part of the
> wedding party and stood up with them. But they
> asked me to read something during the ceremony, and
> that was something I felt I couldn't do. I was very con-
> flicted about it.

Of course, not all instructors feel it is appropriate to engage in such personal sharing. For those who did, however, it seemed to provide a powerful tool for engaging with students and fostering group bonding.

Community Disruptions

Occasionally, the congenial atmosphere of the classroom community
breaks down. Because students are generally supportive and considerate
of one another, it is particularly instructive to see how the class responds to a disruptive student who does not follow the classroom
norms of respect and collegiality. One classroom contained such a student, whose behavior was so different from that of the others that he
stood out as a subset of one. While clearly quite intelligent and engaged
with the material, Joe was often abrasive in class—interrupting teachers,
speaking out of turn, dominating discussions. He also seemed to have

no sensitivity regarding the flow of the class, often raising and pressing tangential points that interrupted and sidetracked the lesson. In one Ethics class, for example, he tried to draw Marc, the instructor, into a lengthy discussion of the nuances of the word "spirit" as used in Maimonides' dictum that a person "should be subdued in spirit and his spirit should be exceedingly low" (*Mishneh Torah*, Laws of Character Traits, 2:3). "In the Hebrew, the word is *ruach*," Marc started to explain. "Well, that doesn't help me!" grumbled Joe, in his typical abrupt manner, and continued to press the point, ignoring signs of impatience from other students and attempts by the teacher to move the discussion along.

As the year progressed, the levels of both Joe's disruptiveness and the other students' frustration increased. In general, interjections and side conversations while other students were speaking were rare, but they occurred much more during Joe's discourses, often about himself specifically. "Where is he going with this?" "Can't we move on?" and "I just wish he'd stop!" were typical muttered comments. Yet no one seemed to feel comfortable confronting Joe about his behavior, including the teachers (although of his two teachers, Sherry and Marc, only the former outwardly showed any frustration with the situation). While the students attempted by more subtle means (comments, facial expressions) to convey to Joe that he was violating classroom norms, he either did not pick up on these signals or chose to ignore them. The situation was thus left unresolved, one of the rare sources of social tension in an otherwise very congenial classroom. However, because Joe was the only one to strongly violate the classroom norms, his impact was muted. Moments of tension surrounding his behavior were common (usually at least once a class), but brief, as other students or the teacher generally managed to get the lesson back on track rather quickly. Had there been more than one student of a similarly argumentative nature, the effect on the class might have been much greater. As one student commented in an interview about the disruptive behavior: "We accept it; it doesn't keep us from coming, it doesn't keep us from being interested, and it doesn't keep us from participating."

Another instance of community disruption surrounding a particular student was not directly observed, but reported in an interview with Debra, a first-year student in an evening class. As Debra described it, the problem was again that a certain student, a woman named Pam, was seen as dominating the class and taking the discussion down too many tangential paths. Unlike Joe, Pam was not described as argumentative or rude, but was seen by some class members as a bit of a know-it-all. Debra, genuinely sympathetic to Pam, tried to understand the situation from both sides: "She knows a lot and always brings her knowledge to class. Sometimes I can see that she's almost too far ahead. People think that she goes down other tangents, but actually she is bringing some very interesting information to us. But at the same time, she is diverting the class and we're not where she is. I can see how it works both ways." This class dynamic made Debra deeply uncomfortable: "I sit opposite Pam, and I can see the faces of the students around her. And I sit there thinking, 'Oh, God. Oh, God.' I have to say that it's a part of the class that I don't like."

More disturbing, Debra became reluctant to speak in class for fear that she would get a similar reaction: "As a result, I stopped putting up my hand. I didn't want them to be making faces about me, too. We are all in our thirties-plus, for God's sake! I thought we did that when we were twelve." While Joe may have been a frustration to his classmates, none of them exhibited or reported a reluctance to participate because of the reactions he elicited. Having not observed the dynamic that Debra described, it is hard to definitively account for the difference. It seems, however, that the difference was that Joe's manner was so different from that of his classmates that his behavior had no impact on how others were treated, while Pam, from Debra's description, seemed to be just enough within the norm that others might have feared being tarred with the same disdainful brush.

Despite these instances of disruption, tensions between students were generally rare in the classroom. There seemed to be a complete lack of competition among the students—no desire to "score points" with the teacher by showing off knowledge or proving another student wrong. Indeed, when a teacher praised a comment as being particularly insightful, the speaker often made a show of looking a bit surprised or embarrassed, waving away the praise of other students. If a past comment was mistakenly attributed to the wrong student, other students (though not the one who actually made the comment) usually offered a quick correction, making sure that credit was properly given. Such incidents suggested that for these students, learning was primarily a communal effort. They seemed to take pride in the advancement of the class as a whole, rather than in individual accomplishments, greatly valuing and appreciating the contributions of their classmates.

The Strength of Social Bonds

While certainly some students were less than thrilled by the social dimensions of their learning experience (as one woman expressed it, "I'm not that interested in hearing about other people's personal journeys"), most seemed to appreciate the opportunity to learn from, as well as with, their fellow students. When reflecting upon their experience in the program, many cited their classmates as a highlight, speaking of them with affection and admiration. "I love the makeup of our class and listening to everyone," enthused Joanne. "It's a great mix of people." Tammy, her classmate, agreed: "I find these are such interesting people, with so many interesting things to say. I've really gotten a lot out of the experience." Sandra was even more enthusiastic about her fellow students: "They're wonderful. They're great people, every one of them. They are all very, very interesting people. People worth knowing, worth listening to." And Bruce, a graduate of a few years before, recalled how much he had learned from the diversity and openness of his classmates: "We learned a lot from one another—not only of things that were in the curriculum but about our backgrounds, and about how we do what we do, and who we are as Jews and how different we are as Jews." As these comments suggest, many students valued one another not only as fellow learners, but as rich sources of knowledge and instruction.

By the end of the year, in both first- and second-year classes, students seemed to have grown deeply attached to their once-a-week learning colleagues. One first-year class displayed a great deal of anxiety over the prospect that they might be split up during their second year in the program, despite assurances by the teacher that this would not happen. They insisted on calling in the site director to hear directly from her authoritative lips that they would remain together as a class. The other first-year class was more easily reassured that they would not be disbanded the following year. However, the fall seemed to be too long for them to wait to continue their learning, so they tried to persuade Hadassah, their teacher, to offer a class for them over the summer. When she told them that she would probably be engaged to teach in a local synagogue's summer adult Jewish learning program, they insisted that this was not good enough. They wanted to continue to learn together as a group, without any intrusion by, in the joking words of one student, "foreigners." The second-year class was equally determined to preserve the group, even though their formal time in the Mini-School was coming to a close. They decided, at the urging of a few enterprising students, to form a book group that would be tailored to meet the interests and time constraints of as many students as possible, thus ensuring that their group experience could continue uninterrupted. Between this group and the optional "graduate" classes, these students may in a few years feel the same as Bruce, who graduated from the Mini-School two years ago, did. When asked whether he still kept up with old classmates, he laughingly replied, "We'll never leave one another."

Conclusion

This chapter has illustrated that several elements of the adult Jewish learning experience operate to produce communities of Jewish learners. Most fundamentally, the classroom setting provides a conducive environment for community building, as can be seen in the learners' attachment to space and location, the arrangement of seating patterns to facilitate discussion, and the use of food and other aids to produce an informal and sociable atmosphere. As a result, learners play out their friendships, be it with preexisting friends or those they have acquired in the classroom; the functioning of friendship cliques can be easily observed, as can a considerable amount of shmoozing before, during, and after the lessons. Learners enjoy sharing personal aspects of their lives and receiving attention, caring, support, and counsel.

The adult Jewish learning classroom, like the traditional Jewish Talmud study group, is rich with fellowship and social interaction. It may be that for students who are just entering the world of Jewish learning, this sense of community is even more crucial than for traditional *lerners* such as those studied by Samuel Heilman. Unlike learners who know that they share high levels of Jewish observance and knowledge, many students may need to know that when they ask questions that could expose their ignorance of Jewish tradition, or share personal stories that reveal their place on the spectrum of Jewish observance, they are doing so among those who are, if not deep friends, at least fellow and sympathetic travelers. Teacher Cindy believed that students felt free to talk about themselves because they knew that their comments would be met with acceptance and respect: "I never heard anyone belittle, or make fun of, or shame someone else. Never. The students are extremely sensitive." Bruce suspected that many of his fellow students had entered the classroom with some hesitation, but quickly developed a feeling of comfort and confidence among their classmates:

> There was a lot of apprehension from a lot of people in the class, especially those who felt as though they didn't come from a particularly rich Jewish traditional background or much education. Those people were probably saying to themselves, I'm going to be overwhelmed here by people who know a lot more than I do. But after a couple of months into the program, everyone felt as if there was something for everyone there. Everybody needs to feel that his own personal Judaism is going to be accepted by not only the teachers, but by the rest of the class.

This foundation of community and acceptance enabled students to comfortably explore dimensions of their "personal Judaism" and together delve further into the meanings of Jewish text, tradition, and culture.

CHAPTER FIVE

The Role of Educational Philosophy in Shaping Curriculum and Instruction

A philosophy shapes the culture of an educational institution and the learning that occurs under its aegis. Since its founding in 1986, the Florence Melton Adult Mini-School has evolved a distinct philosophy of adult Jewish education—how a school should be organized, what the content and structure of the curriculum should be, how teachers should instruct, and what constitutes effective teacher development. In this chapter, we explore how the espoused philosophy of this adult Jewish learning institution evolved and how it influences and is interpreted by teachers, site directors, and students today.

The Making of an Institutional Culture

Each of the sixty-plus Mini-School sites is unique in terms of its administrative leadership, the composition of the faculty, and the makeup of the student body. However, despite geographic, demographic, and staffing differences, sites have much in common. Most obvious is the common curriculum. Equally, if not more significant is the educational philosophy that shapes the culture of this learning environment.

Organizational development theorist Edgar Schein defines culture as "a pattern of shared basic assumptions that the group learned as it solved its problems of external adaptation and internal integration, that has worked well enough to be considered valid and, therefore, to be taught to new members as the correct way to perceive, think, and feel in relation to those problems" (Schein 1992, 12). An institution's culture can foster effectiveness and productivity; improve collegiality and collaboration; facilitate change processes; build commitments to shared ideas and values; motivate staff, students, and community; and help maintain a focus on the primary mission of the institution (Deal and Peterson 1999).

Thomas Sergiovanni points out that the shared assumptions that form the basis of a school's culture are "a negotiated product of the shared sentiments of school participants" (1991, 108). At the Mini-School, this negotiation takes place between centralized leadership in Jerusalem and Chicago, as well as among directors and faculty from the many sites around the globe. The educational vision and philosophy, established at the top of the organizational structure, are conveyed and refined in collaboration with site directors and faculty through annual meetings, written materials, and regular communication via phone, e-mail, and site visits.

The Making of a School

Planning documents from the mid-1980s (before the first pilot site opened) referred to the Mini-School as a project or program.[1] Today, everyone associated with the North American and international offices uses deliberate language, calling it a "school" and not a "program." This image is central to the overall educational philosophy and approach. As Betsy Katz, the North American director, explained:

> It has evolved into a school. When we started, it was just a curriculum. Then it became a series of classes, and then a program—meaning something that's short-term. But now, it has become a school and that's the language I use, a school being a permanent institution in the community.

In addition to this sense of permanence, other features that distinguish the Mini-School from an adult education program include the two-year time commitment, the sequential, structured curriculum that is replicated at every site, and the services provided to the students both within and outside the classroom. These services include extracurricular activi-

[1] Original proposal to the Melton Centre for Jewish Education, Hebrew University, Jerusalem, 1985.

ties and, more important, the attention paid and support given by each site director to the students. These activities contribute to the creation of a learning community and not merely a sequence of centrally designed classes. Though the image that the designers want to convey is that of a school, the preface "mini" is also a deliberate choice. It is intended to reassure and welcome students who may be anxious about the academic pressures and expectations that are typically associated with schooling.

A recently revised and expanded faculty handbook[2] lists goals that center on the importance of building Jewish knowledge in order to build Jewish community. These goals also reflect the value placed on an ongoing critical engagement with the study of Judaism from a pluralistic perspective for students and educators alike. The goals that the top leaders articulate, consistently reinforced with site directors and faculty through written and verbal communication, include:

1. To convey a basic but sophisticated core of Jewish knowledge
2. To create Jewish communities of lifelong learners
3. To stimulate critical thinking and reflection about Judaism in a nonjudgmental way
4. To teach the common roots and experiences of Judaism while affirming pluralism
5. To connect Jewish study and Jewish life in a natural way
6. To stimulate increased participation in the Jewish community
7. To enhance local educational resources and create a cadre of committed, professional adult Jewish educators
8. To build a partnership between Israel and the Diaspora, based on mutual respect and utilizing the strengths of both partners.

A Literacy-Focused Curriculum

From its inception, the central goal of the Mini-School was to increase Jewish literacy among participants. An early planning document described this goal as follows:

[2]*Preparing to Teach: Florence Melton Adult Mini-School Faculty Handbook.* Melton Centre for Jewish Education in the Diaspora, Hebrew University, Jerusalem, 2001.

[The objective is] to give adults mastery of basic Jewish literacy, in a systematic and stimulating manner. Students move from encountering basic Jewish vocabulary, including Hebrew reading, to an intellectual, experiential and spiritual exploration of the four core areas of Jewish knowledge: Bible, history, rabbinics, and the Jewish calendar. (Melton Centre for Jewish Education in the Diaspora 1985, 2–3)

Central to the literacy approach is the acquisition of knowledge, not the exploration of feelings or the development of practical skills. The first Mini-School faculty handbook stated: "Success in this approach is determined by what the student understands and his/her motivation to continue to study Jewish sources."[3] All other consequences, therefore, are secondary to this primary focus on developing a sense of empowerment and commitment to lifelong Jewish learning.

There may be an inherent flaw in this logic, since research suggests that neither identity formation nor literacy is exclusively a cognitive process. Rather, literacy acquisition, including critical thinking, is a complex process of socialization that involves an interaction of social, emotional, and intellectual development (Ferdman 1990; Heine and Lehman 2003; London and Chazan 1990). Recent research has demonstrated that affective learning plays a significant role in prompting critical reflection (E. Taylor 2000; Boyd 1991). Thus, how students feel about their experiences is certainly as important as—if not more important than—the intellectual grappling with how the content is framed by their teachers.

Defining literacy entails deciding what counts as literacy in a given social context (Ferdman 1990). In an objective sense, literacy means attainment of competence, knowledge, and skills (Dubin 1989). However, determining what specific knowledge, skills, competencies, and values are important to teach varies from social group to social group, even within different streams of Judaism. Thus, literacy is always contextualized within a particular culture. Behavioral norms and social values cannot help but shape the assessment of whether someone has attained literacy. The planning and development of a literacy-based curriculum is essentially an ideological process, in that choices must be made in terms of texts and instructional approaches selected, questions raised, and conversations shaped.

[3]Melton Centre 2001, *Preparing to Teach*, 10.

Literacy must be understood in terms of the values, skills, and activities that define the cultural context in which it is situated. As Ferdman (1990) suggests, cultural literacy requires mastering a body of knowledge and developing the ability to interpret the symbols that "codify and represent the values, beliefs, and norms of the culture" (187). He writes: "Literacy goes beyond the superficial transactions with a printed or written page and extends into the ability to comprehend and manipulate its symbols—the words and concepts—and do so in a culturally prescribed manner" (188). Becoming literate means that the learner has greater access to and understanding of the culture, which may trigger changes in thoughts or behavior that shape his or her frame of meaning (Heine and Lehman 2003). Literacy education, thus, is a process of socialization where knowledge is acquired at the same time as values are transmitted in a particular social context (de-Castell and Luke 1988).

The social context at the Mini-School promotes an open exploration of normative Jewish tradition. In this setting, normative is implicitly understood as the set Jewish values, beliefs, and practices that are derived from a system of rabbinic authority as defined by halakhah (Jewish law). Learning focuses on acquiring the intellectual skills to seriously read and interpret sacred texts in order to understand the logic and development of this system. This approach is rooted in a traditional practice called *Torah lishmah*, Jewish study for its own sake. Though *Torah lishmah* is an intellectual process, it also assumes that such study will influence students' commitment to Jewish living, as evidenced by the rabbinic dictum, "Which is greater, study or action? Study, because study leads to action" (Kiddushin 40b).

This approach is also consistent with what Michael Rosenak (1987) describes as "cultural initiation." Here, the principal goal is for learners to master the "language of our culture" so that they can feel comfortable with "its basic assumptions, rhetoric, forms of inquiry, patterns of community, and symbolic expression." Not only should learners be able to express themselves in the language, Rosenak continues; they should also be able "to speak their own *literature;* that is, to be themselves—to use the culture's syntax—but to make their own sentences" (34). Indeed, the fact that the Mini-School promotes dialogue among the learners about the language of "our culture" provides evidence that they are encouraged to engage in a process of writing themselves into the discourse.

Philosophy of Instruction

In our interviews, Katz and Mirvis cited Hawkins (1974) and Hutchins (1954) as particularly influential in shaping their literacy-based philosophy of instruction. Both scholars advocate engaging the learners in dialogue about matters of substance. For Hutchins, the essence of liberal education lies in exposure to the "Great Conversation" that shapes Western civilization. The Great Books contain "not merely the tradition, but also the great exponents of the tradition" (28). The substance of liberal education consists "in the recognition of basic problems, in knowledge of distinctions and interrelations in subject matter, and in the comprehension of ideas" (29).

Hawkins speaks more to the learning process. He describes the learning experience as an "I-Thou" and "It" relationship that takes place in an environment of mutual respect that builds trust and confidence:

> No [learner,] I wish to say, can gain competence and knowledge, or know himself as competent and as a knower, save through communication with others involved with him in his enterprises. Without a Thou, there is no I evolving. Without an It there is no content for the context, no figure and no heat, but only an affair of mirrors confronting each other. (Hawkins 1974, 52)

For Hawkins, the organizing framework for understanding what takes place in a classroom can be seen as a triangle whose three points represent the learner, the teacher, and the subject matter. While each point brings a specific background and context to the experience, it is in the interactions and balancing between the points that learning occurs.

For Katz and Mirvis, the Mini-School's structured, sequential approach distinguishes it from other types of adult Jewish education programs. Some of these other programs focus on practical aspects of ritual life, such as learning to read Hebrew, chant from the Torah, or lead a Passover seder. In this type of course, success is measured by the skills, competencies, and behavioral changes that the participants demonstrate upon completion of the course. Other programs focus on making personal meaning. In facilitating connections between the learners and the texts, these programs revolve around the question, "How do you feel about Judaism?"

In contrast with this student-centered approach, the text-centered approach of the Mini-School retains primary emphasis on the texts, and relevancy is left to the student to construct. Literacy occurs by gaining competence and knowledge through dialogue about specific, substantive content. The common interest and involvement in the subject matter remains central to the relationship at all times. As we will see in chapter 6, teachers function as diagnosticians, responding to their assessments of learners' needs at a particular moment. Here, the question intended to shape instruction must be, "Do you understand the Jewish Conversation that is taking place on a particular issue and can you contribute to this Conversation?"[4]

Evolution of the Curriculum

While always described as literacy or "basic Jewish knowledge," the thinking about what is encompassed under this rubric has evolved significantly over time. In the early days, the curriculum had more of a practical and experiential orientation. In other words, it was explicitly more about answering the question of how to be a Jew. As an internal document from 1987 noted, "The goal is to equip contemporary adults with the knowledge essential to confident *participation in the life of the Jewish family and community in all their dimensions*" (italics added). A teacher-training document from 1989 described the curriculum as basic, though at a high intellectual level and acknowledging students' experience. It further detailed a nondenominational, pluralistic approach that balances the abstract with the concrete, belief and behavior, the private and the communal, as well as spiritual and practical concerns. This orientation toward practice was particularly noticeable in the Rhythms course, which covers the Jewish calendar and life cycle. When the course was revised in the mid-1990s, the focus shifted away from Jewish observance, or the "how-to" of Judaism, toward a more neutral stance of addressing the "why" of Judaism, how traditional practice and beliefs evolved.[5]

[4]"Jewish Literacy: The Preferred Approach of the Florence Melton Adult Mini-School," Melton Centre for Jewish Education, 2001, 10.
[5]Melton Centre 2001, *Preparing to Teach.*

In addition to this shift in orientation, the curricula have become increasingly sophisticated about promoting critical thinking about Judaism. Earlier versions of the courses relied on secondary sources to interpret content for the students. The revised curricula engage students directly in the study of primary texts and raise more questions that challenge students to explore a range of perspectives and approaches to Jewish thinking. The minutes of a national staff meeting in 1995 contrasted the approaches of the old curriculum with the new, saying, "The first curriculum was a 'nice' curriculum, teaching what is nice to do. With some exceptions, it has not been engaging to students or to teachers. The new curriculum is one that deals with contemporary situations that are troubling us today."[6] For example, the introduction to the teacher for the current version of the course, "Purposes of Jewish Living," provides a succinct rationale for how the Bible should be used to demonstrate that the issues and ideas raised in this sacred text still have contemporary relevance:

> The Bible contains profound truths about man and his relationship to God and the world and has served as the basis for much of the literature written subsequent to it. We therefore decided to focus as much as possible on the study of ideas that emerge from the biblical text. Nevertheless, in most lessons, we supplemented the biblical texts from rabbinic and contemporary literature.
> The key elements in our choice of a particular text are:
> 1. That it contain ideas and not just dry facts
> 2. That the ideas of the text are thought-provoking, meaningful, and relevant to the contemporary reader.

Betsy Katz provided a historical context for this evolution in approach:

> In the mid-1980s, the study of primary sources, the Jewish texts, wasn't a priority. Today, you wouldn't think of creating a program for adults that wasn't focused on *Tanakh* and Talmud commentary. Then, there were a lot of secondary sources, and that was the style of curriculum writing.

---

[6]National staff meeting, minutes, February 8–10, 1995, 2.

She noted that because prior to the Mini-School there had never been a systematic, sequential course of Jewish study for adults, there were no adult curricula. Writers of Jewish curricula wrote for children and teachers of children, but not for adults. As the Mini-School has evolved, so too has the demand for more sophisticated material responsive to adult learning styles and needs.

Evolving Views on Teachers and Teaching

As the Mini-School's view of curriculum has evolved, the perspective on how teachers should relate to the curriculum has changed significantly as well. There appears to be a creative and evolving interaction between a curriculum written in Jerusalem and taught at many sites around the world by teachers with a wide variety of backgrounds and perspectives. Early in the institution's history, the curriculum was designed to be almost "teacher-proof," with detailed lesson plans and step-by-step instructions, based on tacit assumptions about what form that literacy-based education should take. Teachers were intended to be a conduit for a set program of learning. An early planning document stipulated the desired qualities of a Mini-School teacher as an experienced Jewish educator who would be able to "teach the curriculum and not themselves" (Melton Centre for Jewish Education in the Diaspora 1985).

Over time, the central leadership came to realize that the learning dynamic was not a dualistic interchange between student and text, but a complex, three-way relationship between teacher, learner, and text, as illustrated by Hawkins's learning triangle. The leadership understood that the content of teaching was inseparable from its form (Handelman 1996). Good teaching demands the teachers' full engagement in the process, interpreting the curriculum to fit with their knowledge, interests, and teaching style. Likewise, a fixed curriculum cannot respond to particular students' prior knowledge, learning styles, life experience, questions, and classroom dynamics. Good teachers get to know their students and use this knowledge in shaping the content and form of instruction. Richer learning also takes place when teachers bring something of themselves into the learning process. The minutes of the second international Mini-School directors' conference in 1996 marked the changing viewpoint, noting that "the curricula follow the new model being utilized in which the curriculum is written for the teacher and not for the student."[7] This shift was designed to provide the teacher with greater autonomy and discretion in choosing how to shape a given lesson. As Katz explained:

> What we provide right now are resources for the faculty. We write for them. They study and then decide what to teach rather than us dictating what to teach, because one thing that we realized right from the beginning was that the style of curriculum writing could be very patronizing, condescending.

Mirvis echoed and elaborated on this understanding when he described the ideal role of the teacher in relationship to the curriculum and the students:

> The curriculum writer in Jerusalem cannot really know what takes place at each individual site. The teachers have to make the bridge between the unfamiliar culture represented by the curriculum and the world of their students. That's why local teachers are so important. They are in tension between where the students are and where the curriculum is. Great teachers feel the tension between them because they are what I call "cultural interpreters." They are teaching the language of a certain literacy to a culture of outsiders.

As currently articulated, the ideal Mini-School teacher has both in-depth Jewish knowledge and a commitment to teaching texts to adults in an interactive style that facilitates the building of a learning community. Faculty members include experienced Jewish educators who represent a balanced mix by gender and denominational affiliation. The Mini-School leadership prefers that site directors hire teachers with professional training in Judaic studies and adult education, as well as, on occasion, lay leaders and informally trained teachers who have acquired

---

[7]Minutes from the second international directors' conference, Israel, January 30–February 5, 1996, 2.

in-depth Jewish learning. Desirable teachers have subject-matter expertise, experience in teaching adults, and a commitment to serving as active role models, in terms of their own ongoing study to deepen their
Jewish knowledge as well as their willingness to express deep Jewish
convictions and act upon them in daily Jewish life. Essential qualities
also include a commitment to pluralism and comfort with discussion
and interactive learning.

Key Components:
Safety, Interaction, Reflection

How the teacher works with and interprets the curriculum is only one
dimension of Mini-School thinking about the teacher's role. In addition,
teachers are expected to help build learning communities within their
classrooms. They are expected to be responsive to adult learning needs
by providing a safe and interactive learning environment, where the
learners' prior experience is valued and the material connects directly to
their lives. In addition, teachers are encouraged to engage continually in
reflecting on their practice in order to improve their teaching.

Creating a safe space is essential to any good adult learning situation. Competent in most of their life skills, adults often feel vulnerable
and insecure about reentering a formal learning environment where subject matter and classroom dynamics are unfamiliar (Brookfield 1986;
Daloz 1999; Vella 1994). As Katz wrote in the faculty handbook: "The
teacher is responsible for the affective/emotional environment of the
class as well as the physical environment. He/she ideally creates a warm,
supportive, nonjudgmental environment where people can question and
grow" (Melton Centre for Jewish Education in the Diaspora 2001, 3).
The faculty handbook frames its discussion on safety with a passage
from Schuster's research on Jewish adult learners: "Although many Jewish adults are eager to learn and are excited about the idea of coming
closer to Judaism, many also feel vulnerable and apprehensive about
taking steps into Jewish learning" (Schuster 1999, 19). In response, the
handbook stresses: "It is vital that the Melton classroom be a safe place
for the learner, where their lack of 'insider' knowledge does not detract
from the joy of studying" (Melton Centre 2001, 17).

Adult learners need to have some sense of control over the learning

process (Vella 1994). Knowledge is constructed through a series of dialogical processes between learners and teachers, between a group of
learners, and through critical reflection, which is a form of the learner's
own inner dialogue. Adult educators generally shape their learning and
teaching objectives around developing in their students a lifelong commitment to continuous learning and self-agency or a sense of responsibility for personal choices, beliefs, and commitments (Taylor, Marienau,
and Fiddler 2000, 32–33). These functions can be seen in the language
used to describe the ideal instructional approach. In addition to text
comprehension, the faculty handbook urges teachers to help students
"interpret the text from one's own perspective, be aware of and open to
alternative interpretations, and understand implications of the text for
one's life" (12). They are also enjoined to demonstrate concern for the
learning of each individual student and to respect the diversity of students' questions and opinions.

Daloz (1999) characterized this facilitative style of teaching as re-
placing "the sage on the stage" with the "guide on the side." Over time,
the curricula have become less directive and more text-based and prob-
lem-centered. Centrally written materials and local site directors explicitly urge teachers not just to lecture and interpret the texts for their
students, but to engage them in a process of inquiry and dialogue about
the texts and the ideas and questions that they raise. A publication from
the late 1990s noted that "active participation and critical thinking are
encouraged by interactive strategies such as text analysis and group discussion. The learners are constantly encouraged to consider the application of the subject matter, sources, and ideas to their own individual
contexts."[8] The faculty handbook devotes an entire section to the topic
of interactive teaching. Using both rabbinic sources and contemporary
writing on adult learning, the handbook (citing educator Paolo Freire)
advocates teaching as a dialogical process where

> knowledge is not the private property of the teacher. Rather, it is
> a medium evoking the critical reflection of both teacher and stu-
> dents. Through dialogue, the teacher-of-the-students and the
> students-of-the-teacher cease to exist and a new term emerges:
> teacher-student with student-teachers. (Freire 1971, 67)

[8]Melton Centre for Jewish Education in the Diaspora, undated booklet, 7.

For the past two decades or more, significant attention has been paid to the role that reflection on practice can have on improving teaching. Donald Schön's now-classic *The Reflective Practitioner* (1983) advocated for "reflection in action," the ability of teachers to continually think about and adjust their teaching in relationship to their students and their texts, advice followed by numerous teachers (e.g., Ashton-Warner 1986; Ayers 1993; Bruffee 1999; MacDonald 1993). With respect to the importance of reflection in learning and teacher development as an interactive faculty dynamic, Lee Shulman wrote:

> By engaging in purposive reflection, documentation, assessment and analysis of teaching and learning, and doing so in a more public and accessible manner, we not only support the improvement of our own teaching. We raise the likelihood that our work is transparent to our colleagues who design and instruct many of the same students in the same or related programs. (2000, 50)

The Mini-School has embraced these principles. Its teachers are encouraged to enter into conversation with the curriculum, to reflect on their practice, and to support one another by sharing ideas and approaches. Betsy Katz remarked: "We have learned that as much as teachers learn from the content of the classes, they learn from the models of teaching presented by [other] faculty" (*InSites* 1996, 2). Likewise, she wrote:

> We want faculty to be capable of Reflective Practice, the ability to teach and then to think about the teaching and learning experiences and learn from it. It is a quality that is highly prized among Mini-School staff who are also faculty. Conversation about the art of teaching can improve the quality of our Mini-Schools.[9]

Professional development of teachers is also a much greater priority than in the past. In 1999, Rabbi Michael Balinsky was appointed director of professional development. His hiring signaled the start of an in-

[9]Minutes of Annual Directors' Meeting, Hebrew University, Jerusalem, February 11, 1998.

tensified approach to help more teachers improve their skills in teaching adults. The faculty handbook, regional conferences, phone consultations, site visits, and an Israel seminar for teachers are examples of recent initiatives in this area. In addition, the Mini-School has taken advantage of new information technology to enhance communication among directors, teachers, and students.

Pluralism and the Learning Agenda

Since its inception, teaching from a pluralistic standpoint has been central to the institutional mission and vision. The consistent message from the top of the organization is that the Mini-School is about literacy education, and not about religious development or enhancing practice. The curriculum explores the many voices represented in Jewish tradition on any given subject. In an interview in 2001, David Harbater, the Jerusalem-based core curriculum writer, stated that his goal is to enable learners to make informed decisions about their lives as Jews. The specific content of those decisions, he said, is not his concern:

> I want a curriculum that enables Jews to be informed so that they can make intelligent decisions about their Jewish life. Even if some Jews—after two years and four courses—find that, based on this knowledge and information, they choose not to be more committed or to be less committed, I don't think we've failed. Because as far as I'm concerned, my goal is for Jews to be informed. Where information could lead an individual Jew is not for me to determine.

Informed choice (intriguingly, a watchword of Reform Judaism, the most liberal denomination) is a core tenet of adult learning theory that the Mini-School espouses. Mezirow (2000) wrote: "Fostering these liberating conditions for making more autonomous and informed choices and developing a sense of empowerment is the cardinal goal of adult education" (26). Central to the process of adult education "is helping learners critically reflect on, appropriately validate, and effectively act on their (and others') beliefs, interpretations, values, feelings, and ways of thinking" (26). Betsy Katz described how the values of pluralism are integrated with adult learning theory when she wrote about teachers' responsibilities to create a classroom culture conducive to adult learning: "The best Mini-School environment encourages students to enter into each other's perspectives and to accept one another as unique and valid. The curriculum and the teacher support the examination of varied expressions of Judaism" (1998, 27).

Mirvis and Harbater both estimated that only 50–60% of faculty teach in a way fully consonant with this well-articulated philosophical stance. They both communicated a sense of urgency in needing to redress this situation, citing the appointment of Michael Balinsky as "the beginning of a whole macro push in this direction" (Mirvis interview). Katz observed that this pluralistic approach seems to grate against a sense of mission held by many Jewish educators who want to teach their students to love Judaism, not just to know about it. They want to respond to their students' questions about beliefs and practice, but may feel constrained by the underlying philosophy of the Mini-School and the design of the curriculum, which discourages them from addressing these questions. As an example, Katz pointed out that many teachers resisted the approach suggested in the recently issued second-generation "Rhythms of Jewish Living" course:

We were interviewing teachers over the past couple months about what they think of it. The teachers are not teaching it academically. Even though the curriculum still emphasizes concepts, not how-to, they're pulled by their students and by their own inclination to teach more about how to observe. Part of it has to do with the makeup of their class. Part of it has to do with the way they are, their own inclinations.

For Harbater, increasing Jewish observance or participation in the Jewish community does not drive the curriculum design:

We have no religious agenda, and I wouldn't even say "the agenda is." Our goal is for Jews to be literate or informed/literate about their Jewishness. In most cases, that leads to a greater commitment to Jewish learning or to Jewish observance. But that is not an explicit, or even an implicit, goal in designing the curriculum.

While the Mini-School does not overtly promote a particular level of Jewish expression, it does leave open the question as to how the curriculum might be construed by individual learners. As befits its pluralistic stance, there appears to be an absence of discussion within the curriculum about what is authentic Judaism. After all, defining authenticity explicitly suggests a particular point of view. However, as noted earlier, there seems to be an implicit message that normative Judaism is grounded in halakhic tradition. So, while the curriculum does not advocate conforming to specific norms, in effect, it could be interpreted as saying that there is a correct way to be Jewish, at least from the perspective of the tradition.

Increasing Literacy and Increasing Participation in the Jewish Community

There appear to be two distinct but related agendas that serve as a hidden curriculum. The first is that participation in the Mini-School will lead to increased participation in the Jewish community; and the second is that study is, in and of itself, a religious and holy act.

The program leadership and many teachers tacitly assume that people enrolling are looking to grow as Jews and that the intellectual study of Judaism will lead to increased commitments to ongoing study and to greater participation in the Jewish community. In other words, the learning experience *is* intended to be personally transformative. In an essay in 1998, Katz acknowledged that teachers must be prepared to help people who look to adult Jewish learning when they are open to, and looking for, change:

> The majority of students who make the commitment to come to learn over a period of two years want to grow as Jews. Research in general literacy education has indicated that studying under these circumstance creates community and is dependent upon community. People change more easily when they share the process with others. The fact that they talk about their accomplishment, their frustrations and their misgivings brings them closer together. There must be intellectual and emotional space in a Jewish classroom devoted to the needs of people in the process of change.

The tension between learning for its own sake and learning for a purpose emerges loud and clear in the faculty handbook issued in 2001.

This document argues that the literacy approach is "intellectually honest," "has no hidden spiritual agenda," and focuses on "intellectual interaction" in the classroom. However, a statement that follows seems to implicitly acknowledge, if not endorse, the expectation that intellectual study will lead to at least some learners reflecting on and changing the level, quality, or intensity of their Jewish practice:

> Although we study *Torah lishmah* as an intellectual endeavor, we are also confident that this learning will influence the students' commitment to Judaism. *Gadol HaTalmud Hamevi Lidai Ma'aseh*—The study of Torah is elevated because it leads to practice. Ultimately, learning should lead to practice and this will increase our students' commitment to Jewish living. (11)

The message about the potential impact that this Jewish learning experience may have on the Jewish community is reflected in the earliest planning documents for the school. In the original proposal, the focus was on educating Jewish parents to ensure that their children would be Jewishly educated and grow up in Jewish homes. The proposal claimed that providing adults with a course in basic Jewish literacy would help "those with children struggling to create a Jewish home, but lack[ing] the basic Jewish education necessary to provide a home environment that has traditionally been a stronghold of Jewish life" (Melton Centre for Jewish Education in the Diaspora 1985, 2). Later, the goal was more clearly stated as: "Learning that is designed to help them achieve the 'literacy' necessary for confident participation in Jewish family and community life" (*InSites* 1993).

In an interview, international director Jonathan Mirvis explicitly described his goals as focused on Jewish education as a means for increasing the numbers of Jews who are active in the Jewish community. He directly attributed the diminished philanthropic and other involvement of Jews in Jewish communal life to a lack of Jewish knowledge. He said: "Being Jewish means community. But you have to understand that first. That understanding doesn't come from anywhere except learning." He continued:

> Our biggest problem today is basically what Florence said ten or fifteen years ago. You have 95% of Jewish adults who are not Jewishly literate who are making the decisions about tomorrow. We can't wait twenty years until our kids come out of day

schools. And if we don't move pretty quickly and teach these people who are making money in high tech about Judaism, we're going to have a whole generation of people who are not going to give money because they have no sense of Jewish belonging. There's this guy in Microsoft who gave a million dollars because he studied in the Mini-School.

Likewise, Florence Melton noted the critical role that adult Jewish learning can have in changing the way communal leaders think and act:

The Mini-School has something so special to offer for leadership because rather than just occupy a seat on the board, and allocate money or direct programming, you have Jews who are committed and understanding of the role of the Jews in the world and how individually they have a role in changing the world.

A Further Goal:
Jewish Study as a Sacred Act

From the outset, one clearly stated program goal was to develop a commitment to continuous learning among the participants. This goal is one of the key instructional objectives that guide the practice of adult educators in general (Taylor, Marienau, and Fiddler 2000). However, an added dimension in the Mini-School's articulation of this goal views Jewish study as a religious act, particularly when it is done in community. This message is grounded in traditional Jewish sources that form the content of the curriculum and is supported by the literature that suggests that successful schools understand their mission as sacred. In describing the qualities required in building a school culture, Sergiovanni notes that leadership "assumes the role of 'high priest,' seeking to define, strengthen, and articulate those enduring values, beliefs, and cultural strands that give the school its unique identity over time" (1991, 104). This set of values and beliefs becomes the official "religion" of the school and gives it meaning and guides its actions (110). Using the language of religion to frame organizational purpose is consonant with the leadership's worldview and sense of purpose about Jewish learning.

Top leadership of the Mini-School routinely attempts to instill a sense of holy mission to those working at the local sites. At the 2001 site directors' conference, leadership from the North American office and the Hebrew University enthusiastically praised the people whom Betsy Katz described as being responsible for the "sacred task" of coordinating the Florence Melton Adult Mini-School. They repeatedly emphasized how crucial partnership and teamwork are to ensuring a successful future. And they directly linked the success of their endeavors to the survival of the Jewish people. Jonathan Mirvis gave an impassioned welcoming speech, emphasizing the potential for the Mini-School to create a global community of adult Jewish learners that focuses on Jewish literacy. He challenged the directors to think of themselves as change agents, charging them to ask themselves, "Have I done what I can to ensure the future of the Jewish people? Will I leave a better Jewish world than the one I came into?"

There is a strong textual basis for connecting Jewish study in community with religious practice. Indeed, the daily liturgy includes a blessing for the study of Torah and actual study of text within the worship experience. Thus, study, in and of itself, is considered a form of religious behavior. Study in the company of others is all the more so, as suggested by the following two rabbinic texts:

> When two people meet and exchange words of Torah, it is as if the *Shekhinah* [divine presence] hovers over them. (*Pirkei Avot* [The Teachings of the Sages], 3:3)

and

> Make yourselves into groups to study the Torah, since the knowledge of Torah can be acquired only in association with others. (Berakhot 63b)

The religious significance of learning in the Mini-School appears in several places. For instance, Katz (1998) noted that an important indicator of success is when students continue to learn beyond the two-year course of study and when they develop a sense of sacredness of connecting to a Jewish learning community. She wrote:

> This indicates more strongly than anything else the fact that a learning community has been formed. The knowledge that one is performing a mitzvah, the joy of learning and the anticipation

of continuous growth all motivate people to continue to learn. The rewards, the comfort and the sense of sacredness of a Jewish learning community is, however, the heart of lifelong Jewish learning.

In another example, an undercurrent of religious significance also is reflected in a session on experiential teaching that is summarized in the minutes from a 1996 directors' conference. Here, it stated that mastering subject matter is not the ultimate goal of the learning; rather, living richer Jewish lives is. In keeping with its pluralistic stance, the minutes do not record a conversation that stipulated the quality, shape, or intensity that those Jewish lives should take, but they do suggest that the learning experience is intended to effect change. The Mini-School is about touching people's lives. Therefore, the content and the process are a means to the end. The end is "touching people's lives" to live Jewishly.

The themes of sacred study and living Jewishly are synthesized in the final remarks of the faculty handbook:

> In the long run, Melton teaching is much more than a successful class, or even engaged adults participating in Torah study. This type of study has the potential to create a learning community in which people enter into dialogue with each other and the texts and voices of the tradition. This learning community can be transformative and students will leave Melton not only as learning Jews, but also imbued with a touch of the holiness of study.

Conclusion

The values supporting the educational philosophy of the Mini-School are informed by two external factors: (1) an assessment of the needs of the adult Jewish community to increase their knowledge of, comfort with, and connection to Jewish texts and Jewish tradition; and (2) the principles of adult education that are drawn from the literatures on adult development and learning, which provide a context for defining expectations about and approaches to teaching. In addition, two internal factors are equally integral to shaping the educational philosophy. These are the institutional commitments to pluralism and literacy-based learning.

The Mini-School advocates a text-based approach to building Jewish literacy based on an open exploration of normative Jewish tradition. It claims to neither promote nor define a particular way of being Jewish. No matter how they ply their craft, teachers are expected to adhere to certain principles. They are to provide a safe setting where learners feel comfortable exploring texts. They are to promote respectful interaction and dialogue among learners. They are to encourage serious reflection about the personal meaning of the texts under study. All this is to take place in a pluralist learning environment that respects individual differences and the different major approaches to Judaism as well.

While Mini-School leaders promote text study as an intellectual endeavor, they also see this literacy approach as the pathway through which Jewish adults will come to increasingly participate in Jewish life at home, at the synagogue, and in the community. They value and promote Jewish study as a sacred act in and of itself, in accord with the rabbinic tradition of *Torah lishmah,* study for its own sake. The leadership hopes that this learning will enable students to make informed choices about their Jewish beliefs and actions. They also hope that this learning will strengthen commitments to ongoing and lifelong Jewish study. In essence, they expect that the learning experience will change people's lives and, as a result, change the Jewish world. These are lofty goals and high expectations. The leaders acknowledge that the Mini-School is a work in progress, needing continual refinement of the curriculum, continual professional development of directors and faculty, and continual caring for the students who enter adult Jewish learning classrooms in search of Jewish knowledge and Jewish meaning to their lives.

CHAPTER SIX
Teachers as Cultural interpreters

The perspectives and experiences of the teachers are a vital component of understanding the extent, nature, and production of Jewish
impact in any adult Jewish learning experience. Indeed, what takes
place in the classroom and beyond appears to result from a complex interaction between the teachers, the curriculum, and the students. At the
Mini-School, as at other adult Jewish learning venues, teachers serve as
"cultural interpreters," translating and interpreting a curriculum that
focuses on building Jewish literacy for people who generally perceive
themselves as lacking adequate Jewish knowledge within their particular
cultural milieu.

What does it mean to serve as a cultural interpreter? The lives of
most American Jews are typically informed far more by the values and
norms of secular American society than they are by any clear articulation of Jewish norms and values. Though highly educated and literate in
terms of American values and culture, few Mini-School students would
describe themselves as highly literate Jews, despite their active affiliation
in the Jewish community. In effect, their attendance at the Mini-School
is a kind of cross-cultural experience where they learn to make sense of
the Jewish part of their lives. In *Israelis and the Jewish Tradition*, Hartman (2000) described the challenge of helping such Jews integrate a
Jewish perspective into their existing cultural meaning system:

> The crucial issue is how Jews who are not prepared for a leap of
> faith and are far removed from a commitment to halakhah and
> rabbinic authority can be encouraged to reengage with Jewish
> traditional texts and feel intellectually empowered to participate
> in Judaism's ongoing interpretive tradition. (160)

The teachers we interviewed perceived that most students come to the Mini-School with a strong, but insufficiently defined or not fully integrated, Jewish identity. They asserted that, for the students, being Jewish is important to them in a visceral sense; accordingly, they engage in adult Jewish learning because they want to add substance to and find personal meaning in Judaism. Students are seeking access to the texts and thought processes that are central to understanding Jewish tradition. Engaging in dialogue with and about these texts strengthens their sense of Jewish cultural identity, the very characteristics that define the self in the context of a particular social group (Ferdman 1990). Teachers serve as interpreter in this process, translating and mediating between the texts and contexts of Jewish tradition and their learners' own lives as Jews.

This chapter addresses several questions about how the teacher plays out the role of cultural interpreter. What are the desired qualifications of a teacher of Jewish adults, and how does the organizational structure support and prepare faculty for teaching in the Mini-School? What are some approaches that teachers take in interpreting the espoused educational philosophy underlying the curriculum? How do they negotiate between teaching about Judaism and helping students make personal meaning? How do they support the Mini-School's pluralistic ideology while simultaneously responding to their students' questions about religious practice? Lastly, what do they say about the teaching experience itself, and what have been the impacts of teaching these adults on the teachers' own knowledge base and professional development?

Characteristics of Teachers

Our insights about the teachers derived from our interviews with learners, the program directors, site directors, and the teachers themselves. The students were not asked to evaluate their teachers, but they regularly made unsolicited comments about the high quality of the teachers and their approaches to teaching. In fact, students consistently reported that studying with supportive, challenging, and diverse teachers was one of the greatest appeals of their learning experience. Their reflections demonstrated great respect and, at times, awe of the knowledge their teachers held. They also expressed deep appreciation for their teachers' ability to create a safe space for learning by allaying insecurities about students not knowing enough. Many were impressed with their teachers' ability to translate complex information into understandable ideas without demeaning or insulting them. They also commented on the teachers' facility in leading group discussions and drawing people into the conversation, asking good questions, prompting reflection about Jewish identity and forms of expression.

The qualities enumerated by students closely fit with what the literature suggests are key elements in effective adult education. Such teachers recognize and accept what adults are bringing to the learning situation—including their insecurities, past experience, intellectual strengths, and immediate learning needs (Schuster 1999). In addition, the literature tells us that effective adult educators foster the learner's independence, helping the learner to become increasingly self-directed (Daloz 1999). They function more as an interactive facilitator than as a detached expert. They help the learner to develop critical reflection and thinking skills as part of the process of perspective transformation (Brookfield 1986; Mezirow 1991). They create learning communities that accommodate diverse points of view and provide opportunities for challenging discourse (Bruffee 1999; Kozol 1985; Senge 1990). They encourage learners to collaborate and learn from one another. And they share their knowledge in a credible and authentic way that helps the learner understand how the teacher has come to a particular worldview (Brookfield 1991).

Interviews with Betsy Katz and several site directors, as well as a review of written material, all point to deliberate and focused adherence to this theoretical foundation. Katz emphasized the importance of having teachers who understand adult learners and can help bring them into the process of learning in a nonthreatening and engaging way:

The students want their teachers to respect them. Even though the students don't have a lot of knowledge of Judaism, they're knowledgeable people otherwise. They want the teachers to be organized and clear in how they present their information. And they want them to be personable. They want to get to know the teachers a little bit.

The site directors described ideal teachers as trained Jewish educators with a commitment to pluralism and to creating a learning environment that focuses on text study but that assures rich discussion and interaction among the students. Ellen Rosen, who both coordinates and teaches at a large, mature site, enumerated three essential qualities in looking for a new teacher: knowledge, charisma, and passion. In terms of knowledge, she stipulated that teachers need to demonstrate deep understanding of their subject matter and be able to teach it in a way that makes it accessible and meaningful to their students. She noted that a modicum of humility is important as well. A cocky teacher who conveys the sense that "I know it all" is less likely to develop a strong rapport with students, she said. She described charisma not only as personality, but also the teacher's ability to reach and teach adults. Ellen's definition of passion encompassed a demonstrable excitement about teaching in general and about teaching course material in particular. According to Ellen, these qualities are far more important than the actual professional training that the teacher might or might not have: "I don't think the students care about the credentials of the teacher. I think that they care about what goes on in the classroom and how they can relate to the teacher and how the teacher relates to the material."

The opportunity to teach adults often attracts prospective teachers. Marcia Jacobsen, the site director at a medium-size site established in 1997, said that, before she had even posted a position announcement, several teachers in the community called her when they heard that a local Mini-School was opening. The selection process included requiring candidates to teach a brief sample lesson to her advisory committee, which they subsequently evaluated before making any hiring decisions. She noted that some teachers did not want to "audition, so to speak," and withdrew from consideration.

Once hired, teachers have the opportunity to engage in a variety of professional development programs. New teachers participate in an orientation process that introduces them to the pluralistic, text-based, sequenced approach of the curriculum. This process helps develop teachers' skills and sensitivities for teaching adults. It also focuses on building a faculty with a shared vision and sense of community. In addition, each site is assigned a liaison from the North American office who visits at least once a year and is available by phone and e-mail for regular consultation. Site directors may hold faculty meetings where teachers can talk about what's taking place in their classrooms, their students, and their teaching. On occasion, the North American office also holds regional professional development programs for faculty from multiple sites in a specific area of the country.

The faculty handbook provides teachers with an overview of the history and educational philosophy of the Mini-School and begins the process of acculturation into the literacy-based approach to teaching. Its detailed explanation of this approach gives primacy to the subject matter and asserts how important it is for learners to enter into and feel part of the "Jewish Conversation" that is integral to Jewish tradition. The handbook also provides detailed guidelines for how to work with the curriculum to prepare interactive, text-based, concept-centered lessons. Additional sections reinforce the importance of reflective practice in teaching and the essentiality of teaching Judaism from a pluralistic frame of reference. The handbook itself tries to model ideal teaching in that it makes use of Jewish texts as well as contemporary educational theory to illustrate and reinforce its approach.

Other initiatives taken by the North American and international offices in the last few years to expand upon and enhance professional development for teachers include the appointment of Rabbi Michael Balinsky in 1999. Much of his work occurs through online and telephone consultations with teachers, as well as periodic site visits and regional seminars. Since that time, the Mini-School has held what are now annual faculty seminars in Israel. These seminars emphasize professional development and *Torah lishmah* (text study for its own sake). Mini-School teachers study with faculty at the Hebrew University and in more experiential modes with tour educators. They also observe classes at various adult education programs and institutions in Jerusalem, in order to participate in the learning and to become familiar with approaches taken by other teachers of adults.

A Varied and Committed Faculty

The experiences of Mini-School teachers stand in marked distinction to many other formal Jewish educational settings that frequently are characterized by reluctant students, curricular materials of inconsistent quality, low status, and limited support for professional development. Studies have chronicled the generally frustrating and draining experience of many teachers in Jewish schools (Schoem 1989; Heilman 1983) who must continuously work to engage their students in the worthiness of the subject matter. Notwithstanding creative initiatives occurring in schools around the country (Reimer 1997; Aron, Lee, and Rossel 1996), most observers and stakeholders in the American Jewish community remain somewhat negative toward Jewish schooling.

In contrast, Mini-School teachers enjoy an environment with highly motivated students, a comprehensive curriculum, respect in the community, and a significant and growing amount of support in terms of professional development. Students lavish praise on their teachers for their Judaic knowledge and sensitivity in teaching adults. Not surprisingly, teachers consistently report tremendous satisfaction in their role as faculty.

The ten female and four male teachers whom we interviewed for this study varied in their personal and professional background, religious observance, and instructional and philosophical approaches. While their tenure as teachers ranged from one to over thirteen years, all were experienced Jewish educators before joining the Mini-School faculty. For many, this was their first experience in teaching adults. For almost all, it was the first time that they had taught adults a sequenced, sustained curriculum.

Seven teachers from the three core sites upon which this study is based were interviewed in person in the spring of 2000. To augment these conversations and expand the database, another seven teachers from six other sites were interviewed by telephone or in person in December 2000. Three of these six were new sites, in their first or second year. Two of the others had been in operation for four years, and the third site for eight. The face-to-face interviews lasted approximately one hour; the telephone interviews ranged from forty to fifty minutes each. Table 4 provides basic information about the teachers interviewed, including names,[1] denominational affiliation, the courses taught and for how long, and their educational and professional backgrounds.

To gain further insight into how teachers interact with and interpret the curriculum, we asked two teachers to keep reflective practice journals over the first ten weeks of the fall 2000 semester. These journals were subsequently shared with the researchers. Included were reflections on their practice, their perceptions of the learning going on, and their own growth and learning as teachers.

[2]All names are fictitious.

| | | | Years at | |
Name	Denomination	Course(s) Taught	Mini-School	Background
Ed Berger	Reform	Dramas, Purposes	2½	Jewish communal professional; 13 years in Hillel, 5 years JCCs
Ted Butler	Reform	Dramas	10+	Physician, lay leader; self-taught
Harriet Friedman	Not available	Rhythms, Dramas	4	25+ years Jewish educator
Miriam Goodman	Conservative	Rhythms, Ethics	7	M.A. Jewish studies; married to Conservative rabbi
Frieda Gottlieb*	Reform	Dramas	5	20+ years Jewish educator; married to Reform rabbi
Charlotte Handelman	Orthodox	Purposes	1	Adult learner; lived in Israel many years
Rich Henry	Reform	Rhythms	2	Jewish communal professional; Hillel and synagogue management
Karla Isaacson*	Renewal	Rhythms	1	20+ years Jewish educator; Jewish Renewal rabbi
Beth Jarret	Conservative	Rhythms, Dramas	4	Conservative rabbi; 18 years Jewish educator
Marci Newhouse	Reform	Ethics, Rhythms	2	Reform rabbi and Jewish educator
Ellen Rosen	Orthodox/ Traditional	Rhythms, Purposes	13	M.A. Jewish education; 20+ years
Arnie Roth	Post-denominational	Rhythms, Purposes, Dramas, Ethics	4	Self-taught Jewish educator; 20+ years
Lucy Seltzer	Not available	Rhythms, Purposes	8	M.A. Jewish studies; 15+ years day school educator
Gail Silver	Conservative	Purposes, Dramas, Ethics	5	Conservative rabbi; 18 years Jewish educator

Table 4: Mini-School Teachers Interviewed

*Kept reflective practice journal

High Commitment

Mini-School teachers care deeply about what they do. For example, Gail Silver, a rabbi, noted that her current half-time congregational job suits her well, because "then I have the other half of my time to teach in the Mini-School, which is what I really love." Similarly, Miriam Goodman, a professional Jewish educator, stated, "I love opening up the eyes and hearts of Jews to see what's inside of them that they have always known but don't really know. I like seeing Jews get excited about Judaism." Frieda Gottlieb, a longtime, self-taught Jewish educator, has taught at two different sites. She extended her observation to the experiences of other teachers as well: "I would say that most of the faculty are doing it because they love it."

Because teachers enjoy their experiences so much, most tend to make long-term commitments to their school. In addition, Betsy Katz observed that on several occasions, when teachers move to another community that has a Mini-School, one of the first things they do is seek out the opportunity to teach. Recently, she said, "A teacher from Florida moved to Des Moines just in time because one of the Des Moines faculty moved to Baltimore. So the Des Moines teacher is teaching in Baltimore. The Florida teacher is teaching in Des Moines, and meanwhile, a teacher from New Jersey also moved to Baltimore and their school is growing, so she's now teaching in Baltimore, too." Katz further noted that two former teachers who relocated to a community without a Mini-School are now working to establish one.

Meaning-Making through a Literacy Approach

As we saw in chapter 5, the Mini-School seeks to develop Jewishly literate adults who feel confident and capable of understanding and engaging in the "Jewish Conversation." Foremost in this approach is the acquisition of knowledge, rather than the exploration of feelings or the development of practical skills. All other consequences, therefore, are secondary to this primary focus on developing a sense of empowerment and commitment to lifelong Jewish learning.

Though literacy is understood, accepted, and embraced by many teachers as the principal goal, there also appears to be an ongoing dialogue about how they can best strike a balance between building literacy and helping learners find personal meaning and relevance in the texts that they are studying. Whether intentionally part of the curriculum or not, the tension between these two foci is inevitable and natural as learners enter into the "Jewish Conversation," which represents a cultural meaning scheme outside of their existing cultural system. Many Jewish educators hope to touch both the hearts and the minds of their learners. They want to instill knowledge *and* love *and* commitment to Jewish learning—ambitious goals, to say the least.

Indeed, Mini-School learners are not interested in just amassing knowledge. They want to understand who they are as Jews and how they fit into the particular social context called Judaism. Rich Henry observed that while the majority of his students were strongly connected to the Jewish community, they were still looking for more. He said, "This is a group of empowered Jews for the most part. But their affiliation has not been that meaningful to them and they want more out of it." Miriam Goodman said that many students are trying to figure out how and why Judaism is important to them, how the various pieces fit together: "I don't know if they are looking for meaning in their lives as much as looking for meaning of Judaism in their lives. It's not the same kind of question. The students say, 'I know I'm Jewish, I know that I do all these things, and what more value is there in what I'm doing?' "

As their Jewish learning progresses, the teachers perceived that learners constantly negotiate between questions of "how to do Jewish" and "how to think Jewish." For example, Lucy Seltzer, who has taught at her Mini-School for eight years, observed, "The old curriculum was lousy. It was too much 'how-to.' I get some people who need to know how to and others who need to know why and what it means. I teach somewhere in between. If people want to learn how, there are lots of good books out there."

Karla Isaacson, an experienced Jewish educator new to the Mini-School, observed the interplay between literacy and identity in terms of her students needing both knowledge and relevance in order to find their place in the Jewish system of meaning. She explained:

> Students come into the program wanting to feel "in," which they would define as knowing certain things. People seem to feel a sense of ownership only when they have both the knowledge and the relevance. And the relevance has to build from their own experience.

When asked to describe their goals for their students, teachers responded that navigating the waters between knowledge and relevance is one way in which they serve as cultural interpreters of Jewish tradition. Gail Silver defined this interpretive role as an encounter between the written text and the human text of her students' lives:

> My role is to be there, guiding, facilitating, directing, introducing new ideas, new ways of helping these people who are the human texts to encounter the written text. Every class, I try to engage them in terms of something from their lives that they bring. That's what they're going to remember if it's ever going to touch them.

Most teachers did not see it as their job to encourage change in levels of religious observance or involvement in the Jewish community. Rather, they hoped that their students would use their newly acquired knowledge to make informed choices on their own. Consistent with the notion of teacher as facilitator and guide, Silver said, "Just the fact that people are thinking and engaging—to me, that's what it's all about." Ed Berger also wanted to develop more literate Jews who can then choose to act or not on their new knowledge:

> My primary goal is to help people who have little or no familiarity with these texts to gain knowledge about them. Even people who have a good knowledge base (and we have quite a few) benefit in using these texts: they can go deeper and work their areas of knowledge and learning not just go with a "Judaism-lite" approach.

In a similar vein, Arnie Roth observed that many students appeared not to know what they were interested in learning when they first started, but that they soon discovered that they would not learn much about the religious practice of Judaism in his classroom:

> I don't think they have worked out what part of Judaism they want to know about. Some are synagogue Jews, and some want to know about the rituals. They quickly learn that that is not what we do. The goal is not to teach theology or make them into religious Jews, though that may happen to a few people. It is to make them *informed* Jews.

Several teachers, however, displayed a less neutral stance, explicitly saying that they did want their students to act on their newly acquired literacy. In most cases, this was expressed in broad, nondirective terms. For instance, Harriet Friedman voiced a desire to have her students increase their comfort with and interest in Jewish learning:

> First and foremost, my goal is to make Jewish learning comfortable and fun, so that they're willing to risk going into uncharted territory. To take them from wherever they are on their personal journey and help them go forward. Also delight in helping students continue learning on their own. Any time a student continues learning, it's a success.

A number of teachers reflected a general aspiration for increased but unspecified involvement in Jewish life. Frieda Gottlieb said: "I would like to feel as though I've made them more Jewishly active." Miriam Goodman expressed similar sentiments when she said that the learning should lead to action: "You've gotten this far, now go and get involved in your congregation and community. Be that model. Don't just keep it in class." Rich Henry would like to see some kind of unspecified behavioral outcome: "We want these students to discover Judaism, the beauty and the passion of how to live a full life and a life of meaning; the fact that Judaism is such a deep value to you—you're going to want to share it with someone."

Sometimes these same teachers more directly articulated a desire for a greater focus on changing practice. For instance, Frieda Gottlieb said: "Part of being a Melton educator is that you buy in to the curriculum. We don't get the opportunity to talk about practice. I would like to see some way in which the curriculum could cover more about how you live your life as a Jew, so that it does affect their lives." Marci Newhouse also commented on what she perceived as the current curriculum's inadequate attention to issues of practice:

> Those who are behind all this need to focus on variations of this program, because we are finding that they are giving us material that may not be right for each class that is coming in, depending on the level of education of the students. There has to be a happy medium between a completely text-based study program and one that helps students figure out how to practice their religion, because many students are coming in wanting to know how to do that.

A few teachers raised questions about whether the primary focus on text-based literacy was appropriate to the needs and interests of their students. Rich Henry thinks that the practical aspects of Judaism are missing from the curriculum and that his students want that information. He balanced this sentiment by saying: "You have to be careful because the practical way that one expresses oneself Jewishly is dependent on your background and what synagogue you belong to and your rabbi and all those other kinds of factors. We have to be careful not to posit a particular way of 'doing Jewish.' "

A Balancing Act between Pluralism and Practice

As we saw in chapter 5, a commitment to pluralism is integral to the educational philosophy of the Florence Melton Adult Mini-School. It is expressed in the mix of teachers who are hired as well as in the curriculum design, which offers a variety of viewpoints on critical issues. It is further reinforced in the strong messages conveyed to faculty through written materials and professional development about not advocating for a particular level of Jewish expression. Students and faculty alike perceive and appreciate the strong value placed on pluralism in the classroom.

Most Mini-School students identify with the liberal movements in Judaism. In the majority of cases, they had never studied with an Orthodox teacher prior to this experience. Many found it stimulating and challenging to hear from teachers who are committed to presenting—and welcoming—diverse points of view. For example, Daniel, the professor profiled in chapter 1, mentioned that one of his teachers was Lubavitch, one was Orthodox, and one was Reform, but that "nobody's trying to sell you their perspective." Daniel was impressed by his teachers' ability to support tolerance and openness: "Everybody needs to feel that their own personal Judaism is going to be accepted by not only the teacher but the rest of the class. That was done very well."

Similarly, Cindy, a former health-care administrator, applauded the pluralistic mix of teachers, and said that she appreciated being exposed to teachers with different orientations: "I had a Conservative rabbi last year and a professional educator who was Orthodox. This year, I have a Reform educator and another Conservative rabbi. It has been a really interesting mix of teachers, and I think that is great."

Wanda, an active member of a Conservative congregation, welcomed the chance to learn directly about Orthodox observance:

The person who taught us was an Orthodox Jew and was talking about his wife going to the *mikveh,* which is totally foreign to my way of life. He explained the spirituality that comes from it and how beautiful certain practices are that I couldn't understand before.

Margaret, a convert from Roman Catholicism, stated that she appreciated having a chance to learn with teachers whose life experience dramatically differed from her own. She commented on how her teacher, Merle, would talk about "going to the butcher shop to get fish heads to make gefilte fish" and "growing up with a grandfather who studied kabbalah," and "having grandparents who perished in the Holocaust." In Margaret's view:

You don't get that from a teacher who has a degree in Judaica who hasn't lived that life. Because she lived that life, she could bring it into the classroom. I wouldn't have the opportunity without Melton to ask someone who came from an Orthodox family, "What was it like growing up with . . . ?" It's a whole side of life I never would have experienced in my religious community or anywhere else. She brought that into the classroom and was so comfortable that you could ask her questions about it.

While there appears to be a genuine commitment to creating a supportive and pluralistic Jewish learning community, as we noted, cultural literacy education takes place within a given social and epistemological context that gives it an inherently ideological agenda (Ferdman 1990). In this case, the agenda appears to be exposure to and an appreciation for Modern Orthodoxy. Several teachers noted what they called either an "Orthodox bias" or an insensitivity to the American Jewish community in the curriculum. Students and teachers both said that the Mini-School provides an opportunity to study with teachers from across the denominational and ideological spectrum. However, what they seemed to be saying was that it exposes liberal Jews to open and tolerant Modern Orthodox teachers, thus providing a counterweight to the increasing antagonism between the various denominations.[2] Based on the survey responses reported in chapter 2, we saw that students indeed became more tolerant of Jews who were more observant than themselves.

Ellen Rosen, who coordinates a large site and also serves as a teacher, observed that the Mini-School works to counter this negative attitude and strife:

> We try to promote the idea that this is the only place in the community where people are going to come together and study, listen to one another, get to know one another, and know that we don't hate one another—that we're not always fighting; we have so many commonalties.

Several teachers who are not Orthodox themselves thought it was important for students to have this exposure. Arnie Roth, a self-described "post-denominational," commented:

> It's important to attract Orthodox teachers to teach. It's wonderful when someone who has always been a Reform Jew with all the Reform biases has a great teacher whom he or she really likes—and the teacher is Orthodox. When a person has a great teacher who is Orthodox, his or her image of Orthodoxy changes forever. They learn to love one Orthodox man, and all their stereotypes go out the window.

Beth Jarret, a Conservative rabbi, echoed these remarks, asserting that students should be exposed to an approachable Orthodox role model. She works to present the full range of denominational perspectives in her teaching, perhaps even taking a deliberately critical position toward her own movement:

> In our community, people have a chance to study with folks whom they might once have thought of as off-limits. They have the opportunity to study with a variety of rabbis. The Orthodox

---

[2]Samuel G. Freedman's *Jew vs. Jew: The Struggle for the Soul of American Jewry* (New York: Simon and Schuster, 2000) is a recent documentation of this growing tension between the movements, which is also a frequent topic of coverage in the Jewish press.

rabbi in this community plays a key role. They love studying with him because he's approachable and "normal." People know I'm a Conservative rabbi, but I'm perceived of as a community rabbi. It's easy to talk critically of the movement that you're affiliated with, so the Conservative movement gets a bit of a bad deal. I'm particularly interested in comparative ideologies of the movements, so my students get a lot of that.

Teacher-Curriculum Interactions

In any educational setting, teachers influence and shape the curriculum in two ways: they provide ongoing feedback to the curriculum writers for modification of the formal, written materials; and they adapt and augment the materials for use in their own classrooms. This is expected and perhaps even encouraged by the Mini-School leadership. In fact, the current curriculum includes no set lesson plans. That level of detail is left to each teacher to decide. The faculty handbook describes the curriculum as a kind of *hevruta* (study partner) for teachers, to aid them in constructing their own lessons based on the texts and rationale provided.

Examples from our interviews with teachers shed light on how they use the provided texts and guidelines to build lessons that fit their teaching style and their students' interests, motivations, and experiences. For example, Gail Silver explained that the texts presented in the written curriculum constitute the raw material for her lessons, so instead of spending time searching for relevant texts, she can focus on figuring out how to make the texts come alive for her students:

> I appreciate having the texts there, but I also appreciate the flexibility that we have to find other texts to fill in what we might consider gaps or to make more contemporary, up-to-date material. Even though the curriculum is set, there are still many opportunities for creativity.

Another teacher, Arnie Roth, noted that selection of texts provided and developing an instructional approach that fits their students' needs and their own teaching style: "Each teacher is unique. You have to allow for that. Melton gives them the basic material and instructs them to take their personal experiences, take their way of teaching and incorporate it."

Miriam Goodman commented as well on the flexibility present in the curriculum. Though she claimed to adhere to the content of the curriculum, she also makes accommodations to fit the learning needs of her students:

> Parts of the curriculum don't fit well with the makeup of the class. Since there is so much material in there, one is able to focus on pieces of it. So you can streamline for the class what you want to talk about; that enables the teacher to pick what fits for her students.

Ellen Rosen, a site director as well as a teacher, appreciates the rich textual resources provided in the curriculum. She places the authority in the classroom in the texts themselves, rather than on her as the mediator between student and text:

> I'm not the kind of a teacher who stands up and talks about spirituality, talks about issues without tying into something. Having something text-based makes it more comfortable for me and for them. They have something to go back to. It's not just me saying this or, "Oh, it sounds like a good idea." There's a textual basis for what I'm saying.

Teachers' Methods of Instruction

To better understand how teachers think about and plan their instructional methods, we asked two teachers to keep reflective practice journals for one semester. Frieda Gottlieb, an experienced Mini-School teacher, showed a fairly consistent approach to preparation and sensitivity to issues of adult development and learning. Frieda's students needed organizational tools such as timelines, maps, and key questions to provide a context for each class session. She frequently introduced her class with a brief review of the previous week, and then distributed the organizational tools to keep the class oriented and focused. She also made note of the importance of what the Mini-School calls "road maps" (summary sheets that provide key vocabulary and highlight the main points of each lesson).

As a general rule, each of Frieda's classes focused on one core concept, idea, or question. After introductory remarks, the choreography of a typical class consisted of reading aloud a series of selected texts followed by the teacher asking framing questions to facilitate and shape discussion. Following Bloom's taxonomy of progressively more complicated questions, Frieda's first questions were designed to ensure that students understood the content. Next, Frieda would ask the students to interpret and at times apply the texts to issues of contemporary relevance. In her journal, Frieda wrote that in each lesson, she asked her class to concentrate on the stated objective for the lesson. However, she acknowledged that her students frequently redirected the conversation from textual analysis to personal meaning-making. For instance, she commented several times on how, in various lessons the conversation turned to God at unexpected places. In such cases, she conveyed a willingness to forgo the text-centered nature of the lesson to allow her students to grapple with ideas and questions of immediate relevance and concern. Her notes suggested that she demonstrated care for her students and a clear sense of their preferences in terms of instructional modalities and needs for organizing concepts and contextual frames. The following journal passage written after a class on messianism reveals Frieda's sensitivity to her learners—a sensitivity that belies the notion of an exclusive focus on text. It also displays her attempts to adapt her teaching to address students' interests and needs:

> I thought this was a very good lesson. I spent time talking about belief. I think they are struggling with their own beliefs and I am encouraging them not to feel frustrated if they are not sure what they believe. This class is very interested in talking about God and wanting to have easy answers. I thought today that the students who were comfortable with their Judaism were supportive of those who were searching. There was a lot of participation from students who had not spoken before. I am going to try to incorporate more questions dealing with personal dilemmas. It seems to be effective in their learning.

While the in-class process outlined above is typical, it is by no means the only one that teachers follow. Karla Isaacson, an experienced

Jewish educator teaching in the Mini-School for the first time, was also commissioned to keep a journal. Her journal reflected a struggle with finding a satisfactory balance between her personal style, her instructional goals, and the curriculum. She frequently wrote about how she negotiated between her interpretation of the literacy goals of the curriculum, and her sense of what her students wanted and needed. During a unit on prayer she wrote:

> I feel the "why" of prayer (not the fact that *Shaharit* was set by Abraham), or "How do I use this text to do soulful expression" is a much more urgent issue than whether praise and thanks are the same or different or whether *Minha* was set by Isaac or the Temple service. I continue to feel that there are developmental issues for adults that we only touch upon in passing.

Karla's reflective practice journal indicates that she was having some difficulty interpreting just how far she could diverge from the curriculum and still be teaching a lesson that fit within the principles of the Mini-School. She wrote: "The curriculum is too cumbersome. Each text tells a story that I could elaborate on. I'm not sure I like the story that the curriculum overall is trying to tell (i.e., the selection of texts), or at least, I think sometimes there are better stories to tell." In another instance, she reflected on the tension between what she perceived as the intellectual focus of the curriculum and her own belief "that the information in this class is destined for the mind, heart, body, and for action." Karla's frustration appears related to her struggle to adjust her own style of teaching to a fixed curriculum. Indeed, her desire to attend to the emotional and spiritual needs of her students is not inconsistent with what the Mini-School professes as an important value. For instance, during a conversation among teachers that took place on the Mini-School Listserv in November 1999, Michael Balinsky, director of professional development, spoke to this same issue, noting that the Mini-School classroom can and should address issues of the heart and the mind:

> I do not believe that Melton is an academic program. The approach can be taught with heart. Having sat in the *shiur* [lesson] of many rabbis, I think the experience is anything but academic. We are not teaching theology, but Torah, in all its many voices and complexities. That is as much an experience of the heart and the mind.

Teachers who have been in the Mini-School for a longer period do seem to find the balance that Karla Isaacson was still seeking. As teachers become more comfortable and familiar with the subject matter, they tend to be less concerned about covering the material presented in the curriculum and more flexible and creative in their selection of texts and approaches. For example, Marci Newhouse, whom we interviewed when she was teaching the same class for a second time, said: "I'm having more fun this year. I'm less caught up in whether we cover everything. I never followed the recommended order, anyway—it didn't work. But I thought I had to cover the text. Now I'm less concerned. I'm letting go of it more, relaxing more." Beth Jarret, a rabbi and experienced teacher, described the difference between teaching Dramas for the first time as compared with Rhythms, which she has taught for several years and has now completely rearranged and augmented:

> I stick pretty faithfully to the Dramas curriculum. It's my first time doing it. So I figure that you can't know much about it without doing it at least once. But with Rhythms, I have to bring in a lot of other stuff. People have lots of questions about women and tallis, tefillin, and *kippot*. We spend more time on prayer as well.

Though new Dramas teachers "stick pretty faithfully" to the curriculum, more veteran teachers do not. Ed Berger, who was teaching Dramas for the third time when he was interviewed, perceived that the curriculum doesn't provide sufficient historical context in which to situate the themes that it explores:

> I bring in other texts. I find that people have a limited background in Jewish history and of Jewish time, both chronological and in terms of events. They need more context. People have no idea of where to place King David in history, or when the first Temple was destroyed. I love to see how through sacred and other texts we can move back and forth in time and memory. That's an important part of Jewish methodology.

Ted Butler has taught Dilemmas/Dramas for over ten years. He built his own curriculum using various pieces of each of the three different versions of the course. Over the years, he has also developed several additional lessons that are not part of any of the curricula. One of these is

a simulation of the First Zionist Congress, for which the students prepare over several weeks.

Making It Relevant

The teachers we interviewed appeared to intuit a principle of adult
learning theory that posits that adults must feel a sense of control or
self-direction over their learning (Knowles et al. 1984; Vella 1994). Reflecting on how students spent more time than planned or expected discussing a particular topic, Frieda Gottlieb commented: "I want them to
have some control over their learning." Gail Silver cited an example of
how much more engaged her students are when the subject matter has
direct relevance to them:

> We had a lesson in Purposes two weeks ago on leadership. I
> went out of my way to elicit from the people in the class who
> are leaders in the community what their experiences are, how
> they understand the leadership structure of the Jewish commu-
> nity, and so on. They decided that was the greatest lesson be-
> cause they had a chance to share who they were.

Our interviews with students showed how much they appreciated
their teachers' ability to make course content compelling and relevant.
For Linda, a lawyer who became a stay-at-home mom, "the subject
matter comes to life through the teacher." She recalled that her initial
ambivalence about learning the laws of kashrut gave way because of the
way it was presented by her teacher:

> It was presented in an enthusiastic, interesting, stimulating way.
> I remember calling up my father and saying, "Do you know
> why kashrut is the way it is and what it means?" I told him all
> about different kinds of law, and different kinds of thinking
> with the rationale of why it got started, and why different peo-
> ple might look at it as still important.

In another example, Edna, a retiree, praised her teacher, Ron, for his
ability to make the material relevant, in contrast with adult education
teachers she had experienced elsewhere. She observed, "Ron brings
things more into today's context so that the relationship between where

we're coming from is relevant." Roger, a physician, mentioned that his teacher, Rachel, offered text interpretations that gave him new ways of thinking about his own life:

> Every subject that Rachel taught, she gave a spiritual context to it, not just the actual event. For example, Passover: it isn't just leaving Egypt. *Mitzrayim* means "limitations" or "a narrow area." So it's about us leaving our limitations—in other words, growing. So Rachel takes the Passover story and makes it into something that's relevant to us now for our growth.

Sensitivity to Adult Learners

One of the most consistent compliments students paid concerned their teachers' ability to assess students' needs and make appropriate accommodations. The students liked that their teachers could take complex ideas and make them accessible to novices, while not insulting the learners' intelligence or embarrassing them for their ignorance. Mindy, a foundation administrator, commented:

> Our teachers made it very palatable for us. They explained things that may have been explained to me before but that had gone right over my head. But they bring it down to a level where, for a person who was certainly not well educated as far as Judaic studies, it's possible to learn and enjoy learning. The questions that we may ask or that I may ask: nothing is unimportant. That makes a person feel comfortable.

Likewise, the way the teachers recognized the vulnerability of the learners especially impressed Daniel, the college professor. Despite his strong Jewish educational background, Daniel noted that he and many of his fellow learners felt unusually insecure when they began their two-year course of study. He commented that the teachers proved adept at mitigating the students' anxiety: "They know how to listen and how to make people not feel that they were ignorant." Daniel also said that whenever something came up that was "very basic," the teachers "dealt with it on a straightforward level and made sure that the answers to basic questions did not make people feel as though they were being belittled or that they were being embarrassed or, more important, that they shouldn't have asked the question."

Sharing Personal Beliefs

The teachers interpret the pluralistic vision of teaching multiple perspectives in diverse ways. They recalled a wide range of responses when students asked them what they personally believe, or what a denominational position is on a particular issue. As we saw in chapter 3, many teachers naturally share their personal beliefs and assumptions about God and various aspects of ritual observance and prayer. Others seem more reluctant to delve into this personal realm. For instance, Ted Butler simply stated, "I try not to let them know how I feel about this thing or that thing." Frieda Gottlieb directs students to their rabbi when they have theological or faith-related questions. A student sent her an e-mail asking whether she believed that the Temple was destroyed because the people had sinned. She replied, "I e-mailed her back and said that she needed to talk to her rabbi. What she was asking was what I believed, and I won't go there. I don't like to talk about what I believe because that isn't what it's about. It's about what *you* believe."

Other teachers feel comfortable sharing their personal beliefs, but they do so in a qualified manner. For instance, Beth Jarret said:

> I always start by saying something like, "Remember, you're asking Rabbi Beth Jarret, a Conservative rabbi. If you were to ask someone else, you'd get a different answer. My answer is only right for me and my family. I don't have a congregation. Nobody has to listen to me." I work hard to make sure that everybody understands that I'm giving my personal perspective.

Ed Berger gave a similar reply: "I tell them what I believe, but I put it in a context. People usually ask me outside of class. Or, if I do get asked in class, I try to make a separation and say that this is not quite pertinent to what we're trying to do. I try to bracket my answers."

Harriet Friedman generally does not proffer her opinion until after the students have expressed theirs. Sometimes, however, she does begin by stating her opinion when the topic is difficult or potentially controversial in order to make it safer for her students to reflect on and express their own points of view. For example, she handled a tense situation around teaching about the *mikveh* (ritual bath) to illustrate how she addressed personal issues of belief:

Some of our students didn't want to study about *mikveh* at all. I said that we would be leaving a huge hole in our study of Jewish experience without studying it. I had originally scheduled a trip to a *mikveh*. There's a political backdrop to this: the Orthodox rabbis had stopped allowing Conservative and Reform conversions in our local *mikveh*. In the end, the class chose not to go. Instead, I brought in texts and we watched some video excerpts. We had a rich conversation on a very touchy area. It was one of the best classes we had all year.

Some teachers initially struggle with the pluralistic approach. Miriam Goodman, a Conservative Jew, was uneasy at first, until she realized that the commitment to teach in a pluralistic manner enabled students of any level of Jewish identity and practice to feel safe and included in the conversation:

In the beginning, I wasn't comfortable, but then I realized that it is easy to teach a class and say that Jewish law says such and such. I can teach pluralistically because I can say that if I look at mitzvot like this on a ladder, all people have their own space and we are all still one people, and it's an individual thing. I'm very comfortable with that because people should love Judaism where they are at in terms of their own beliefs and practices and they should follow through with whatever commitment they made.

In a later remark, however, Miriam (who is married to a congregational rabbi) appeared to have lingering ambivalence about her responsibility to encourage increased commitment to Jewish practice, particularly as it relates to synagogue involvement: "I think that if there were a way to get people to give out more of what they've learned and share it, the whole community could benefit. I know that the Federation community gets some of this, but shuls don't."

The Use of Dialogue and Other Instructional Strategies

Adult learning that focuses on adult development or growth is typically dialogical in nature, where the teacher functions in a facilitative rather than directive role, where internal conversation with the self and external conversation with others are integral to the instructional process.

Dialogue goes beyond discussion of the content to explore the meaning underlying it. It challenges learners to identify, test, and adjust their interpretations relative to others. As described by Taylor, Marienau, and Fiddler (2000), in dialogue "learners *inquire into and respond openly to others' ideas,* at the same time thinking about and being willing to *surface and question assumptions underlying their* own and others' statements" (emphasis in original, 34). Our evidence suggested that dialogue is a regular feature in many Mini-School classrooms. We saw examples of this in the ethnographic analysis presented in chapters 3 and 4. In addition, several students we interviewed commented on their teachers' ability to engage the class in reflective thinking and discussion of diverse perspectives. Mindy, the foundation administrator, gave a specific illustration:

> Many times, our teachers will start out with such questions as "What do you think this is?" "What do you do on . . . ?" or "What are your five most favorite holidays?" So it gets you thinking. Then we go around the room: "What did we write and why did we write that?" and "How do you feel on Rosh Hashanah?" and "Why Yom Kippur?—things that I would not have thought of myself. That's what I think is so interesting about having twenty-five people in the room.

In a similar vein, Linda, a lawyer-turned-homemaker, described her teacher, Merle, as "better than any rabbi I ever met" when it came to inviting conversation:

> We had many beautiful discussions. I guess it was like being in a yeshiva! It was that secret side of Judaism: the highs and the beauty of thinking about the ideas. Merle had a way of drawing it out of each person and getting us to think about it methodically. She never led us to a conclusion but led us along so that we could really think about things.

Judy, a clinical psychologist, said that with her teachers, "there are always questions that are posed to the group and opportunities for students to make comments." Community leader Leslie's teacher would have the group read aloud and then would ask, "What do you think it means?" Leslie said that as more and more people offered interpretations, she could see where her own ideas fit in.

However, students and teachers also lamented the limited amount of time that they had to engage in such a rich dialogical approach. Judy, the psychologist, noted that discussion often focused more on clarifying the readings and did not allow for significant reflection:

> There are always questions that are posed to the group and opportunities for students to make comments. But the comments take you back to the readings, as opposed to having more time to sit and mull it over and think about it from your own point of view, and question and argue, and so on. We don't have time to do *that*, which would be fun.

Some teachers thought that such an approach would be inappropriate to the learning agenda. For example, Lucy Seltzer does not explicitly challenge her students to reflect on their assumptions: "I try to help people find their place. I don't push for cognitive dissonance."

In addition to promoting dialogue among the learners, several teachers also try to move beyond lecture and discussion to employ a wider variety of learning modalities in the classroom, such as role-playing, music, and cooperative learning activities. For example, Arnie Roth frequently uses *hevruta*, a form of cooperative learning familiar in Jewish text study circles, which entails students studying a text independently in pairs before joining a larger group discussion. He varies his approach from week to week because "I don't want them to predict exactly what I'm going to do. I vary the format because that is a way of stimulating them. I always try to have a surprise. If I think they are getting into a rut, I change my technique."

In addition to the mock Zionist Congress, Ted Butler gave several other examples of how he has adapted the curriculum to suit his teaching approach. He crafted a lesson on Shabbetai Zvi that involved a role-playing exercise that he thought would be more engaging than simply reviewing the written material provided in the curriculum:

> I invited a couple of students to present the material in their own way. They simulated a modern newscast describing the career of Shabbetai Zvi and broke off just at the moment when he's faced with the choice of apostasy or Islam. With fifteen minutes to go in the class, they dumped it back in my lap and said, "You can tell them the rest"—with no warning. It was great chemistry in there.

Another teacher, Gail Silver, uses music to help make the themes of the text study in her Purposes class more accessible to her students:

> Maybe once every three weeks, I bring my guitar and teach songs that are relevant to the topic. Sometimes, I also bring things from popular culture. The week that the curriculum topic was miracles, we began the class by singing "Wonder of Wonders, Miracle of Miracles," from *Fiddler on the Roof* and then used that song to define the various kinds of miracles in Judaism. It was something that they were familiar with, so it was a great entrée.

As noted, time seems to be a key inhibitor to expanding this kind of creative teaching. Teachers often feel constrained by their need and desire to cover the material thoroughly in just one hour a week. Rich Henry commented: "I always seem to be short ten minutes." In her reflective practice journal, Frieda Gottlieb frequently wrote that she "ran out of time" in a lesson. Her comments reflected her internal conflict between covering the material in the curriculum and allowing time for students to make meaning. After one lesson, she wrote: "I thought there was too much material to cover in one class. I am constantly trying to meet the students' needs and be true to the curriculum. I wish we had more concise choices." Likewise, Ellen Rosen noted:

> There's always this terrible tension. We have one hour. How can that hour best be spent? The curriculum doesn't deal with that at all. Curriculum deals with "the facts, ma'am." These are the readings. These are the ways that you can look at the readings. So the curriculum doesn't help you in that way at all. It takes creativity, thought, and also figuring out what you are going to take out in order to fit this activity in.

Impact on the Teachers Themselves

Regardless of tenure, background, or other teaching experience, the teachers we interviewed consistently reported how much they enjoy teaching in this adult Jewish learning setting. Several comments echoed the sentiments of one teacher: "I think this is the thing in the week I enjoy the most." Ted Butler said that one of the pluses of retiring from his full-time job as a physician is that he now has the chance to teach a daytime class in addition to his evening one. Lucy Seltzer said that the first of her teaching jobs she returned to after an illness a few years ago was the Mini-School. Marci Newhouse, a rabbi in her second year of Mini-School teaching, noted that this experience affirms her calling:

> This experience has helped me realize that teaching is the most important thing I do—no matter what age, what context. This has helped me realize that this is what I was born to do. This pulls out of me what I'm best at and what I love most. I love watching lights go on all over the room and learning myself.

Perhaps one reason that these teachers love this experience so much is that they feel they are growing, both in terms of their own Jewish content knowledge and as teachers. As Charlotte Handelman said, "I feel like a student myself preparing for class. It's opening a new way of learning." Harriet Friedman, a twenty-five-year veteran Jewish educator, described how she has both grown and been validated by teaching Dilemmas for two years and the new Dramas curriculum this year:

> This is the most exciting teaching I've done in my life. I've taught many three- to four-week classes. I do teacher training, lectures to churches, student groups. I see Melton as creating a community of learners. The students become my teachers while I teach them. It changes with each group. When I first started teaching Dilemmas, there was a sense of satisfaction. It was very comforting to find many, many texts that the curriculum writers in Jerusalem chose that I have been using for years.

The teachers' understanding of their connection to and role in the Jewish community also has broadened as a result of their association with the Mini-School, as suggested in a remark by Beth Jarret:

> It has probably made me more community-minded. You always learn when you teach. That's always a good thing to do. Being a part of the system has made me aware of a larger cross-section of folks than I would have if I had been in a congregation. Everyone I'm around cares about Judaism. If I were a congregational rabbi, I would have different challenges and headaches. I've learned a lot.

Many teachers also expressed tremendous respect for the adults who have made a two-year commitment to serious Jewish study. They recognized how busy people are and are impressed by the many students who attend class consistently. They also reported enjoying the opportunity to teach adults who have a range of backgrounds and perspectives as learners and as Jews. Lucy Seltzer, whose "day job" is in a Jewish day school, observed that teaching adults challenges her in different ways from teaching children:

> I like teaching adults. It has stretched me in terms of things I've learned. Teaching Purposes is a stretch, because it's less my area of expertise. There's something nice about teaching grown-ups. It comes at the end of a very long day for me. I schlep in but walk out energized. There's something different about presenting ideas to grown-ups.

Virtually all of the teachers interviewed echoed this refrain about the pleasure and excitement in teaching heterogeneous groups of adults. They learned themselves as they grappled with the curriculum and their varied students. Many felt continuously challenged to respond to the wide range of learners who enroll. Rich Henry had to do the same lesson three times for three different classes: "Every one was different. I had to be very, very prepared to be able to think on my feet." Frieda Gottlieb also commented on the need to be flexible: "My teaching style is very much connected to my students. How I teach one class isn't how I teach another, because I'm concerned that they learn. I'm constantly reevaluating every lesson." Gail Silver also reflected on the challenges of teaching a diverse group of adults with a wide range of knowledge and experience: "There are people who come in with various strong backgrounds. Then there are people on the other end, coming from no background, a little background, or since they were children, people who haven't engaged in this kind of study."

These challenges require teachers to be thoughtful about their teaching. As mentioned earlier, Ted Butler maintains files of all three versions of the Dilemmas/Dramas curriculum on his computer and builds his own course using various components of each. For Miriam Goodman, student feedback has helped her to revise and adapt her teaching style:

> Louise, our site director, gives us copies of the students' evaluations. Some of the things they said helped me adapt the ways

that I teach the students. I found myself taking my tapes home and listening to them to find out, after the students commented, if I could hear myself from a different perspective.

For Karla Isaacson, another experienced Jewish educator, teaching in the Mini-School made her shift her entire instructional approach:

> Before teaching in the Mini-School, I was either teaching people who were more literate, or those not interested in becoming literate. In those settings, I would create motivation first and use texts as supporting material. In this class, where building literacy is primary, I have to reverse my orientation by starting with texts and then building relevance. I'm realizing how important it is to help people feel grounded in the context of the texts.

Conclusion

Teaching is an art of translation. The teacher's job is to help the learner encounter and interpret unfamiliar subject matter and build a base of knowledge. In literacy-based education, the further task is to help the learner assimilate the cultural values, norms, and symbols into their own identity as an individual and as a member of the group. As one teacher put it, "The teacher serves as guide or facilitator, helping people who bring their own 'human texts' to their learning experience encounter the multiple written texts of the Jewish tradition." Most Mini-School teachers do not directly try to persuade their students to change their lives in any particular way. Yet for many, it is not simply an exercise in knowledge acquisition. They come motivated to learn about where and how Judaism fits in to their lives. The curriculum and instruction starts with building knowledge. However, as students grapple with these texts and the experiences their teachers facilitate, the pieces of Jewish history, thought, and practice fall into place, questions form, and meaning is sought. For many students, this encounter results in their recasting the narrative of their lives in some way. It may be through a newfound enthusiasm for Jewish study. It may be through increased levels of observance, or through finding deeper meaning in the practices they already do. It may be through greater involvement in Jewish communal activities, or it simply may be finding a greater level of comfort or sense of self as a Jew.

The teachers are part of a dynamic and fluid interaction between learner, instructor, and text. Their job requires them to constantly mediate between the curriculum's text-based approach to Jewish literacy and their students' search for personal meaning. It requires them to teach Judaism in an open pluralistic manner, while still attending to students' questions about observance and practice. In short, teachers of Jewish adults navigate between knowledge and relevance, while avoiding advocacy of increasing levels of religious observance or community involvement. Almost all teachers confront the question of where and when to give the sort of religious guidance that might be better suited coming from a congregational rabbi, or that they themselves might otherwise provide in a learning environment less committed to pluralism.

The curriculum provides the basic frame for instruction, but the students and teachers determine the ultimate shape of the learning experience. The teachers provide the road map. The speed and direction that the students take in traveling the path is ultimately left to each individual to decide. Teachers supply the first level of interpretation by providing the context, by making the texts coherent and accessible, and by raising questions that prompt students to discover meaning. They adapt the curriculum to fit with their own personal teaching styles and their students' needs as they perceive them. At times, they forgo the text-centered nature of the lessons to give students the chance to grapple with issues of immediate relevance. Some experiment with a wide array of instructional approaches such as role-playing, music, and cooperative learning.

The experience inevitably affects not just the learners, but the teachers themselves. Clearly, they enjoy teaching at the Mini-School. They also report that they are growing, both as Jews and as educators. They gain a deeper familiarity with Jewish texts and ideas, and they feel a stronger link to the Jewish community. As teachers, they experience a special relationship with their learners and are challenged to become reflective practitioners, giving more (or different) thought to their teaching than in other contexts.

CHAPTER SEVEN
A Moral Imperative:
The Role of Educational Leadership

Scholarship about school leadership and practice tells us that successful schools need strong leaders to achieve excellence. School leaders inspire, motivate, coordinate, supervise, and support teachers. They develop and implement curriculum, guide teachers in developing skills and instructional strategies, and monitor student learning and well-being. Effective school leaders also build a sense of shared purpose and community. The need for such leadership is a given in Jewish education, at least in schools that serve children. Even the smallest congregational school will have a principal. However, the assumption of the essentiality of such a leadership role has not yet taken hold in the burgeoning world of adult Jewish learning.

In contrast to the prevailing reality, each Mini-School does have such a role, in the form of the site director. This individual provides the connective tissue that builds relationships, holds the community together, and makes the Mini-School far more than just a series of classes in adult Jewish learning. In effect, the site director functions as principal or head of the school. The importance of this role was recognized in 2001 with an official name change from "site coordinator" to "site director."

In *Moral Leadership*, Sergiovanni notes that "transforming schools from organizations to communities may be a key to school improvement" (1992, xiv). Although his focus is on the public school system, the parallel to the Florence Melton Adult Mini-School is striking. The Mini-School provides more than a learning environment; it creates a learning community. The bonds that participants build between themselves and the texts, their teachers, Jewish tradition, the process of learning, and among one another belie the two short hours a week that they meet. How this program transforms itself into a school, and from a school to a learning community, rests largely in the hands of the site directors.

Site directors' responsibilities fall into two main categories: program administration and educational supervision. Their administrative tasks include marketing and student recruitment, making logistical arrangements regarding classrooms, meeting dates and time, budgeting, and organizing extracurricular activities. Site directors frequently work with a lay-led advisory board on fund-raising and strategic planning. Supervisory responsibilities include the recruitment and hiring of teachers. Site directors monitor instructional quality as well, by ongoing coaching, mentoring, and evaluation of teachers.

Though the people who fill the director positions come from diverse backgrounds, they share several qualities that are consistent with what the school literature describes as essential for effective leadership. Few sites have difficulty in finding directors, which, curiously, contrasts with the chronic shortage of qualified day and congregational school leaders (Council on Initiatives in Jewish Education 1999). Yet the skill set required is remarkably similar.

This chapter explores reasons for why this may be the case. It examines the specific skills, motivations, and experiences directors bring to their positions and how they create a learning community. It also explores the challenges that directors face in their jobs and the impact that the experience has had on their own personal growth as Jews and as Jewish educators.

Like their students, the overwhelming majority (89%) of directors are women. Of the fifty-seven directors listed in the site directory, only six are men. Data for this chapter come from in-depth interviews with directors at four sites, as well as notes from three days of participant observation at the international conference for Florence Melton Mini-School directors in February 2001. At the conference, Lisa Grant attended programs and workshops, spoke informally with directors, and in one session asked participants to reflect in writing about how their experiences have changed them, if at all. Individuals who were formally interviewed are cited by name.[1] In addition, some informal conversations are reported that are not attributed to a specific individual. The written remarks were anonymous and are presented as such.

[1] All names are fictitious.

Site Director Motivations and Qualifications

Site directors fall into two general categories. One group consists of a sizable number of lay people who were attracted to the position because of their own involvement and excitement about adult Jewish learning, either in a Florence Melton Adult Mini-School or other venue. Some of these people may have had training in general education or other types of program administration, but the main factor that drew them to the position was the product itself, namely, a comprehensive experience in adult Jewish learning. A strong secondary attraction for this group appears to be the flexibility that allows many directors to work on a part-time basis, and thus pursue other interests and obligations.

Career Jewish professionals constitute the second group of site directors. These directors are more likely to work full-time, though often, the site director role is only one of many that they fill in their communities. They include rabbis, educators, and Jewish communal service professionals. Many people in this group serve both as director and teacher at their site.

While directors travel different routes to their job, they have much in common. They frequently described their jobs with a sense of mission or calling. They expressed the belief that adult Jewish learning in general, and their own job in particular, makes a difference in their own Jewish community and the Jewish world in general. They spoke with a deep sense of commitment to their students and to the international enterprise of the Mini-School. And, like the teachers, directors consistently reported how much they enjoy their jobs.

Site directors also shared a commitment to their own ongoing learning. Both those with professional training and those with lay backgrounds described their jobs as a learning experience. They noted that they learn from their students, from the teachers, and from the challenges of learning such managerial aspects of the job as marketing, budgeting, fund-raising, and long-range or strategic planning.

In the same way that the Mini-School can have a profound influence on the lives of its students, many of the lay directors reported that they felt transformed through their own Jewish learning in general, or their association with the Mini-School in particular. Denise Feldman, a recently appointed director at a new site, was illustrative of this group of lay people who were inspired to reenter the workforce or change professional focus as a result of their participation in Jewish learning. She described herself as a "Jewish late bloomer":

I became bat mitzvah at age thirty-nine. I was raised in a secular household. When our oldest child turned seven and was getting ready to attend Hebrew school, I decided to take the adult Hebrew class so that I could help her. After that experience, the rabbi said to me, "You need to keep studying." So I did!

Shortly after her adult bat mitzvah, three years prior to our conversation, Denise began teaching second grade at her synagogue and became co-adviser of the junior youth group. When she learned about the position of site director, she was interested because it was part-time and would afford her the opportunity to work in the Jewish community. "The position was flexible, and I would be working with wonderful people. It would allow me to spend time with my kids. The Jewish community offers a lot to us. We need to give back." Now, Denise said:

I feel good about being involved in something so positive. I think people don't realize how lucky we are to have a Melton school here. We did a great job getting it started. I feel like one of the students. I really like the classes. It's also helping my teaching in religious school.

Other lay directors echoed Denise's positive feelings. Roberta Kaplan was one of the significant number of directors who began their association with the Mini-School as students and ended up as professionals. She was a student in one city and continued her Jewish learning after graduating. When she moved, she became the director in her new community. "This is the best job I've ever had in my life," she stated emphatically.

In other cases, directors came from different fields and were drawn to the Mini-School because of its focus on adult Jewish learning. Tara Miller was an example here. With a master's degree in basic education, Tara worked predominantly in literacy education in the secular community. However, when someone from her synagogue recommended her for the director position, she took the job because of its connection to the Jewish community and its part-time flexibility, which suited her needs as a mother of a young child. Though she noted it was a less political job than most of her other work, she also said how much she enjoyed helping Jewish adults make learning connections.

In addition to these emerging Jewish professionals, many other site directors have strong Jewish educational backgrounds and experiences.

Various directors have served in congregations as pulpit rabbis and educators, on college campuses as Hillel directors and program planners, and in a range of communal organizations such as Bureaus of Jewish Education and Jewish Community Centers. Many of the more experienced directors also teach at their sites in addition to fulfilling these key administrative functions. Ellen Rosen is representative of this type of director. She has a master's degree in Jewish education, more than twenty years of teaching in congregational and day schools, and has served as an educational administrator in a central agency. In addition to her role as director at a large site, she also teaches classes. Ellen also serves as director of adult Jewish learning at the Bureau of Jewish Education in her community. The Mini-School is sponsored by this agency, and she considers it a flagship program of the organization.

Site Director as School Leader:
Moral Authority, Caring, and Stewardship

Site directors are passionate about their work and deeply committed to adult Jewish learning. This passion is manifested through a sense of moral authority about the purpose of the Mini-School, caring for the students, and stewardship for their particular site. As we will see below, these qualities conform to findings about moral leadership in schools.

Moral Authority

The literature on leadership distinguishes between several forces that contribute or detract from the school effectiveness. Sergiovanni (1992) writes that school leaders typically rely on a combination of five possible sources of authority: bureaucratic, psychological, technical, professional, and moral. Each is important in the smooth management of a school, but the professional and moral sources, he argued, are those that separate "well-managed" schools from those most often identified as "excellent."

In Sergiovanni's view, bureaucratic authority is grounded in rules and procedures to ensure the smooth functioning of the school on a day-to-day basis. This form of authority requires mastering managerial tools such as planning, organizing, coordinating, and scheduling. Psychological authority is based on the power of personality and persuasion, the leader's ability to motivate and inspire. Technical authority is derived from knowledge illuminated through scientific research.

The will to follow leaders whose source of authority is bureaucratic, psychological, or technical is extrinsically motivated. Compliance and cooperation are obtained through a school leader's managerial skills, but do not necessarily create in teachers a commitment to the enterprise itself. Sergiovanni's two other sources of authority—professional and moral—engender desire and commitment that are intrinsically motivated, that is, based on a sense of doing what is good and right. Professional authority relates to the leader's expertise and practice. Here, power is not derived from rules, research findings, or anticipation of psychological rewards. Rather, professional authority is rooted in the knowledge base of teachers, which is the combination of many factors, including, but not limited to, scientific and procedural knowledge as well as personal experience. Professional authority must be built through dialogue among teachers that establishes collective norms of practice.

Moral authority is based on a sense of obligation and responsibility derived from shared values, ideas, and ideals. When moral authority predominates in a school culture, it becomes a learning community where "what is considered right and good is as important as what works and what is effective, [where] people are motivated as much by emotion and beliefs as by self-interest, and [where] collegiality is a professional virtue" (Sergiovanni 1992, 39).

Moral authority is conveyed largely through what Sergiovanni describes as symbolic and cultural forces of leadership. Here, the school leader instills a sense of purpose and commitment to the principles and values of the school. While bureaucratic, psychological, and technical aspects of leadership are important for managing the structures and substance of the school, symbolic and cultural forces affect the faith that people have in the school and in one another as collaborators in the building and sustaining of the enterprise (Sergiovanni 1991).

The site directors' interactions and relationships with faculty and students seem to embody the principles of moral leadership. This inference derives from the overall tone of formal and informal conversation at the directors' conference. Participants spoke with enthusiasm and sincerity about the opportunity that their role affords them to help others become more confident and comfortable as Jews. While not without criticism of the curriculum, the directors spoke of the pride they share in their connection to the national and international endeavor to bring pluralistic, literacy-based, comprehensive Jewish learning to adults around the world. They conveyed a shared sense of purpose and a conviction that they were involved in something right and good and essential to the future of the Jewish people.

The site directors' sense of moral authority also was reflected in two specific ways: their commitment to the pluralistic, text-based approach to Jewish learning; and their desire and determination to create learning communities. Ellen Rosen remarks about creating an open atmosphere for pluralistic, nonjudgmental exploration of Judaism were representative of sentiments heard again and again in different ways. She noted: "One of the things we have to keep explaining to them over and over again is that the classical sources are for everyone. We all go back to the same place, regardless of what movement we situate ourselves in. It's what we make of it as we widen the circle."

Sergiovanni notes that "important messages and high ideas" are often communicated through "simple routines and humble actions properly orchestrated" (1991, 107). Much of what the site directors do can be seen as these small actions that create a powerful sense of culture. For example, many of the supposedly administrative tasks that the director performs support the creation of a warm and welcoming environment for adult learners. This includes small, but significant, things such as putting tablecloths on the tables where the students study, making name cards for students, tape-recording sessions for students who may have to miss a class, and providing or organizing snacks during the break between classes. Each of these actions transforms what might otherwise be an undifferentiated elementary school classroom or a meeting room in a Jewish Community Center or other public space into an adult learning environment where the learners' needs for comfort and respect are anticipated.

Site directors attend to the whole experience of the learners, not just that which occurs inside the classroom. The text-based, literacy-focused, pluralistic curriculum affords minimal opportunity for exploring the more experiential side of Jewish practice. In many sites, directors augment this intellectual approach with a variety of extracurricular programs, such as a Friday night dinner, a field trip to a *mikveh* (ritual bath) or funeral home, a model seder, or a Purim feast. The most extensive and far-reaching of these programs is the Florence Melton Adult Mini-School Israel seminar, a short-term study tour that attracts students, graduates, and their spouses or significant others. These kinds of programs give students an opportunity to explore other avenues of Jewish expression outside of the text-based classroom study that makes up the bulk of their learning experience.

At Denise Feldman's site, a sense of community among students is growing through activities outside of the classroom and additional learning:

> We've tried to do other events with them, such as holiday celebrations. We met in someone's home once. We bring in outside speakers and encourage Mini-School people to attend, and many do. Now, groups are meeting separately from the class, little *havurot*. They're studying together. We do a Thursday *Parashat Hashavuah* get-together. Some of the other teachers do that, too. The people in these groups are still enrolled in the program.

Caring for the Students

The moral authority that appears to drive the site directors in their interactions and attention to students is embodied in an ethic of care. Since most of the directors are women, it is not surprising that this value clearly resonates with the core principles of feminist pedagogy that focus on the "importance of connection, relationship, and the role of affectivity in learning" (Tisdell 2000, 156). This quality of caring seems to be integral to their commitment to building relationships within and beyond the classroom.

Research on women as school leaders in particular (Shakeshaft 1987) suggests that three leadership characteristics are far more prevalent among women than among men: (1) the emphasis on building relationships and connections with people; (2) a commitment to teaching and learning as a core component of their job; and (3) the attention paid to building community. Site directors' comments reflected a strong focus on each of these characteristics.

While all of the functions that the site directors perform are important for the smooth running of the school, perhaps the most essential role she (or he) serves is that of "dean of students," or guidance counselor. Most adult Jewish learners have been away from formal classroom learning for a long time. While they may be quite expert in most areas of their lives, many come to this experience feeling inadequate, if not illiterate, as Jews. It is the job of the director, along with the faculty, to create a safe environment to ensure that the students' experience of learning is supportive, positive, and enriching. For the director, this typically means monitoring the classroom interactions between students, teachers, and texts. It means allaying students' anxieties about not knowing enough, and regularly following up on students with irregular attendance. At times, this means simply offering a sympathetic ear to the complexities in life that may impinge on regular attendance. At other times, it requires actively soliciting feedback about teachers, classroom interactions, or other barriers to participation.

The site directors speak directly with each prospective student to hear the reasons that they want to enroll and what they hope to attain. They sit in on classes, phone students at home, and chat with them during the breaks. They work deliberately with faculty to foster a culture where students can learn from one another as well as from their teachers. Marcia Jacobsen stated, "Part of the success, beyond the curriculum and the teachers—both of which are very, very important—is the *hevrah* that they formed in that class." In an essay published in *Beineinu*, the Mini-School newsletter, a director wrote about the transformation of her school into a community:

> When the first graduating class of the Florence Melton Adult Mini-School held its commencement ceremony in June of 1997, it was clear that we had built more than a school. We had built a community: A community grounded in meaningful Jewish study. A community which has promoted deep, personal and abiding friendships. A community where we will always feel safe asking questions about our Jewish traditions, rituals, ethics, history, and thought. A community that has brought us closer to ourselves, to each other, our Jewish community, and our faith. (Lederman 1997)

The site directors' care and attention provide the thread that weaves the distinct classes together. Without these efforts, each class would stand alone. The task is somewhat seamless for directors who also teach. Ellen Rosen makes sure that she gets to know all of the first-year students by teaching them. She added:

> Some I get to know much more than others. Some will come over and talk after class; others will not. Others you don't hear from in class. But one thing that many teachers do—and I try to

do as often as I can—is have them do certain readings in *hevruta* so that they at least can talk among themselves.

Even those who do not teach routinely sit in on classes to remain visible and accessible to students. At small sites, a director may become a regular participant in the class. At larger sites where multiple classes are held, the director more typically makes rounds, visiting different classes at various points in the year. At the February 2001 conference, several newly appointed directors mentioned that it was important for them to sit and study with the students, both as site directors and as learners themselves.

The site directors also take many proactive measures to ensure that students remain comfortable and excited about learning. These included soliciting periodic written evaluations on the teachers, as well as making routine phone calls or sending e-mail to ask students for more general impressions and feedback. Marcia Jacobsen, a director at an established medium-size site, stated: "I call people regularly. If they're absent once, sometimes I don't call. But two times, they get a call: 'I hope you're okay.' 'Is there anything I can do?' 'Is everything all right?' They appreciate being called." Later, when thinking about how she might want to improve in her role, she added:

I want to be able to communicate to people who have some hesitance about Jewish study. If they feel somewhat tentative, or insecure, or threatened, I would like to be able to communicate more successfully to them that people are there for them. It's not a test. I have to do a better job in reaching these people and then urging them to come to try to study.

Students come to see the director as an enthusiastic supporter of their learning. Louise Milstein noted that current students and graduates call her often, eager to share news about their lives and learning activities. Often this news is about how their studies have changed them. She said:

I happen to be in a wonderful position where people want to come back and tell me how Melton has affected their lives. It has changed the lives of so many people. Many of them became members of synagogues as a result. We have had several students who have converted to Judaism as a result of this program.

Louise also related an incident that demonstrated the importance of the director to the well-being and support of her adult students. She received positive and dramatic feedback from a particular student whom she decided to let enroll a month after the class had already begun:

> A student came up to me this year and thanked me, and when I asked her for what, she replied, "You did something that completely changed my life. When I called you, it was already four weeks into the program, and registration had been cut off, but I really wanted to become a part of this program. You allowed me to register, anyway. Your wisdom has guided me through this program to the point where I am now considering the rabbinate."

While relationships with site directors do not always result in such profound transformations, the ethic of caring pervaded directors' descriptions of relationships with students. Many mentioned receiving regular e-mail and phone calls from students and former students with book reviews or comments about an experience. Beth Jarret, a site director as well as a teacher, noted: "What I love most is when students stop me in the parking lot and ask me questions. I have a lot of students who don't ask questions because they're ambivalent or shy. I try to take note of that dynamic. I do follow-up with people."

Site directors also help students reflect on their growth in informal conversations throughout their learning and through more formal exercises as well. Ellen Rosen developed an idea suggested at a directors' conference that asks the students to write a short essay entitled "My Thoughts as I Begin" at the beginning of their first year. She told students to write for themselves and then to give their essays to her in a sealed envelope. At the end of their second year of studies, when students are asked to write a closing reflection about their learning experience, she returned the earlier piece to give students a basis for comparing their growth. She noted:

> Last year's class was the first class that had written these essays, and I returned their materials to them. It's very interesting for them to see their reactions. Most of them had forgotten that they'd even written this. Some of the responses are very, very emotional. My secretary is graduating this year and is converting to Judaism.

We learned in interviews that the students seem to deeply appreciate the efforts that the site directors make to help them succeed in their learning. For example, during her first trip to Israel, in the summer between her first and second year of studies, Sharon regularly related what she was seeing to something she learned in class with Ellen Rosen, who serves as both teacher and director at her site.

Stewardship: True to Purpose

The leadership that site directors practice is subtle and understated. Though their title was officially changed to "director" at the international conference held in February 2001, they are still more likely to describe their role as facilitative rather than directive. They seem to understand that their job is to serve their students through supporting the values and ideas that shape the culture and content of the learning experience. This type of leadership is described as a form of stewardship (Bolman and Deal 1993; Kofman and Senge 1993; Sergiovanni 1992). Such leaders focus on remaining true to the purposes that are the heart of their mission. They work hard at developing and nurturing and protecting community. They build relationships with faculty and students that are based on mutual respect and a shared commitment to the values and principles that define the school. In a sense, they work together through a "morally based contractual relationship that can bond people together" as a "covenantal community" (Sergiovanni 1992, 102). According to Sergiovanni: "The leadership that counts, in the end, is the kind that touches people differently. It taps their emotions, appeals to their values, and responds to their connections in other people. It is a morally based leadership—a form of stewardship" (1992, 120).

In essence, site directors seemed to be reflecting an ideal form of Jewish leadership, where motivation comes not from self-aggrandizement, but rather through a sense of service to something larger than themselves. This sense of service is clearly conveyed in one director's written remarks:

> To be in a small community and be able to have a program that is so welcoming to our entire Jewish community is exciting. Our program is small, and I'm relatively new. Students don't see me as the one who makes it happen, but they are enthralled with the teachers. (I'm also a student.) It's a wonderful feeling to know the joy and sense of satisfaction that various

students and graduates have expressed for taking the time for Jewish learning.

Marcia Jacobsen's description of who should consider enrolling in the Mini-School reflects the idea that a covenantal relationship is inherent in the adult Jewish learning process. Time and interest are the two main criteria, she said. Beyond that, however, is the sense of partnership between the learner and learning. She noted:

> Nobody's going to force you to be an active learner. You have to express interest. You have to walk part of the way by yourself, but we'll walk down that path and take you by the hand. I think that for most people, the Mini-School offers a variety of learning possibilities within the classroom setting. And the camaraderie, the *havurah* builds as you're in the class. All of it works beautifully.

Challenges to Directors: Competing Demands

Almost all site directors work part-time, usually holding other jobs, sometimes in different settings and sometimes within the agency that hosts the Mini-School in their community. They may work in central agencies for Jewish education, at Jewish Community Centers, in synagogues, or the Jewish Federation. They typically have a number of tasks that compete for their time and attention. Most of these other tasks are generated and sustained at the local level, which is immediate and ever present. Their Mini-School connection is more remote and diffuse. As we saw in the discussion about the Mini-School's educational philosophy in chapter 5, the central leadership continually conveys a sense of a team with a sacred mission to spread Jewish learning throughout the world. Surely these efforts have a galvanizing effect for many of these site directors who spend much of their time working on multiple tasks with limited resources.

Directors described facing a variety of challenges that can be sorted into several categories: challenges regarding supervision of faculty who may be far more knowledgeable and experienced Jewish educators than the directors themselves; challenges that arise as a result of split responsibilities and multiple reporting lines; challenges over role definition and responsibilities; and challenges regarding negotiating the delicate balance between supporting and encouraging the creativity of individual teachers and remaining true to the curriculum and ideology of the Mini-School.

Challenges in Supervising Faculty

The site directors most frequently mentioned challenges linked to their responsibility for hiring and supervising faculty. Teachers are expected to be accomplished adult Jewish educators who demonstrate a commitment to pluralism in the Jewish community and accept the range of students' Jewish practices and beliefs as valid. As one director said: "I did not want teachers who would shuffle through the material and say, 'I could do something better than this Melton stuff.' This would make the students wonder, 'What is this Melton curriculum?'" Further, teachers are expected to "model deep convictions and ideas about their Jewishness and express those ideas in daily Jewish life." They are also expected to be excellent communicators who are comfortable with classroom discussion and interactive learning.

Site directors must assess these qualities at the initial hiring and monitor them on an ongoing basis. Those directors with limited educational experience often find this task quite daunting. The directors' manual offered the following guidelines to help define this task:

Even without a strong educational background, a director can spot certain difficulties. A director may not be able to catch a mistake in content, but there is a lot s/he can see:

- Are students engaged?
- Are they interested?
- Are they participating?
- Is the teacher lecturing and not involving students in any discussion?
- Are there signs that the teacher has not prepared? No road maps? Not teaching the curriculum—but rather what they have usually taught about the general subject?
- Is the teacher disorganized and/or hard to follow?
- Does the teacher show disrespect in any way for the students, their lack of learning, their Jewish identity? (Katz and Shapiro, 1998)

Challenges of Multiple Roles and Responsibilities

Juggling the competing demands of different jobs is another challenge noted by many of the site directors who hold multiple Jewish educational positions in their communities. Eve Epstein, who also serves as principal of the community high school in her area, related one example of the potential conflicts posed by her multiple responsibilities and dual role. The high school meets on the same night in the same location as one of her Mini-School classes. She felt spread too thinly and unable to meet the needs of either group well enough on that night, but was extremely reluctant to change the day or time of the Mini-School class, since she felt this would be disruptive and inconvenient to the students. Nevertheless, she decided to do so, announcing her decision more than six months in advance of the change in order to give people time to prepare.

Most directors do not have extensive background or experience in marketing and fund-raising, though these aspects are an important part of the job. Many directors are uneasy about performing these tasks, especially when they wear multiple hats and have multiple demands on their time. In some cases, directors embrace the opportunity to expand their skill set. One director wrote: "My experiences as a site director have transformed me professionally, as I am also being pushed to grow into new areas as a professional—most recently, in the areas of business management, fund-raising, and marketing." However, some directors saw this role as conflicting when their jobs required them to raise funds for a variety of programs or initiatives. In response, some communities have shifted the responsibility for fund-raising to a lay advisory committee, rather than relying on a director who may have competing demands.

Curriculum and Teacher Need to Mesh

The North American office and the Institute at the Hebrew University focus on building and sustaining a common culture, in partnership with their sites. They want a student in Houston to have basically the same learning experience as someone in Cincinnati, Portland, or Memphis. At the same time, they also want their teachers to go "off the page," to interpret and adapt the curriculum to their own personal style. Michael Balinsky, director of professional development, said that his sense of an ideal instructional mix would be 75% of the structured curriculum and 25% what the individual teacher brings from his or her experience, perspective, and talents. As noted, the curriculum neither provides lesson plans nor direction on how to teach the material. It provides only content and themes. Teachers receive sample "road maps" that outline a suggested approach to covering the material, but they are encouraged to develop strategies that fit with their own conversation with the material.

One of the directors' responsibilities is to monitor this interaction between the teachers and the curriculum. They do this by regularly sitting in on classes. This helps them get to know the students as well as observe the classroom dynamic. Where necessary, they offer constructive feedback to teachers about the interactions between students, teacher, and material. Betsy Katz described this critical role:

> We have the directors, no matter what their background, sit in on all the classes. Many of them become what I call "master students." The director can be helpful in getting a sense of the pacing of the class and level of engagement on the part of the students. They know if they themselves are engaged by a teacher. The director can be valuable in providing constructive feedback to the faculty if they're boring, lecturing too much, or disorganized.

Denise Feldman interpreted this national directive: "I am the watchdog. I sit in on every class. I watch the teachers to make sure they are teaching according to the Melton approach. I have a sense of what they're supposed to cover and how: Do they provide a road map? Are they engaging the students?"

The site directors cited a number of obstacles that impede teacher performance, including inadequate preparation for the class, overreliance on lecturing, criticizing students or the curriculum, and an inability to relate to adult learners. Directors must take proactive measures to coach teachers to help them adapt their teaching styles to adult learning and to the principles of pluralistic, text-based study. One of Carol Levin's teachers was paying too much attention to a particular student, who often took the class on a tangent unrelated to the theme of the lesson. The teacher said, "I like to argue with Larry. Not everyone is as sharp as he is." The director reminded the teacher that his job was to reach everyone, not to let one student monopolize the teacher and direct the class conversation.

Directors also described occasions where a teacher needs to be coached because of an inability to teach in a pluralistic, text-centered, systematic approach. Ellen Rosen recounted a case of a charismatic teacher who was not using the Ethics curriculum: "She wasn't teaching it in a systematic way because she had her own ideas about it. And for that she was not very successful, even though she was a very good teacher."

After hearing feedback from the site directors, some teachers decide that the Mini-School is not a good fit with their skills and interests. One director gave an example of a college history professor teaching Dramas at her site. He focused only on the history, not the dilemma presented as central in the curriculum. It wasn't a good match for him or the students. He taught only one year and then quit.

Melanie Green described a similar situation at her site, that had a more positive outcome. She was able to work with her Dramas teacher, who was also a professor of Jewish history at a local university. First, he taught as if it were a university-level course. The students found it too complex and overwhelming and frequently got lost, though they were impressed by his vast knowledge. Melanie coached the teacher by giving him the feedback she was hearing from the students. She suggested that he simplify his approach and tell the students up front his plan for the lesson and its central themes, so that the students could see the beginning, middle, and end of his presentation. He was able to adapt his style, and the class proceeded much more smoothly.

Another director described a similar difficulty with one of her teachers responsible for teaching the Ethics curriculum. This teacher was frequently critical of the curriculum in front of the students, complaining that the material was being quoted out of context. The director understood that her job was to encourage him to put the material into context.

From other director reports, it is clear that coaching does not always work, and the teacher is ultimately dismissed. This dismissal may be due either to student complaints, the director's assessment of teacher quality, or a combination of both factors. Ruth Phillips had to dismiss a weak teacher midyear. This process was painful and difficult for her, but necessary to protect the reputation of her site. Another site director cited an example of a teacher who was dynamic, personable, and popular with many students, but whom she felt was not teaching the curriculum in an open and pluralistic fashion:

> The teacher was enormously successful. But early on, I began to have problems with some of the things she was saying in class. She was creating her own Hasidim—not literally, but figuratively. She was very much promoting the Hasidic life. I spoke to her about that, but it wasn't easy to deal with her. She was resistant to any kind of suggestion and very aware of how much power she wielded over people because she had her own group.

Eventually, the director made the difficult decision to dismiss the teacher. "The fact that she can be such a fervent Lubavitch person, it's wonderful, it's good. But this is just not the setting."

Directors Transforming Themselves

The moral leadership exercised by site directors was most evident in their personal reflections about how the position has affected their own lives. In interviews and conversations at the February 2001 conference, site directors were much more likely to share stories of its impact on students rather than on them personally. They also spoke about how teachers grow and change through their experiences teaching adults. However, the frequently heard refrain of the Mini-School being the best job ever suggests that their experience as directors has had an impact on their own sense of Jewish self as well. At a conference session, directors had the opportunity to reflect in writing on their own experiences and growth. Four general themes emerged from the responses of the twenty directors who submitted responses. A small number wrote that they did not feel personally transformed. Consistent with their commitment to caring, several directors wrote about the deep satisfaction they experienced in seeing others grow, rather than about their own transformation per se. A similar number of people wrote about their satisfaction in developing personal and professional relationships with students and faculty. About half described their connection with the Mini-School as a transformative experience. Many of these individuals were both directors and teachers and wrote that they have grown in both roles. A selection of comments representative of these four themes follows.

No Change

Three respondents wrote that their role as site director had not transformed their lives at all. However, all conveyed a strong sense of commitment to what they perceived as an extremely rewarding job. One of these people was newly appointed at a start-up site, so she had little experience upon which to reflect. However, she also did not rule out the potential for future change:

> Having not gotten to the point of an existing Mini-School, I can only use the conference as my frame of reference. I can certainly anticipate the likelihood of transformation due to the experiences of others described to me. Only time will tell if this will come to fruition.

While the other two dismissed feeling changed by their experiences, their comments reflected pride of association and a strong sense of the contribution that the Mini-School makes to their community. One wrote, "I don't see this as transforming my life. I am happy and proud, and it gives me a sense of worth to serve the community in all aspects of my job." Similarly, the other wrote, "Melton provides a service to our community, and I'm proud to have a job that does something positive for our city."

Satisfaction in Seeing Others Grow

Consistent with the ethic of caring that permeates much of what the directors do, several wrote that they were enriched by the experience of watching and helping others grow. One director echoed Betsy Katz's statement that a director performs a sacred task: "I certainly feel my work has a spiritual value because I'm involved with people's souls. I feel a fluctuating but growing sense of my own capacity to impart both information and enthusiasm when I see students getting excited about a Jewish idea." Along similar lines, one site director wrote how gratified she was to be part of a process of exciting people about Jewish study:

I take great pride in the fact that I have been able to bring that group of learners together and start them on a road that enables them to take a very special Jewish educational journey. It further delights me when they graduate and tell me that they want to continue this journey.

This sense of satisfaction about seeing others grow extends beyond the students to the professional development of teachers as well. As one site director wrote:

I've had the remarkable opportunity to watch my teachers grow as educators of adults right before my eyes from week to week, whether because they are "growing" with the curriculum or because they are becoming so connected to their students' changes and changing needs. What a joy to be the third point on this relationship triangle and to know that what I do as a site director is so pivotal to this shared Jewish journey. As I pursue personal growth, how lucky I am to be part of the growth of so many others.

Satisfaction in Developing Personal and Professional Relationships

Several directors described the personal and professional relationships that they have developed. Frequently, they blurred the lines of distinction between their personal and professional lives, as each of the following three passages suggests:

This has been my most rewarding professional experience. The feeling I get when I walk around my site, watching ninety people totally involved in Jewish learning, is overwhelming. The personal relationships I have established with the students and teachers are meaningful and enriching.

* * *

Coming into an established Jewish community is a difficult transition. Being a director has brought me friends and contacts and access to the community. As it has been an entry point for my students into the Jewish world of study, so, too, has the Mini-School given me an entry into the Jewish community.

* * *

My job at the JCC, especially Melton, has helped me accomplish many of my life goals: understanding Judaism, working with a community, having my children raised in a community. Melton has enriched my life professionally and personally.

Personal Transformation in Terms of Professional Growth

A significant number of people wrote about the impact on their own growth as learners, citing the joys of continually learning from their colleagues. One person wrote: "Melton has caused me to think about my own practices and has challenged me to learn more and know more." Another added: "My transformation has been from constantly learning in order to teach, to learning as I teach." Similarly, a third noted: "The greatest transformation for me was in observing instructors and incorporating their joy and passion into my own teaching."

Others learned from their students. "Melton has opened my eyes to the whole field of adult Jewish learning—and the power and impact of adults learning Jewishly either for the first time or as a director," one said. Another wrote: "To teach adults encourages me to hone my teaching skills. Adults demand it. Adult learners encourage me to keep learning. I must be sharp to keep their interest and encourage their progress." One comment noted the potential for an adult Jewish learning experience to touch peoples' lives, whether they are directors, faculty, or students:

> Everything I have done in my life personally and professionally has led me to this point. My educational goals were to become a knowledgeable Jew. My professional goals are to help others find their Jewish path. I have always been a teacher of one thing or another: swimming, Israeli dance, Hebrew, Torah; I have always loved learning.
>
> I have to use everything I know, and I never know enough—it's a constantly rejuvenating and self-generating process. Of all the positions I have had as a Jewish professional, being a Mini-

School director has given me the greatest sense of fulfillment
and satisfaction.

Conclusion

The site directors are the linchpin in the Mini-School system. If the
teachers are cultural interpreters, the directors may be seen as cultural
arbiters. They serve as the bridge between the North American and international offices and their local sites. They determine whether their individual site fits into the ideological and pedagogical framework of the
Mini-School. The site director functions as head of the school in all its
roles, as chief administrative officer, dean of students, and conveyor of
the vision of what a quality adult Jewish learning experience can and
should be. Whether professional Jewish educator or lay leader turned
professional, directors appear to embrace their position with a sense of
moral purpose and a deep appreciation, respect, and care for students,
past, present, and future. Most define their leadership role in language
of stewardship or caretaker rather than in organizational or technical
terms. As women committed to building relationships and building
community, most directors appear temperamentally and ideologically
suited to fill this role. They do not have to "buy in" to this approach to
leadership because it makes good business sense. Rather, it seems to
come from deep within their nature as women and as Jews committed
to Jewish education and the Jewish people.

While the ideological commitment seems firm, directors are nonetheless confronted with many challenges. For most, this role is only part
of their professional lives. They work in local communities, with more
immediate demands and concerns than those that may come from a centralized office in Chicago or Jerusalem. Some struggle with developing
new administrative skills such as marketing, budgeting, and planning.
Others struggle with finding the right teachers, who are open to and
supportive of the philosophy of pluralistic, literacy-based adult education. They also are challenged to coach and guide these teachers to
adapt the recommended interactive instructional techniques and to continually reflect upon and improve their practice.

Despite these demands and challenges, site directors love what they
do. They feel enriched by their responsibilities and supported in their
growth as professionals. They are fully committed to the enterprise of

adult Jewish study, to the Mini-School approach in particular, and to their students most of all. Almost all describe their involvement in the Mini-School as professionally and personally rewarding. For many, this goes beyond a sense of satisfaction to a sense of transformation. As they help to touch the Jewish lives of their students, their lives are touched as well.

CHAPTER EIGHT
A Journey of Heart and Mind:
Transforming the Adult Jewish Learning Experience

Teaching for Jewish literacy must be a process that engages both the hearts and minds of the learners and teachers in adult Jewish learning settings. Rabbi Zadok ha-Cohen of Lublin wrote that one does not internalize Torah study without an emotional attachment to the text. This lesson from the past resonates with more contemporary adult learning theory and reflects the balance between intellectual and emotional engagement with Jewish study that contemporary educators and communal leaders strive to achieve.

> Words of Torah which pass through the heart, that is, that the heart feels and is affected by, are defined as a "tree of life" and an "elixir of life." For the heart is the source of vitality, as it is written: "Above all thou guardest, keep thy heart, for out of it is the issue of life" (Prov. 4:23). This is the principle: When one's heart is actively inspired by the study of Torah, then it has vitality and is internalized. (*Zidkat ha'Zaddik*, no. 225 [1973/74])[1]

Our study sought to explore how one adult Jewish learning program affects the hearts and minds of its students. We believe that the impact of the learning experience at the Florence Melton Adult Mini-School—and optimally, other adult Jewish learning enterprises—may be understood

---

[1]Norman Lamm, ed. and trans., *The Religious Thought of Hasidism: Text and Commentary* (New York: Michael Scharf Publication Trust of Yeshiva University Press, 1999; distributed by KTAV Publishing), 234.

in terms of three dimensions: making meaning; building connections; and enriching, but not necessarily adding to, practice. These dimensions provide a framework for explaining how the experience enriches and expands the meaning of Judaism through an intellectual process of building Jewish knowledge and an emotional process of strengthening participants' connections to the Jewish community and experiences of Jewish learning.

The three central areas of impact of the experience—making meaning, building connections, and enriching practice—correspond to the three primary characteristics that social scientists use to define religious commitment—beliefs, belonging, and behaviors. Our analysis suggests that people who enroll in adult Jewish study clearly are seeking greater connection to and meaning in Judaism. Their outward expression of this meaning-making process may or may not be manifested in explicitly religious language, or everyday behavior, or even participation in Jewish communal life; overall, however, adult Jewish learning does appear to significantly strengthen, deepen, and broaden the learners' understanding of how Judaism and Jewish values fit into their lives.

Revisiting Our Conceptual Frameworks

At the beginning of this book, we posed a series of questions as an organizing framework to understand what begins for learners in the classroom and extends beyond it to their interpretations of Jewish texts and commitments to Jewish living. These questions focused on the Mini-School in particular, but are germane to broad and significant issues in adult Jewish education today. We now return to these questions as a means of summation and to enrich our understanding of the impacts of a systematic, long-term adult Jewish learning experience. First, we place the Mini-School into a broad cultural and sociological context. What accounts for the popularity of adult Jewish learning, and the Mini-School in particular, in the current climate? Next, we consider a series of questions about the processes of teaching adults, and the interactions between teachers, learners, and the curriculum: How do the teachers relate to their students? How do they mediate and interpret a curriculum developed in Jerusalem for their American learners? What role does the educational philosophy of the Mini-School play in shaping teaching decisions in local classrooms?

Finally, we return to the core question of impact of the learning experience on the students. What happens to these learners in terms of their sense of Jewish identity, Jewish meaning, Jewish practice, and engagement in Jewish life? We conclude this discussion by considering implications for the field of adult Jewish learning and the American Jewish community as a whole.

Reflections on the Mini-School's Appeal

The sheer number of Mini-School sites continues to expand, from three pilot sites in 1986 to sixty-five in five countries in 2003 (over fifty sites in the U.S. alone), with plans for further expansion under way. In addition, established sites continue to draw steady, if not often increasing, numbers of learners, suggesting that the Mini-School does not quickly exhaust its potential constituency even after several years of operation in a particular locale. This ongoing appeal demands explanation.

Perhaps we can better understand the appeal when we consider it in the context of trends in American religion in general, as well as within cultural currents specific to American Judaism. With respect to society at large, social scientists have noted the inward turn of many Americans for at least two decades. *Habits of the Heart* (Bellah et al. 1985) was not the first work of this nature, and far from the last. According to this scholarship, Americans have become more individualistic and less communitarian, more engaged in tending to the self and less active in civic and community affairs. Whether community involvement has in fact declined (as Robert Putnam argues in *Bowling Alone,* 2000) or has been merely transformed into the sorts of behavior that are less regular, visible, and countable (as Robert Wuthnow claims in *Loose Connections,* 2002) is a matter of some debate. Nevertheless, almost all learned observers agree that Americans have turned away from membership and activity in larger, more institutionalized organizations (national organizations with local chapters) in favor of participation in small groups. Wuthnow concludes that as many as 40% of all Americans are involved at any one time in a self-help group, and that perhaps half of these groups are affiliated with houses of worship. Membership in such groups is fluid, time-bound, and task-oriented, aimed at addressing specific issues and concerns.

Commensurate with these trends, Americans have turned in large number to various forms of adult education and enrichment, religious in orientation and otherwise. In so doing, they have sought those sorts of venues that combine social experiences with intellectual stimulation and that address their personal agendas as developing adults. Moreover, when they turn to these educational opportunities, they often do so as demanding and sometimes sophisticated consumers, seeking "performative value," that is, a product or service whose educational and social worth justifies the cost in terms of time and money.

Clearly, the Mini-School, emerging in the 1980s and flourishing thereafter, picked up and comported well with these trends in joining education and consumption. Among its features are its intimate, small-group quality; its orientation to affirming individuals and helping them grow in ways that they determine; its time-bound quality (two years); and the character of its activity, which is both religious and educational. Moreover, the policies, practices, and elements of organizational culture are drawn directly from the business world. It is no accident that Jonathan Mirvis, the chief professional, developed the Mini-School explicitly along theoretical lines advanced in the literature on business franchises, modeled after Florence Melton, who is herself a successful entrepreneur.

The growth in "customer base" can be attributed, in part, to the very targeted appeal of the "product." Although the Mini-School presents itself as an opportunity available to anyone seeking an introduction to Jewish life and text, it appeals to a relatively well-defined market, as our survey and interviews demonstrated. The demographic and Jewish identity profile of the learner is fairly well circumscribed. For the most part, learners are parents or grandparents, married, female, well educated, reasonably affluent, free of high-pressure job responsibilities, engaged in Jewish life, and with a history of adult Jewish learning. Certainly, we find variations on this theme, and not all individuals fit this composite characterization. However, with all their variety, Mini-School learners in the aggregate constitute a particular market niche—they share many characteristics, as Americans and as Jews, that set them apart from the larger population from which they are drawn.

Here we find a telling parallel with the strategies adopted by many religious congregations seeking to survive and flourish in the turbulent, dynamic, and highly competitive spiritual marketplace (Roof 1999). Some churches seek to provide a wide range of services aimed at appealing to the diverse populations in their immediate neighborhoods. Others eschew this neighborhood-based model and aim at a religious market niche, appealing to a certain type and style of religious adherent across a much broader geographic region (Ammerman 1997). The niche-marketing strategy, of course, characterizes businesses as well as churches. It means developing products and services, as well as methods for marketing and delivering them, that exert strong appeal for a highly defined potential market.

The Mini-School, though genuinely open to all, follows a well-honed recruiting strategy, both in early and succeeding stages of operation. Sites are disproportionately located in Jewish communities with above-average rates of synagogue affiliation. Early recruitment often focuses upon communal leaders, members of the boards of Jewish Federations, synagogues, and Jewish Community Centers. The course of study demands a two-year commitment to weekly classes, a readiness to engage in the study of Jewish texts, and to enter into dialogue with teachers and fellow students. All these circumstances work to shape the potential constituency, by appealing to those with a certain configuration of characteristics and by failing to appeal to others who may be less than ideal in terms of their Jewish involvement and background, employment status, or social class. More precisely, those who are only minimally involved in Jewish communal life are not likely to devote hours to Jewish text study; at the same time, those with extensive background in text study would find the curriculum too elementary.

The curriculum itself reflects the niche-marketing strategy. The Mini-School promises a learning experience that is Jewishly pluralistic and provides a curriculum to support it. But to say that the curriculum is pluralist is not to say that it is a course on comparative Judaism. Rather, the curriculum, as well as the learning experience it supports, clearly advances a religious conception of Judaism. Moreover, as we have suggested earlier, at least implicitly, the Mini-School approach implies a normative stance toward the Jewish tradition, one embedded and embodied in the halakhic tradition.

It is religious in the sense that among the several streams of Judaism represented in the curriculum, all are religious. Thus, someone whose principal Jewish interest lies in any number of areas outside of religious life might well not find the Mini-School curriculum of particular interest. Examples might include those whose primary interests are in political affairs (of the Left or the Right), Zionism and pro-Israel activity, cultural pursuits (literature, art, music, and so on) and social justice. In fact, although the Mini-School purports to represent the major religious streams equally, the curriculum is much more consistent with the Modern Orthodox and Conservative emphases on rabbinic Judaism, Jewish law, ritual, kashrut, and related matters than with Reform ideology. Although the Mini-School staunchly promotes informed decision making, a pillar of Reform Judaism, it resonates less with other emphases of Reform Judaism, such as *tikkun olam* and the prophetic tradition. In point of fact, the ideological mix of the curriculum is consonant with the way that most involved American Jews of Conservative or Reform affiliation would conceive of Judaism. A choice of some sort is unavoidable and even desirable; but it is a choice to represent a religious conception of Judaism over others and, quite possibly, to privilege a normative or halakhic view of religiosity over others as well.

If this underlying conception of Judaism comports well with prevailing conceptions among the American Jewish public, so, too, does its emphasis on text study as the centerpiece of its instruction. Text learning has been central to Jewish life and culture for centuries. However, throughout much of the twentieth century, the study of Jewish texts (Bible, Talmud, and others) remained popular and widely practiced only among American Orthodox Jewish men. At some point, perhaps in the 1980s, text study began to attract interest and cachet among involved Jews of both genders, across the denominational spectrum, including— somewhat significantly—Jewish philanthropic leadership.

This development is but part of a larger shift in the organized Jewish community. Since the late 1960s, that leadership welcomed increasing involvement in traditional Jewish activities. Conventions of Jewish Federation leaders introduced kosher food, the obligatory recital of prayers before and after meals, Judaic scholars, Sabbath and havdalah services, *divrei Torah* (short commentaries on the Bible), and eventually, text study itself. The Mini-School drew upon this turn toward traditional Jewish cultural elements, reflected it, and may well have helped promote it. Not coincidentally, the last third of the twentieth century witnessed the emergence of a number of efforts for change, aimed at intensifying the Jewish commitment and Judaic knowledge among Jewish philanthropic elites. CLAL (the Center for Learning and Leadership) and the Wexner Foundation's Heritage Program are among the best known of such efforts. The Mini-School's appeal and growth, then, owe something to the zeitgeist—specifically the more widespread growth in interest in Jewish learning, particularly among leadership in organized Jewish life.

Teacher-Learner-Curriculum Interactions

All education aims at eliciting some sort of change. Along with teaching specific knowledge, skills, and competencies, schools and the teachers within them attempt to inculcate the norms, values, and ideals of their culture. Neither the selection of what is to be learned, nor the context in which it is to be taught is value-free. These values are represented first by the formal, written curriculum. They are then interpreted, modified, and enacted by individual teachers who bring their own goals, beliefs, understanding, and skills to the learning experience. At the Mini-School, the enacted curriculum is a product of negotiation between a more content-centered teaching about Judaism and a more learner-centered teaching to facilitate personal meaning and engagement with Jewish tradition.

Effective teaching of adults requires maintaining a delicate balance between presenting information and eliciting understanding. As we discussed in the introduction, it requires a careful blending of mimetic learning (wherein knowledge is presented from authoritative teacher to dependent learner) and transformative learning (in which the learner actively "makes meaning" from content and experience) (Jackson 1986). Adults want their teachers to be credible, in terms of their subject-matter expertise, and authentic, in terms of the relationships with their learners (Brookfield 1991). Good adult educators must be accountable to and respect their learners. This means transmitting relevant and meaningful information and providing opportunities for learners to voice opinions, to reflect on assumptions, and to engage in active conversation with the texts and with one another.

The interaction between Mini-School teachers and curriculum is grounded in a pluralistic approach toward the study of Jewish texts and tradition. We frequently heard the phrase, "We teach Jewish literacy through the study of texts." Almost as frequently, we heard words to this effect: "Our goal is to make people more informed as Jews, not to make them more Jewish." On the surface, this suggests that the principal focus of the Mini-School is on the transmission of knowledge about Judaism. Indeed, much of what takes place in these classrooms did appear to follow this content-centered, mimetic approach. However, we also saw that teaching cultural literacy goes beyond teaching for mastery of subject matter. In fact, few students interviewed could remember specific details or content from a lesson. What they did remember was how much better they thought they understood Judaism and how engaged they felt in the conversation. For some, it was an initiation, though for most, it was about deepening their already binding connections.

The formal curriculum of the Mini-School is rich in content. It aims to teach the "language" of Jewish culture (Rosenak 1987). As Jonathan Mirvis stated, "If you don't understand content, we can't talk about anything." However, despite this avowed content orientation, the goal of teaching Jewish literacy cannot be achieved strictly through a mimetic approach. Effective teaching of adults (and, one could argue, of children as well) requires engaging them in making meaning and owning the content for themselves. As Rosenak wrote, this means teaching learners not just to understand the language of Judaism, but how to use it to make their own literature. This demands a transformative approach. The Mini-School grapples with this tension on many levels. Strong messages are conveyed about the importance of a pluralistic, text-based approach to teaching. Equally strong messages, however, are conveyed about what it means to be an effective teacher of adults. The former fits largely within Jackson's mimetic tradition, while the latter fits mostly within the transformative.

The teachers we observed and interviewed described a broad range of instructional philosophies and approaches. They all seemed to be conscious of the need to balance between the mimetic and transformative. Most thought that their teaching was consistent with the values and intentions conveyed by the curriculum. However, some struggled with certain aspects—feeling that there wasn't enough in the curriculum to help learners grow spiritually or help them increase their practice.

We would argue that successful teachers of Jewish adults make it their business to help their learners sort out what Judaism means in their lives. Indeed, the most profound impacts all relate to finding greater meaning in Judaism, in terms of an increased excitement and commitment to Jewish learning, a greater tolerance and appreciation for differences in religious expression, and the feeling of a deeper personal meaning in whatever Jewish practices one may choose to observe. The content is the language of instruction, but the literature, in Rosenak's terms, becomes the meaning that the learners derive from it.

Religious Education

Making, exploring, and expressing meaning are at the heart of any enterprise of religious education. Since meaning-making is the core impact for the majority of students, we might automatically infer that the Mini-School is an experience of religious education. Yet Jewish education does not neatly fit with the religious rubric, at least in the way Americans generally define "religious." Being Jewish classically combines what Western culture has divided into distinct and separate religious and ethnic spheres. In contrast to the implicit focus on religious growth and God found in the literature on Christian education, the world of Jewish education seems more varied and complex. Jewish education can have a multidimensional focus on history, culture, literature, practice, and belief. We saw that religious growth per se is neither articulated nor advocated as a goal of the learning experience. As teacher Arnie Roth stated: "The goal is not to teach theology or make them into religious Jews. It is to make them *informed* Jews." Nonetheless, the goals of building Jewish literacy and helping to make personal meaning naturally prompt many participants to reflect on and even change their religious lives. Adult learning experiences, especially those that attend to learning with both the heart and mind, can and do have obvious impacts on one's inner, spiritual life.

Leona English identified three components of spiritual development that can be fostered through adult religious education: "A strong sense of self; care, concern, and outreach to others; and the continuous construction of meaning and knowledge" (English 2000, 30). Each of these components is an integral part of the Mini-School. By far, the most commonly reported impact was a strengthened self-awareness of what it means to be Jewish. Students also spoke of the social bond established among the learners. This sense of care and concern extended beyond the classroom as well, as students frequently mentioned that their learning gave them an opportunity to learn about various ways of being Jewish. In some cases, the new or reinforced social bonds affirmed their own preexisting religious practices; in a few instances, the bonds prompted students to change. In all cases, however, it enhanced their acceptance and respect for others. Further, students regularly noted that their studies enriched their understanding of Judaism and the meaning that they drew from being Jewish. According to English, "The search for meaning is bound up in the understanding of everyday life" (30). Adult learners who seek meaning within Judaism seem to be doing just that. Most are not looking to change their lives in any profound way, but are looking instead to deepen their understanding of who they are.

In their approach to religious education, English and Gillen (2000) noted that adult learners are "compelled to become active agents in constructing meaning" (531). We saw how learners were helped to construct meaning by teachers who functioned as facilitators and co-learners, rather than definitive sources of knowledge. We saw how meaning was constructed in the classroom through dialogue and critical self-reflection. As self-understanding grew, we also saw how learners grappled with reassessing or redefining their relationships with the Jewish community, both local and global. In addition, the pluralistic, non-judgmental approach to study helped many develop a broader tolerance for, if not embrace of, the varieties of religious expressions possible within Jewish life.

Teaching for Jewish Identity

Identity is generally understood as one's self-definition, in terms of values, attitudes, interests, behaviors, and self-image. It is how one defines one's sense of unity, coherence, and purpose (McAdams and de St. Aubin 1998). Identity also is understood to be a social construct, meaning that it cannot be defined outside of the society in which the individual resides. Studies on identity development show that one's self-definition varies significantly throughout the life span as different priorities, life challenges, needs, and interests take root. The Florence Melton Adult Mini-School aims to effect such a redefinition of Jewish self through a process of educating for cultural literacy. It seeks to ensure that an active engagement with Judaism is at the core of how participants define themselves. The Mini-School hopes that a deeper understanding of and connection to Jewish texts and traditions will inspire ongoing Jewish learning and continued active participation in the Jewish community.

Students found meaning in their studies when the teachers helped make the text relevant to their lives. Affirming and building on learners' experience was valued as part of the learning process. As adults move through the life cycle, reflecting on their experiences helps them reinterpret, reimagine, and reintegrate past knowledge with new insights. In effect, this means that there is the potential for the development of new understandings that lead to a recasting of one's life story and a reshaping of identity. At the Mini-School, this process centered on the study of Jewish texts that is designed to strengthen the learners' sense of self as Jews, as well as their connections to Judaism and the Jewish people. At its best, the learning process provided participants with the opportunity and setting to reassess and reinterpret the narrative of their lives.

Mini-School students enroll in a two-year course of Jewish study. For adults with multiple responsibilities and demands on their time, this is a significant commitment. It should not be surprising, therefore, that most of these students are already strongly affiliated in terms of their connections to synagogues, Jewish communal and cultural organizations, and informal Jewish social networks. Most students who enroll are not ambivalent about their identification as Jews. They are already involved as members of synagogues and as adult learners. What they are seeking is formal Jewish knowledge, in part to close the gap between what they think they know and what they think they ought to know, given their relatively high levels of involvement in Jewish life. They want to know what it means to be a member of this particular group. They want to enrich their lives as Jews. As teacher Miriam Goodman said, "I don't know if they are looking for meaning in their lives as much as looking for the meaning of *Judaism* in their lives." Or, as a graduating student put it, "I now know why we do what we do."

Though already engaged as Jews, one clear effect of the learning process was a deepening and strengthening of participants' Jewish identity or, more specifically, their sense of belonging within the social or cultural group called Judaism. Women, in particular, create their identities at the intersection of competence and connection (Brooks 2000a). Given that around 80% of the Mini-School students are women, it should come as no surprise that an enhanced sense of competence and greater connection to the Jewish people, both in terms of the global and more intimate community, was among the most frequently described consequences of the learning experience.

Jewish identity inextricably blends religious and ethnic components (Glazer 1972). However, as London and Chazan (1990) noted, "In most uses of the phrase 'Jewish identity,' the word 'Jewish' does not refer to any agreed-upon or universal set of Jewish beliefs or behaviors, and the phrase does not imply what Jewishness itself means" (13). Jewish identity education, according to London and Chazan, should promote greater involvement in and commitment to the Jewish community without directing people to one particular set of beliefs and behaviors that constitute the right way to be Jewish.

Mini-School students manifested stronger Jewish identity in a variety of dimensions. Some students spoke about increased pride and comfort in being Jewish. Many focused on how their increased knowledge of Jewish texts, Jewish history, ethical precepts, and values made them feel more capable and confident as Jews. For many students, the learning experience motivated them to continue Jewish studies.

While most students did not attribute significant changes in religious observance or communal participation to their studies, the overwhelming majority described their learning experiences as positive, if not inspirational. Far more students reported changes in how they think and feel as Jews than those who reported actual behavioral changes. Many more students made statements such as, "It has caused me to re-think many of my own values," or "It has provided a better context for my Jewishness," than those who said, "I now celebrate Shabbat whereas I didn't before." However, even those who remarked, "I don't feel my actions have personally changed that much," also said, "It has taught me a lot more about the *reason* we believe things." In other words, students developed deeper insights and understandings of Jewish thought and traditions, which in turn made them more secure in the Jewish expressions and practices that they had chosen.

In addition to increased personal connection and meaning, many students also described a greater appreciation of and sense of responsibility to the Jewish people. At the most intimate level, students felt they were better Jews because they could now enrich the Jewishness of their families. Many also expressed a greater tolerance toward Jews with different beliefs, practices, and denominational affiliations.

Teaching for Perspective Transformation

Though cultural literacy is clearly the central mission of the Mini-School enterprise, faculty, site directors, and students would readily agree that something deeper than the transfer of information is taking place. To be sure, students are engaged in a rational intellectual activity of study and discourse. Yet they also draw upon and make connections to deeply rooted symbols, feelings, and memories of their own Jewish lives. This experience strengthens Jewish identity and can result in religious growth as well.

Another way of looking at this learning experience is to ask whether it is transformational learning, by which we mean a fundamental change in how a person makes meaning. This type of learning is more a function of *how*, rather than *what*, we know (Kegan 2000). It relates to the inner experience of knowledge, rather than outer behaviors or the quantity of knowledge that one attains. Before people can change their structures of meaning, they need to identify the assumptions and feelings that shape their current sense of self. The reality of most adult students' lives is that they have not yet "developed the capacity for articulating and criticizing the underlying assumptions of their own thinking, nor do they analyze the thinking of others in these ways" (Belenky and Stanton 2000, 73).

Though most Mini-School students are strongly identified Jews, they themselves acknowledged that prior to enrollment, they lacked indepth knowledge of Jewish history and thought. The first step for many was simply to understand the sequence and structure of the development of Judaism. While the experience prompted a significant number of students to reflect on "the reasons we do believe things," only a small proportion seemed to take this reflection to the point where it would challenge their assumptions or change their behavior. For most students, their learning reinforced their preexisting positions, making them more comfortable where they were.

It seems that a literacy-focused, pluralistic approach has the potential to trigger a number of responses. All learners seemed to engage in some degree of a reframing of narrative, not necessarily in terms of explicit behavioral change, but in terms of developing deeper understandings, new beliefs, and new or strengthened commitments. For certain people, this occurred through a rational process of critical reflection. Others responded more to the emotional or spiritual process reflected by Boyd's "soul-centered psychology." After all, as we have seen, the Mini-School faculty is urged to teach to the hearts and the minds of their students. However, the one-hour time frame, the focus on texts, and the students' primary need to put the pieces together before they can begin to think critically about them all may delimit opportunity for reflective discourse or exploration of the emotional or spiritual dimensions of the learning experience. Many teachers ascribed to the ideal of promoting dialogue and employing a range of creative teaching techniques, but they also acknowledged that time constraints meant that instruction was often through frontal delivery of information, with minimal time available for conversation that might raise questions, challenge assumptions, and evoke feelings. Also, teachers represented a range of opinions about their role as a change agent, from Lucy Seltzer's "I try to help people find their place. I don't push for cognitive dissonance" to Miriam Goodman's call to action: "You've gotten this far; now get involved in your congregation and community. Be that model. Don't just keep it in class."

While an exclusively rational model of transformative learning does not really fit with what happens, looking at transformational learning as a narrative process of recasting one's life story (Randall 1996; Brooks 2000b) is more consonant with the impacts we discovered. This perspective is based on the assumption that the experience and intensity of transformation depends on where one situates oneself within the community. For example, most Mini-School students are situated in the mainstream of the Jewish community by virtue of their affiliations and involvements. These types of people may experience transformation as a growth toward recognizing multiple systems, as Kegan claims (1994), or toward increasingly complex and inclusive structures, as Mezirow writes. They become more sophisticated in their understanding and more tolerant of differences. These types of changes enrich and deepen an already established identity. However, for people who are more marginally situated or uncertain about where they fit, the transformation may be toward a stronger and more consolidated narrative of identity (Brooks 2000b, 167).

In an ideal sense, the Mini-School encourages its learners to reflect seriously and critically on their Jewish identity and to make informed choices about their Jewish practices. What actually takes place in classrooms and with individual students, however, varies greatly. While what some researchers have labeled "transformative learning" may not be the explicit intent, such learning does occur with some students, and with some teachers and site directors as well. Certainly, some key elements of a transformative learning experience are in place—dialogue, respect, and accountability (Vella 1994). By virtue of their commitment to a two-year process of learning, it is apparent that students are seeking answers and looking to fill a void in their lives. Many teachers observed that for a good number of learners, knowing more naturally leads to questions of whether the newly acquired knowledge should produce changes in beliefs and behaviors. Teachers understood that students grow by moving beyond knowledge acquisition and understanding, into questioning assumptions, values, and perspectives (Cranton 1997).

Implications for Adult Jewish Learning

Our study offers many insights into a particular experience of adult Jewish learning. We believe that many of the principles and practices developed by the Florence Melton Adult Mini-School may be adaptable to other substantive programs of adult Jewish education. The Mini-School's philosophy of promoting ongoing personal engagement with Jewish tradition from a pluralistic perspective fits with the values of individual choice and autonomy that are so prominent in American life in general and American Jewish life in particular. This approach works effectively with American Jews, who constitute the great majority of Mini-School learners, but we wonder how transferable these values may be around the globe. The Mini-School operates sites in Australia, Great Britain, Canada, and Israel. These sites were not included in our inquiry, however. Further exploration of the applicability of a particularly American view of pluralism certainly could be a subject of further inquiry.

The Mini-School embodies principles of adult development and adult learning through its commitment to creating safe, nonjudgmental, and interactive environments where the learning builds on and is relevant to individuals' life experiences. Like adult learners everywhere, students are engaged through a mix of social interaction, intellectual stimulation, and social prestige. These principles and practices are unquestionably germane to any program of adult Jewish learning. We saw the variety of approaches that teachers use to educate for cultural literacy and how they mediated between the curriculum and their students, making it safe, inviting, and exciting to learn. We also saw the range of ways in which teachers navigated the tensions between pluralism and normative tradition, and between teaching about Judaism and promoting Jewish engagement. These multiple approaches appeared not only to increase access to the language of Jewish culture, but also to enable learners to use that language in making personal meaning and enrich their lives. The model of cultural literacy appears to be a particularly good match with students who are seeking greater depth of connection to the language of Judaism through its texts and traditions. However, as we noted in chapter 1, the Mini-School is not suited to every type of adult learner. One size does not fit all. What other programs of adult Jewish learning can learn is the importance of knowing their audience and designing curriculum and instruction to meet their particular motivations and needs.

Although these students are among the most highly engaged Jews in their communities, they are not that different from their peers in terms

of what they hope to get out of their learning experience. Adults participate in learning for intellectual and personal development. This holds
true for all forms of adult education and all the more so for religious
learning. Mini-School students may be ready to commit to a more in-
tense and sustained program of learning than others, but all adult Jewish learners are seeking, in varying degrees, a way to strengthen, deepen,
and broaden their sense of how Judaism fits into their lives. They are
looking for meaning and connection.

Perhaps motivations for adult Jewish learning differ most significantly in the area of practice. Hebrew classes, learning Torah trope,
adult b'nai mitzvah programs, and other "how-to" kinds of learning are
likely to attract people who are more primed for changes in practice.
Participants understand, up front, that such change is the goal of the
program. Like their counterparts in other adult Jewish learning activities, these learners are also seeking deeper meaning and connection to
Judaism, but they have made an explicit commitment to behavioral
change.

In addition to meeting the needs of their learners through curriculum and instruction, the site director is important to the health and
well-being of the individual students and each individual site. We saw
how principles of moral authority and symbolic leadership inform and
inspire site directors to create caring and supportive environments that
can foster development of learning communities. In parallel with the
best practices of educational leaders, the site directors go beyond mastery of administrative skills to embrace a mission of stewardship for
their sites. Here, too, the lessons that other adult learning programs
might draw from this approach to nurturing the learners and creating
learning communities are compelling.

Implications for the Contemporary
Jewish Community

Our study explored the motivations and impacts of participation from
the perspective of the students, teachers, and site directors in one adult
Jewish learning program. We described how this program attempts to
teach the common roots and experiences of Judaism in a nonjudgmental, pluralist environment. We saw how the experience helps enrich and

expand the meaning of Judaism through an intellectual process of building Jewish knowledge and through an emotional process of strengthening participants' connections to the Jewish community and fostering a passion and dedication to lifelong Jewish learning.

As noted earlier, the three central areas of impact of the experience—making meaning, building connections, and enriching practice—correspond to the dynamics of "beliefs, belonging, and behavior" that traditionally define religious commitment. From this perspective, "religion" is a multidimensional concept. One aspect of religion is its doctrine, or the concomitant set of *beliefs* to which an adherent ascribes. From another perspective, a religion is something to which a person *belongs*. A third element of religion is *behavior*, that is, participating in public or private activities considered to have religious importance (Mockabee, Monson, and Grant 2001, 675).

While these characteristics derive from the study of religion in a society that is predominantly Christian, all three elements interact to shape Jewish identity as well. Belonging to the Jewish community has always served as the primary means of identification. Jewish texts and traditions emphasize the importance of the collective in Jewish life. The Bible intones that Jews are (or ought to be) a "holy people," a phrase that immediately intertwines the sacred with the tribal. Ruth tells Naomi, "Your people shall be my people. . . . Your God shall be my God." Although American Jews may not be able to cite these biblical verses, the sense of the collective is ingrained through cultural and societal practice. Belonging to the Jewish people extends beyond communal ritual and individual religious practice. Such concepts as the Jewish people, the State of Israel, Jewish institutions, the minyan, and the *kehilah* afford opportunities for expressing one's belonging to the Jewish community. Personal matters of faith are bound with and subsumed under what has been called "historical familism" (Liebman and Cohen 1990).

Judaism (like Catholicism and Eastern Orthodoxy) places greater emphasis on behavior than belief, in distinction to Protestantism. Sociologist Marshall Sklare (1979) referred to the "sacramental character" of Judaism, that being Jewish is more about action than about faith. In traditional Judaism, the observance of ritual is of inherent importance, and pleasing to God, above and apart from whatever spiritual or moral lessons that may be attached to specific rites and ceremonies. As noted in Kiddushin 40b, when debating the relative merits of study and practice, the Rabbis agreed with the opinion of Rabbi Akiba that study is "greater" because "it leads to practice."

Mini-School students are predominantly American and therefore are influenced by American trends and values as much as, if not more than, Jewish ones. For the most part, they are strongly identified and active Jews. They not only belong to the community, but are frequently entrenched. Their level of ritual practice is already much higher than that of average American Jews, even among the affiliated. For them, however, the rote performance of ritual is not enough. What they seek through learning is substance and meaning to support their strong identification and behavior. As such, making meaning is their central motivation.

In broad strokes, this educational experience seems to produce profound and widespread changes in the derivation of meaning, understanding, appreciation, empowerment, and contextualization. At the same time, it seems to generate only small and isolated changes in behavior, with the clear exceptions of participation in and support of Jewish study itself. Learners widely reported an increased likelihood of continuing to study Jewish subject matter, even when they infrequently reported changes in such bellwether indicators as ritual practice, holiday observance, prayer, organizational involvement, and volunteer activities.

A long line of educational and social psychological research tells us that learners change their images, beliefs, and attitudes far more often than they change their behavior. As we noted repeatedly, the sorts of changes reported—and not reported—by learners comport well with the implicit contract between the Mini-School and the learners. For sound reasons connected to educational philosophy and recruitment of students, the Mini-School eschews a focus on behavioral change. While challenging one's beliefs and understanding in a respectful and accepting fashion is a central feature of the learning experience, the educational staff refrain from directly addressing matters of practice, or even appearing to question the patterns of practice followed by their students. Moreover, the learners' families, friends, synagogues, and organizations generally remain outside of the purview of the learning experience and provide little incentive for behavioral change on the part of the learner. If anything, abiding social ties prove to constrain and inhibit change in actual behavior.

Our study documents a close correspondence between the Mini-School's educational philosophy and its educational outcomes. In this respect, we can understand that we did not discover a greater incidence of change in conventional measures of Jewish involvement and practice. After all, the Mini-School does not deliberately promote behavioral change. Nonetheless, the question remains worthy of consideration, given the fact that Judaism emphasizes the centrality of specific behaviors, both in the ritual and interpersonal spheres. Against this background, an educational program that fails to produce dramatic shifts in sanctioned behavior may be viewed as disappointing by some.

One explanation for the behavioral stability is that, as a group, these learners are already highly involved in Jewish communal life (both statistically and relative to the American Jewish population). For most students, the main function of the Mini-School is to bring their Jewish intellectual, emotional, and spiritual development in line with their prior level of relatively active involvement. And this they appear to achieve quite well. At the same time, notwithstanding the minimal changes in ritual practice, we also cannot ignore what appears to be a significant impact on attitudes among Jewish communal leaders. Since so many learners are active in organized Jewish life and institutions, their widely reported new support for Jewish learning generally and day schools specifically may bring about an elevated place of Jewish learning in the organized Jewish community.

Many of these adult learners who preceded their Mini-School experience with a trajectory of Jewish growth will undoubtedly continue to grow and increase their active Jewish involvement at home, in the synagogue, and in other organized Jewish environments. This two-year period is but one portion of a lifelong Jewish journey. A snapshot at the end of two years may fail to reveal prospective changes in behavior some years down the road. What is clear and profound at this point is that these adult learners find their Judaism, however they choose to practice it, far more meaningful after their two years of study than they did before. At the same time, the early evidence of behavioral change, or lack thereof, ought to inspire ongoing questioning and deliberation.

Ultimately, our study focused on the individual adult Jewish learners. Though we raised the question of its impact on the American Jewish community as a whole, detailed exploration of this topic was beyond the scope of our mission. Nevertheless, this would be an important topic of inquiry. Much is at stake for the future of the Jewish people. The Mini-School leadership believes that Jewish learning is the key to Jewish engagement and, ultimately, to the survival of the Jewish community. Our findings suggest that they may indeed be correct in this assumption. Yet our evidence is incomplete, and questions remain about the enduring impact on individual lives as well as the life of the Jewish community. Further exploration of these questions should be of significant concern to Jewish educational leadership and all those involved with promoting the intensification of involvement on the part of Jewish adults in the United States and throughout the Jewish world.

The Hebrew University Study of the Florence Melton Adult Mini-School Graduating Class, 2001

Looking back over the last two years, to what extent were you satisfied with each of the following aspects of your Florence Melton Adult Mini-School experience? (Circle numbers)

Your teacher in the course:	Very dissatisfied	Somewhat dissatisfied	Not sure	Somewhat satisfied	Very satisfied
Rhythms of Jewish Living	1	3	1	17	78
Purposes of Jewish Living	1	4	5	21	69
Ethics of Jewish Living	2	3	5	17	74
Dramas/Dilemmas of Jewish Living	1	2	4	15	79
The mix of lecture and discussion overall	0	4	1	36	59
The responsiveness of teachers, generally, to students' questions	0	3	3	22	72
The ability of the teachers, generally, to make the texts accessible and meaningful	1	1	4	25	69
The content of the courses	1	3	6	45	46
The value of the readings	1	5	12	48	33
The coordinator's (or site director's) handling of students' needs	1	2	4	15	78
The coordinator's (or site director's) handling of administrative matters	1	1	4	18	75
The other students, first year	1	2	6	23	68
The other students, second year	1	1	4	19	74
Your experience overall	1	1	1	29	68

How Have You Been Affected?

Listed below are several possible outcomes of studying at the Mini-School. To what extent would you say that you have been affected, if at all, in each of the following ways? As best as you can, try neither to overestimate nor underestimate the impact of your educational experience.

As compared to before I studied at the Mini-School,	Not at all	Some-what	To a great extent
I more often see ethical implications in a lot of my ordinary activities	11	57	33
I have become more comfortable studying Jewish texts (in English)	8	43	49
I have undertaken more Jewish learning on my own	20	48	32
I know more Hebrew than I did before	57	32	11
I have become more active in my community as a Jewish resource	42	44	15
I have become more active in my family as a Jewish resource	21	51	29
I see myself more as a Jewish role model for my family or friends	24	49	27
I have become more attached to the Jewish community	23	49	28
I contribute more than before to Jewish charities	48	41	11
I have become more attached to the Jewish people	30	39	31
I have become a more committed advocate of community support for Jewish education	22	38	40
I have become more in favor of Jewish day school education	40	36	23
I have developed a new set of friends	24	53	23
I have acquired new networks of people in the Jewish community	23	54	23
I have become more spiritual	32	43	25
I have deepened my faith in God	37	41	22
I have developed a greater appreciation for Jews who are more observant than I	24	41	35
I have developed a greater appreciation for Jews who are less traditional than I	39	45	17
I feel more strongly than before that there is a right way to be Jewish	68	20	12
I have become more of a Jewish "pluralist"	34	45	21
I have become more observant	51	37	12
I celebrate Shabbat more than I used to	55	30	16
I have become more observant of kashrut	71	18	11
I have become more active in a synagogue	60	29	11
I now take on more roles in synagogue worship services	59	27	14
I find prayer more meaningful than before	36	42	22

Some By-Products? Possible Changes during the Last Three Years

As compared with three to four years ago, how would you rate your current levels of activity in each of the following areas? (Circle numbers of your answers)

	Much less active	Somewhat less active	About the same	Somewhat more active	Much more active
Celebrating Jewish holidays	0	1	50	34	15
Contributing to *tzedakah*	1	1	63	27	8
Studying Jewish texts	0	1	31	45	23
Engaging in social action	1	1	72	22	4
Teaching family members about being Jewish	1	2	41	43	14
Working on committees, boards of Jewish organizations	3	4	72	14	7
Working on committees, board of a synagogue	5	4	71	13	7
Attending synagogue services	2	3	59	23	13
Other synagogue activities	4	2	67	19	8
Celebrating Shabbat	2	1	58	25	14
Observing kashrut	5	1	74	13	8

In your own words, how has the Florence Melton Adult Mini-School affected you?

_____

_____

_____

What, if anything, would you change about the Mini-School experience?

_____

_____

Your Jewish Learning Activities

Listed below are several adult Jewish learning experiences. In each case, please indicate whether:

1. you participated in these experiences in the five years prior to enrolling in the Florence Melton Adult Mini-School;
2. you participated in these experiences in the two years you were attending the FMAMS;
3. you intend to participate in these experiences in the coming year.

	During the 5 years prior to FMAMS		During the last 2 years		Next year	
	Yes	No	Yes	No	Yes	No
Attended a talk or lecture on a Jewish theme (not a sermon)	82		84		85	
Took a class on a Jewish theme (*other than* FMAMini-School)	60		56		74	
Participated in an ongoing study group on a Jewish text or theme	35		41		57	
Read a book (other than the Torah or Bible) on a Jewish theme	76		80		82	
Studied Hebrew	34		27		38	

Some Jewish Concerns

How important is being Jewish in your life? (Circle numbers of your answers)			
1 Very 90	2 Somewhat 10	3 Not very 1	4 Not at all —
Compared with three years ago, has your level of Jewish activity generally . . .			
1 Increased 57	2 Decreased 2		3 Stayed the same 41
Have you ever been to Israel?			
1 Yes, twice or more 44	2 Yes, once 31	3 No 25	
How emotionally attached are you to Israel?			
1 Very 52	2 Somewhat 38	3 Not very 9	4 Not at all 1

Your Jewish Involvement—Current and Recent

Below you'll find questions referring to several Jewish beliefs and practices. In each case, please answer with respect to your current situation *this year* (2000–01), and then also answer with respect to your situation in *the year before* you enrolled in the Florence Melton Adult Mini-School (1998–99). (Circle numbers of your answers)

During the past year (or 3 years ago), did you:	This year		3 years ago	
	Yes	No	Yes	No
Read a Jewish newspaper, magazine, or other publication?	93		81	
Read a book, other than the Bible, because it had Jewish content?	92		83	
Use the Internet for Jewish-related information?	71		35	
Are/were you or is/was anyone in your household a member of a synagogue or temple?	90		87	
Do/did you or does/did anyone in your household usually light Sabbath candles on Friday night?	73		67	
Do/did you keep kosher in your home?	29		26	
Do/did you keep kosher outside your home?	15		12	
On Yom Kippur, did you fast all or part of the day?	87		86	

Thinking about Jewish religious denominations, do/did you consider yourself to be . . .	This year	3 years ago
Orthodox	6	3
Conservative	48	47
Reform	34	36
Reconstructionist	3	3
Secular	2	2
Just Jewish	7	9

How often do/did you go to any Jewish services . . . (Circle numbers of your answers)	This year	3 years ago
Only for weddings and bar mitzvahs	5	5
Only on the High Holidays	7	10
A few times a year	26	32
About once a month	18	18
2 or 3 times a month	20	17
About once a week or more	23	18

How well can/could you read Hebrew, such as in a prayer book, regardless of the amount you understand? (Circle numbers)	This year	3 years ago
Not at all	22	31
Can sound out words slowly	49	45
Can read words fluently	29	25

How many of the people you consider to be your closest friends are/were Jewish? (Circle numbers of your answers)	This year	3 years ago
None	1	3
Some	11	14
About half	16	17
Most	57	52
All	15	15

	This year		3 years ago	
	Yes	No	Yes	No
Have you done any volunteer work for, or sponsored by, a synagogue, Federation, or other Jewish organization?	83		76	
During the past year/3 years ago, have you been a dues-paying member of a Jewish Community Center (JCC) or YM/YWHA?	45		43	
Have you attended any program or activity at a Jewish Community Center (JCC) or YM/YWHA?	82		79	

Your Children

Do you have any children? (If you have no children, please proceed to the next page.)	Yes	No
	75	
(IF YES:) How old is your oldest child? *Median = 25* (0–17 = 33)	(18–29 = 27)	

(IF YOUR OLDEST CHILD IS AGE 7 OR OLDER:) Which of the following types of Jewish education did your oldest child receive?	Yes	No
A one-day-a-week Jewish education program, such as a Sunday school	43	
A part-time Jewish school that met more than once a week, such as an afternoon school, Talmud Torah, or heder	38	
A full-time Jewish day school or yeshiva	21	
Private tutoring	10	
Other type of school	7	

If you had a 4- or 5-year-old child now, would you send him or her to a Jewish day school next year?	Yes	No
	39	

If you had a child who were to marry, how important would it be to you, if at all, that your child's future spouse be Jewish?			
1 Very important 73	2 Somewhat important 23	3 Not very important 4	4 Not at all important 0

Your Jewish Upbringing

Thinking about how you were raised, were you raised as . . .		
1 Orthodox 8	3 Reform 21	5 Secular Jewish 10
2 Conservative 37	4 Reconstructionist	6 Just Jewish 11
7 Not Jewish 12		

When you were about 10 or 11 years old, did anyone in your family usually or always light Sabbath candles on Friday night?	Yes	No
	50	

When you were 10 or 11 years old, about how often did you personally attend synagogue or temple services?		
1 Not at all 13	2 Only the High Holidays 27	3 A few times a year 21
4 About once a month 10	5 Two or three times a month 14	6 About once a week or more 16

Which of the following types of Jewish education did you receive in grades 1 to 7?	Yes	No
A one-day-a-week Jewish education program, such as a Sunday school	45	
A part-time Jewish school that met more than once a week, such as an afternoon school, Talmud Torah, or heder	37	
A full-time Jewish day school or yeshiva	3	
Private tutoring	6	
Other type of school	5	
Did you have a bar/bat mitzvah at age 12 or 13?	40	
When you were in college (or graduate school), did you take any courses specifically focusing on Jewish subjects, such as Jewish history, Hebrew, or the Holocaust?	25	

Your Demographic Characteristics

You are . . .	
1 Male 20	2 Female 80

Your age				
0–39 = 11	40s = 30	50s = 30	60s = 16	70+ = 12

Your zip code

Are you currently . . . (Circle numbers of your answers)

1 Married 77	2 Single/Never married 6	3 Divorced 8
4 Separated 2	5 Widowed 5	6 Living with someone 3

Are you currently . . .

1 Employed full-time 37	2 Employed part-time 18	3 Retired 24
4 A student 1	5 A homemaker 18	6 Something else 3

What is the highest level of education you have attained?

(IF YOU ARE MARRIED:) What is the highest level of education your spouse has attained? (Circle numbers)	You	Your Spouse
Grade school, high school	1	0
High school graduate	1	3
Some college	8	9
B.A., B.S., college degree	43	32
Master's degree or equivalent	30	27
Doctorate, M.D., or equivalent	15	29
Other	2	1

**What was your household's total income, before taxes, for 1999?
Median = $115,000**

1 Less than $35,000 7	5 $100,000 to $150,000 22
2 $35,000 to $50,000 8	6 $150,000 to $200,000 12
3 $50,000 to $75,000 11	7 $200,000 to $300,000 9
4 $75,000 to $100,000 17	8 $300,000 or more 14

Thank you for completing this survey!

References

Ammerman, Nancy. 1997. *Congregation and Community.* New Brunswick, NJ: Rutgers University Press.

Apps, Jerold. 1991. *Mastering the Teaching of Adults.* Malabar, FL: Krieger.

_____. 1994. *Leadership for the Emerging Age: Transforming Practice in Adult and Continuing Education.* San Francisco: Jossey-Bass.

Aron, Isa. 2000. *Becoming a Congregation of Learners.* Woodstock, VT: Jewish Lights.

Aron, Isa, Sara Lee, and Seymour Rossel, eds. 1996. *A Congregation of Learners.* New York: UAHC Press.

Ashton-Warner, Sylvia. 1986. *Teacher.* Reissue edition. New York: Simon and Schuster.

Aslanian, Carol B., and Henry Brickell. 1980. *Americans in Transition: Life Changes as Reasons for Adult Learning.* New York: College Board.

Ayers, William. 1993. *To Teach: The Journey of a Teacher.* New York: Teachers College Press.

Bateson, Mary Catherine. 1989. *Composing a Life.* New York: Atlantic Monthly Press.

Belenky, Mary F., Blythe Clinchy, Nancy Goldberger, and Jill Tarule. 1986. *Women's Ways of Knowing.* New York: Basic Books.

Belenky, Mary F., and Ann V. Stanton. 2000. "Inequality, Development, and Connected Knowing." In *Learning as Transformation: Critical Perspectives on a Theory in Progress,* ed. Jack Mezirow et al. San Francisco: Jossey-Bass.

Bellah, Robert, et al. 1985. *Habits of the Heart: Individualism and Commitment in American Life.* Berkeley: University of California Press.

Ben-Peretz, Miriam. 1990. *The Teacher-Curriculum Encounter.* Albany: State University of New York Press.

Bolman, Lee G., and Terrence E. Deal. 1993. *The Path to School Leadership: A Portable Mentor.* Newbury Park, CA: Corwin.

Boshier, Roger. 1977. "Motivational Orientation Revisited: Life-Space Motives and the Education Participation Scale." *Adult Education* 27, no. 2: 89–115.

Boyd, Robert D., ed. 1991. *Personal Transformations in Small Groups: A Jungian Perspective.* London: Routledge.

Boyd, Robert D., and J. Gordon Myers. 1988. "Transformative Education." *International Journal of Lifelong Education* 7, no. 4: 261–84.

Bridges, William. 1980. *Transitions*. Reading, MA: Addison-Wesley.

Brookfield, Stephen. 1986. *Understanding and Facilitating Adult Learning*. San Francisco: Jossey-Bass.

_____. 1987. *Developing Critical Thinkers*. San Francisco: Jossey-Bass.

_____. 1991. *The Skillful Teacher*. San Francisco: Jossey-Bass.

_____. 1995. *Becoming a Critically Reflective Teacher*. San Francisco: Jossey-Bass.

Brooks, Ann K. 2000a. "Transformation." In *Women as Learners: The Significance of Gender in Adult Learning*, ed. Elisabeth Hayes and Daniele D. Flannery. San Francisco: Jossey-Bass.

_____. 2000b. "Cultures of Transformation." In *Handbook of Adult and Continuing Education*, ed. Arthur A. Wilson and Elisabeth E. Hayes, 161–70. San Francisco: Jossey-Bass.

Bruffee, Kenneth A. 1999. *Collaborative Learning: Higher Education, Interdependence, and the Authority of Knowledge*. Baltimore: Johns Hopkins University Press.

Caffarella, Rosemary S. 2002. *Planning Programs for Adult Learners*. San Francisco: Jossey-Bass.

Cohen, Steven M. 1983. *American Modernists and Jewish Identity*. New York: Routledge.

_____. 1988. *American Assimilation or Jewish Revival?* Bloomington: Indiana University Press.

_____. 1995. "The Impact of Varieties of Jewish Education upon Jewish Identity: An Inter-Generational Perspective." *Contemporary Jewry* 16: 68–96.

_____. 1998. *Religious Stability, Ethnic Decline*. New York: Florence G. Heller / JCC Association Research Center.

_____. 2000. "Assessing the Vitality of Conservative Judaism." In *Jews in the Center: Conservative Synagogues and Their Members*, ed. Jack Wertheimer. New Brunswick, NJ: Rutgers University Press.

Cohen, Steven M., and Gerald B. Bubis. 1998. "'Post-Zionist' Philanthropists: Emerging Attitudes of American Jewish Leaders Toward Communal Allocations." Jerusalem: Center for Public Affairs.

Cohen, Steven M., and Aryeh Davidson. 2001. *Adult Jewish Learning in America: Current Patterns and Prospects for Growth*. New York: Florence G. Heller / JCC Association Research Center.

Cohen, Steven M., and Arnold M. Eisen. 2000. *The Jew Within: Self, Family, and Community in America*. Bloomington: Indiana University Press.

Council on Initiatives in Jewish Education. 1999. CIJE Leaders Report. New York: Mandel Foundation.

Cowan, Rachel. 1994. "The New Spirituality in Jewish Life." *The 1994 Annual Report of the Nathan Cummings Foundation*. New York: Nathan Cummings Foundation.

Cranton, Patricia. 1994. *Understanding and Promoting Transformative Learning*. San Francisco: Jossey-Bass.

———, ed. 1997. "Transformative Learning in Action: Insights from Practice." *New Directions for Adult and Continuing Education*, no. 74 (summer): 89–96. San Francisco: Jossey-Bass.

Cross, K. Patricia. 1981. *Adults as Learners: Increasing Participation and Facilitating Learning*. San Francisco: Jossey-Bass.

Daloz, Laurent. 1999. *Mentor: Guiding the Journey of Adult Learners*. San Francisco: Jossey-Bass.

Deal, Terrence, and K. Peterson. 1999. *Shaping School Culture*. San Francisco: Jossey-Bass.

Deboy, James D., Jr. 1979. *Getting Started in Adult Religious Education*. New York: Paulist.

deCastell, Suzanne, and Allan Luke. 1988. "Defining 'Literacy' in North American Schools." In *Perspectives on Literacy*, ed. Eugene R. Kintgen, Barry M. Kroll, and Mike Rose, 159–74. Carbondale, IL: Southern Illinois University Press.

DellaPergola, Sergio. 2001. "Jewish Women in Transition: A Comparative Sociodemographic Perspective." In *Jews and Gender: The Challenge to Hierarchy*, ed. Jonathan Frankel, Studies in Contemporary Jewry 16, 209–42. New York: Oxford University Press.

Dirkx, John M. 2000. "Transformative Learning and the Journey of Individuation," *ERIC Digest* no. 223. Columbus, OH: ERIC Clearinghouse on Adult Career and Vocational Education, Center on Education and Training for Employment, College of Education, Ohio State University.

Dubin, Fraida. 1989. "Situating Literacy within Traditions of Communicative Competence." *Applied Linguistics* 10, no. 2: 171–81.

English, Leona. 2000. "Spiritual Dimensions of Informal Learning." In *Addressing the Spiritual Dimensions of Adult Learning*, ed. Leona M. English and Marie A. Gillen, 29–38. San Francisco: Jossey-Bass.

English, Leona M., and Marie A. Gillen. 2000. "A Postmodern Approach to Adult Religious Education." In *Handbook of Adult and Continuing Education*, ed. Leona M. English and Marie A. Gillen, 523–38. San Francisco: Jossey-Bass.

Ferdman, Bernardo. 1990. "Literacy and Cultural Identity." *Harvard Educational Review* 60, no. 2 (May): 181–205.

Freire, Paolo. 1971. *Pedagogy of the Oppressed*. New York: Seaview.

Glazer, Nathan. 1972. *American Judaism*. Chicago: University of Chicago Press.

Gudmundsdottir, Sigrund. 1991. "Story-maker, Story-teller: Narrative Structures in Curriculum." *Journal of Curriculum Studies* 23, no. 3: 207–18.

Halbertal, Tova Hartman, and Steven M. Cohen. 2002. "Gender Variations in Jewish Identity: Practices and Attitudes in Conservative Congregations." *Contemporary Jewry* 22: 37–64.

Handelman, Susan. 1996. "The Torah of Criticism and the Criticism of Torah: Recuperating the Pedagogical Moment." In *Interpreting Judaism in a Postmodern Age*, ed. Steven Kepnes, 221–39. New York: New York University Press.

Harbater, David. 2000. "Drama of Jewish Living through the Ages." New Curriculum. Jerusalem: Florence Melton Adult Mini-School Institute, Hebrew University of Jerusalem.

Hartman, David. 2000. *Israelis and the Jewish Tradition*. New Haven: Yale University Press.

Hartman, Moshe, and Harriet Hartman. 1996. *Gender Equality and American Jews*. Albany: State University of New York Press.

Hawkins, David. 1974. *The Informed Vision: Essays on Learning and Human Nature*. New York: Agathon.

Hayes, Elisabeth. 2000. "Voice." In *Women as Learners: The Significance of Gender in Adult Learning*, ed. Elisabeth Hayes and Daniele D. Flannery, 79–110. San Francisco: Jossey-Bass.

Heilman, Samuel C. 1983. *The People of the Book: Drama, Fellowship, and Religion*. Chicago: University of Chicago Press.

Heilman, Samuel C., and Steven M. Cohen. 1989. *Cosmopolitans and Parochials: Modern Orthodox Jews in America*. Chicago: University of Chicago Press.

Heine, S. J., and D. R. Lehman. 2003. "Move the Body, Change the Self: Acculturative Effects on the Self-Concept." In *Psychological Foundations of Culture*, ed. M. Schaller and C. Crandall, 305–31. Mahwah, NJ: Erlbaum.

Hoffman, Lawrence A. 1996. "*Al Chet Shechatanu* . . . for All the Sins That We Committed Willingly or Unintentionally . . . : Four Unintentional Sins of Synagogue Life." http://www.uahc.org/living/letuslearn/s15alchet.shtml

Holtz, Barry. 1999. "Reading and Teaching: Goals, Aspirations, and the Teaching of Jewish Texts." In *Abiding Challenges*, ed. Israel Rich and Michael Rosenak, 401–26. Tel Aviv: Freund Publishing and Bar-Ilan University.

Horowitz, Bethamie. 2000. *Connections and Journeys: Assessing Critical Opportunities for Enhancing Jewish Identity*. New York: UJA-Federation.

Houle, Cyril. 1961. *The Inquiring Mind*. Madison: University of Wisconsin Press.

Hutchins, Robert M. 1954. *Great Books: The Foundations of a Liberal Education*. New York: Simon and Schuster.

Imel, Susan. 1998. "Transformative Learning in Adulthood." *ERIC Digest* no. 200. Columbus, OH: ERIC Clearinghouse on Adult Career and Vocational Education, Center on Education and Training for Employment, College of Education, Ohio State University.

InSites: Newsletter of the Florence Melton Adult Mini-School Institute. 1993 (winter). Jerusalem: Hebrew University.

InSites: Newsletter of the Florence Melton Adult Mini-School Institute. 1996 (winter). Jerusalem: Hebrew University.

Jackson, Philip. 1986. *The Practice of Teaching*. New York: Teachers College Press.

Jewish Education News. 2001 (winter). New York: Coalition for the Advancement of Jewish Education.

Johnstone, J. W. C., and R. J. Rivera. 1965. *Volunteers for Learning: A Study of the Educational Pursuits of Adults*. Hawthorne, NY: Aldine.

Jordan, June, et al. 1991. *Women's Growth in Connection.* New York: Guilford.

Josselson, Ruth Ellen. 1987. *Finding Herself: Pathways to Identity Development in Women.* San Francisco: Jossey-Bass.

Katz, Betsy Dolgin. 1990. "A Model of Successful Educational Practice." *Journal of Jewish Education* 58, nos. 1 and 2 (spring/summer).

———. 1998. "Creating a Learning Community: It Just Doesn't Happen—Case Study of the Florence Melton Adult Mini-School." *Jewish Education News* (spring): 26–28.

Katz, Betsy, and Jane Shapiro. 1998. *Madrich: Coordinator's Manual—The Florence Melton Adult Mini-School.* 2d ed. Jerusalem: Florence Melton Adult Mini-School Institute, Hebrew University.

Katz, Jacob. 1961. *Tradition and Crisis: Jewish Society at the End of the Middle Ages.* New York: Schocken.

Kegan, Robert. 1994. *In Over Our Heads: The Mental Demands of Modern Life.* Cambridge, MA: Harvard University Press.

———. 2000. "What 'Form' Transforms? A Constructive-Developmental Approach to Transformational Learning." In *Learning as Transformation: Critical Perspectives on a Theory in Progress,* ed. Jack Mezirow et al., 35–70. San Francisco: Jossey-Bass.

Kim, Kwang, and Sean Creighton. 2000. "Participation in Adult Education in the United States: 1998–1999." *Education Statistics Quarterly* (spring).

Knowles, Malcolm S. 1980. *The Modern Practice of Adult Education: From Pedagogy to Andragogy.* 2d ed. Chicago: Follett.

———, et al. 1984. *Andragogy in Action: Applying Modern Principles of Adult Learning.* San Francisco: Jossey-Bass.

Knox, Alan B. 1977. *Adult Development and Learning.* San Francisco: Jossey-Bass.

———. 1986. *Helping Adults Learn: A Guide to Planning, Implementing, and Conducting Programs.* San Francisco: Jossey-Bass.

Kofman, Fred, and Peter Senge. 1993. "Communities of Commitment." *Organizational Dynamics* (autumn): 15–43.

Kosmin, Barry, et al. 1991. "Highlights of the 1990 National Jewish Population Survey." New York: Council of Jewish Federations.

Kozol, Jonathan. 1985. *Illiterate America.* Garden City, NY: Doubleday.

Krych, Margaret A. 1997. "The Gospel Calls Us." In *Lifelong Learning: A Guide to Adult Education in the Church,* ed. Rebecca Grothe, 12–32. Minneapolis: Augsburg.

Lazerwitz, Bernard, Alan J. Winter, Arnold Dashefsky, and Ephraim Tabory. 1998. *Jewish Choices: American Jewish Denominationalism.* Albany: State University of New York Press.

Lederman, Amy Hirschberg. 1997. "It Takes a Community to Build a School." *Beineinu: Newsletter of the Florence Melton Adult Mini-School* (fall): 5.

Liebman, Charles, and Steven M. Cohen. 1990. *Two Worlds of Judaism: The Israeli and American Experiences.* New Haven: Yale University Press.

London, Perry, and Barry Chazan. 1990. *Psychology and Jewish Identity Education.* New York: American Jewish Committee.

MacDonald, Joseph. 1993. *Teaching: Making Sense of an Uncertain Craft.* New York: Teachers College Press.

McAdams, Dan P. 1993. *The Stories We Live By.* New York: Guilford.

McAdams, Dan P., and Ed de St. Aubin. 1998. *Generativity and Adult Development: How and Why We Care for the Next Generation.* Washington, DC: American Psychological Association.

McCutcheon, Gail. 1988. "Curriculum and the Work of Teachers." In *The Curriculum Studies Reader,* ed. David J. Flinders and Stephen J. Thornton, 188–97. New York: Routledge, 1997.

McKenzie, Leon. 1986. "The Purposes and Scope of Adult Religious Education." In *Handbook of Adult Religious Education,* ed. Nancy T. Foltz, 7–24. Birmingham: Religious Education Press.

The Florence Melton Adult Mini-School: A Quality International Jewish Adult Education Network. Jerusalem: Florence Melton Adult Mini-School Institute. Undated booklet.

Melton Centre for Jewish Education in the Diaspora. 1985 (spring). "The Florence Melton Adult Mini-School Project." Internal document. Jerusalem: Hebrew University.

_____. 1987 (February). "The Melton Adult Curriculum." Internal document. Jerusalem: Hebrew University.

_____. 1989. "Florence Melton Adult Mini-School Teacher Training Outline." Internal document. Jerusalem: Hebrew University.

_____. 2001. *Preparing to Teach: Florence Melton Adult Mini-School Faculty Handbook.* Pilot version. Jerusalem: Hebrew University.

Merriam, Sharan M., and Rosemary S. Caffarella. 1999. *Learning in Adulthood: A Comprehensive Guide.* 2d ed. San Francisco: Jossey-Bass.

Mezirow, Jack. 1991. *Transformative Dimensions of Adult Learning.* San Francisco: Jossey-Bass.

_____, et al. 1990. *Fostering Critical Reflection in Adulthood.* San Francisco: Jossey-Bass.

_____, et al., eds. 2000. *Learning as Transformation: Critical Perspectives on a Theory in Progress.* San Francisco: Jossey-Bass.

Minutes of the Annual Directors of the Florence Melton Adult Mini-Schools Meetings. 1998. February 9–16. Hebrew University, Jerusalem.

Mockabee, Stephen, Joseph Quin Monson, and J. Tobin Grant. 2001. "Measuring Religious Commitments among Catholics and Protestants: A New Approach." *Journal for the Scientific Study of Religion* 40 (December): 675–90.

Morstain, B. R., and J. C. Smart. 1974. "Reasons for Participation in Adult Education Courses: A Multivariate Analysis of Group Differences." *Adult Education* 24 (2): 83–98.

Osmer, Richard R. 1992. *Teaching for Faith: A Guide for Teachers of Adult Classes.* Louisville, KY: Westminster / John Knox.

Poupko, Yehiel. 1999. "Response." *A Statement on Jewish Education: Text and Responses.* New York: American Jewish Committee.

Putnam, Robert D. 2000. *Bowling Alone: The Collapse and Revival of American Community.* New York: Simon and Schuster.

Randall, William. 1996. "Restorying a Life: Adult Education and Transformative Learning." In *Aging and Biography: Explorations in Adult Development,* ed. James Birren et al., 224–47. New York: Springer.

Reimer, Joseph. 1997. *Succeeding at Jewish Education: How One Congregation Made It Work.* Philadelphia: Jewish Publication Society.

Roof, Wade Clark. 1993. *A Generation of Seekers: The Spiritual Journeys of the Baby Boom Generation.* New York: HarperCollins.

———. 1999. *Spiritual Marketplace: Baby Boomers and the Remaking of American Religion.* Princeton, NJ: Princeton University Press.

Rosenak, Michael. 1987. *Commandments and Concerns.* Philadelphia: Jewish Publication Society.

Sarna, Jonathan. 1995. *A Great Awakening: The Transformation That Shaped Twentieth-Century American Judaism and Its Implications for Today.* New York: Council for Initiatives in Jewish Education, CIJE Essay Series.

Schein, Edgar. 1992. *Organizational Culture and Leadership.* 2d ed. San Francisco: Jossey-Bass.

Schlossberg, Nancy. 1999. *Overwhelmed: Coping with Life's Ups and Downs.* New York: Lexington.

Schlossberg, Elinor Waters, and Jane Goodman. 1995. *Counseling Adults in Transition: Linking Practice with Theory.* New York: Springer.

Schoem, David. 1989. *Ethnic Survival in America: An Ethnography of a Jewish Afternoon School.* Providence, RI: Brown Judaic Studies Series.

Schön, Donald. 1983. *The Reflective Practitioner: How Professionals Think in Action.* New York: Basic Books.

Schuster, Diane Tickton. 1999. "Jewish Adult Development: New Lessons for Educators of Adult Jewish Learners." *Agenda: Jewish Education* 12: 16–21. New York: JESNA.

———. 2003. *Jewish Lives, Jewish Learning: Adult Jewish Learning in Theory and Practice.* New York: UAHC Press.

Schwab, Joseph. 1977. "Translating Scholarship into Curriculum." In *From the Scholar to the Classroom: Translating Jewish Tradition into Curriculum,* ed. Seymour Fox and Geraldine Rosenfield. New York: Melton Research Center for Jewish Education, Jewish Theological Seminary.

Senge, Peter M. 1990. *The Fifth Discipline: The Art and Practice of the Learning Organization.* New York: Doubleday.

Sergiovanni, Thomas J. 1991. *The Principalship: A Reflective Practice Perspective.* 2d ed. Boston: Allyn and Bacon.

_____. 1992. *Moral Leadership: Getting to the Heart of School Improvement.* San Francisco: Jossey-Bass.

Shakeshaft, Charol. 1987. *Women in Educational Administration.* Newbury Park, CA: Sage.

Sheehy, Gail. 1996. *New Passages: Mapping Your Life Across Time.* New York: Ballantine.

Shrage, Barry. 1996. *Building a Community of Torah and Tzedek: A New Paradigm for the Jewish Community of the 21ˢᵗ Century.* Boston: Combined Jewish Philanthropies.

Shulman, Lee S. 1990. "Foreword." In Miriam Ben-Peretz, *The Teacher-Curriculum Encounter.* Albany: State University of New York Press.

_____. 2000. "From Minsk to Pinsk: Why a Scholarship of Teaching and Learning." *Journal of Scholarship of Teaching and Learning* 1: 48–53.

Sklare, Marshall, and Joseph Greenblum. 1979. *Jewish Identity on the Suburban Frontier: A Study of Group Survival in the Open Society.* Chicago: University of Chicago Press.

Soloveitchik, Hayim. 1994. "Rupture and Reconstruction: The Transformation of Contemporary Orthodoxy." *Tradition* 28: 64–130.

Taylor, Edward W. 2000. "Analyzing Research on Transformative Learning Theory." In *Learning as Transformation: Critical Perspectives on a Theory in Progress,* ed. Jack Mezirow et al., 285–328. San Francisco: Jossey-Bass.

Taylor, Kathleen, Catherine Marienau, and Morris Fiddler. 2000. *Developing Adult Learners.* San Francisco: Jossey-Bass.

Tennant, Mark, and Philip Pogson. 1995. *Learning and Change in the Adult Years: A Developmental Perspective.* San Francisco: Jossey-Bass.

Tisdell, Elizabeth. 2000. "Feminist Pedagogies." In *Women as Learners: The Significance of Gender in Adult Learning,* ed. Elisabeth Hayes and Daniele D. Flannery, 155–84. San Francisco: Jossey-Bass.

Tough, Allen. 1979. *The Adult's Learning Project: A Fresh Approach to Theory and Practice in Adult Learning.* 2d ed. Toronto: Ontario Institute for Studies in Education.

U.S. Department of Education, National Center for Education Statistics. 2002. "Participation Trends and Patterns in Adult Education: 1991–99," NCES 2002–119, by Sean Creighton and Lisa Hudson. Washington, DC: U.S. Department of Education.

Vella, Jane. 1994. *Learning to Listen, Learning to Teach: The Power of Dialogue in Educating Adults.* San Francisco: Jossey-Bass.

_____. 2000. "A Spirited Epistemology: Honoring the Adult Learner as Subject." In *Addressing the Spiritual Dimensions of Adult Learning,* ed. Leona M. English and Marie A. Gillen, 7–16. San Francisco: Jossey-Bass.

Vogel, Linda. 2000. "Reckoning with the Spiritual Lives of Adult Educators." In *Addressing the Spiritual Dimensions of Adult Learning,* ed. Leona M. English and Marie A. Gillen, 17–27. San Francisco: Jossey-Bass.

Watzlawick, Paul, John Weakland, and Richard Fisch. 1974. *Change: Principles of Problem Formation and Problem Resolution.* New York: Norton.

Wuthnow, Robert. 1994. *Sharing the Journey: Support Groups and America's New Quest for Community.* New York: Free Press.

_____. 1999. *Growing Up Religious: Christians and Jews and Their Journeys of Faith.* Boston: Beacon.

_____. 2002. *Loose Connections: Joining Together in American's Fragmented Communities.* Cambridge, MA: Harvard University Press.

Yoffie, Eric. 1997. Presidential sermon, UAHC 64th Biennial Convention, Dallas, October 29–November 2, 1997.